BLACK TRIUMPH

A Novel of Alien Resistance

BLACK TRIUMPH

A Novel of Alien Resistance

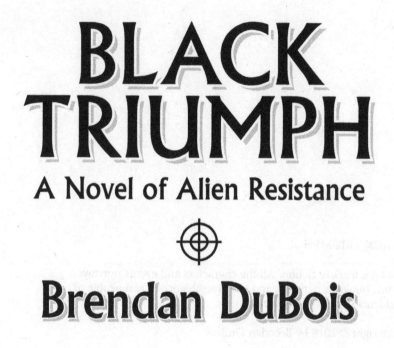

Brendan DuBois

A Baen Books Original

Baen Publishing Enterprises
P.O. Box 1403
Riverdale, NY 10471
www.baen.com

ISBN: 978-1-4814-8343-8

Cover art by David Seeley

First Baen printing, October 2018

Distributed by Simon & Schuster
1230 Avenue of the Americas
New York, NY 10020

Printed in the United States of America

10 9 8 7 6 5 4 3 2 1

This is for:

Iraq combat veteran Chris "Chez" Chesak

Former U.S. Army Captain Vincent O'Neil, Company Commander,
1st Battalion (Airborne), 508th Infantry Regiment

And all those who have served.

Acknowledgments:

I'd like to extend my thanks to Toni Weisskopf and Tony Daniel of Baen Books—great editors both—and to the entire Baen publishing team, including copyeditor Scott Pearson. Thanks, too, to artist Dave Seeley, who produced superb cover art based on my imagination. As well, appreciation to my wife, Mona Pinette, my first reader, and final thanks to the science fiction community for welcoming me back after a decades-long absence.

BLACK TRIUMPH

A Novel of Alien Resistance

"Our sun is one of 100 billion stars in our galaxy. Our galaxy is one of billions of galaxies populating the universe. It would be the height of presumption to think that we are the only living things in that enormous immensity."

—Wernher von Braun

CHAPTER ONE

One of the many things one learns over the decade-long war against the alien race known as the Creepers is how one's academic schedule is geared to learning about wars past and present. Even though we don't know where the Creepers come from or why they are here— besides killing millions of people and tossing us back into a nineteenth-century way of life, there are a lot of theories and not many facts—the powers that be in our school systems make sure we learn about war in all its deadly aspects.

For example, one semester back at Ft. St. Paul in Concord, New Hampshire's capital, I spent an entire semester as a corporal in the N.H. National Guard, learning about the famed Siege of Leningrad, which had taken place more than a century earlier. Nowadays those drowned ruins are called by their original name, St. Petersburg, but back in late 1941, elements of the German Army Group North attacked and surrounded the city in a long, grueling siege that wasn't lifted until nearly nine hundred days later. In nearly three years the city was shelled, bombed, and slowly starved to death, until millions had died.

Yet life went on.

In a tattered history book that was passed from hand to hand in a cold classroom two or three years ago, our instructor showed us a sign that had been painted on walls along part of the downtown of Leningrad:

"Citizens! During artillery bombardment this side of the street is especially dangerous."

That meant that even with the constant shelling, the battered citizens who went to work at the tank factories, or the food ministry, or in the city government, were still expected to go to work, and just make note of which side of the street was safer.

With the Creepers, there's something similar whenever their orbital battle station is in view, even if it's just for a few minutes. That had been the home base of the Creepers, overseeing the continued occupation and destruction of Earth, and even though it didn't make much difference when it was visible or not—the killer stealth satellites in orbit were capable of hitting you or your building or your vehicle, day or night—people hunkered down, or walked along a wall or under the trees.

But in other times, we crazy kids in the military would just sit out in the open.

Like right now.

I'm stretched out on a stretch of grass kept mowed by Navy personnel here, at Naval Support Activity Saratoga Springs, a small military base in upstate New York I never knew existed. My dog Thor, a Belgian Malinois who is supposedly a descendant of Cairo, the dog that went in with the SEALs when they zapped Osama bin Laden some decades ago, is stretched out, his head resting on my full belly. Around me are members of my platoon—Lileks, Balantic, Melendez—and all of us have full bellies, and are sharing a cold bottle of Coca-Cola.

Balantic, a young girl barely in her teens, holds up the Coke bottle and takes a swig, then passes it over to Lileks, another young girl that has burn cream on half of her face from yesterday's battle. "These Navy squids . . . they sure live large. What the hell are they doing up here in New York?"

Melendez says, "Research."

"What kind of research?" she asks.

"Research in how best to piss you off," he says, and there's some laughter at that.

It's a sweet blue day in October and I shouldn't be here, I should be with my crew back in New Hampshire, at Ft. St. Paul, but this is as good as place as any. I scratch Thor's ears and he whines and settles in some more, and then a quiet voice says, "There they are, the buggy bastards."

We all look up and yes, there it is, the orbital battle station for the

Creepers, silently moving across in the sky. Even in low Earth orbit it's big enough to be visible in the daylight, and the jagged oval structure slips by as we stare up at it.

When it finally disappears between a distant line of trees, Lileks says, "Who knew they had a second one."

"Who knows anything," Balantic says. "Hey, Sarge."

"Right here," I say.

"You said something, back at the Air Force base, the . . ."

"Stratton," I say. "It was Stratton."

"Yeah, right, well, you said something about how the Air Force destroyed the original orbital battle station two months back. Can't they do it again?"

"I doubt it."

Melendez says, "Sarge, why not? If they can do it once, they can do it again."

I rub Thor's ears some more. He twitches. I wonder what he's dreaming. I hope he's dreaming about chasing rabbits or squirrels, and not mechanized monsters that came light-years just to kill and drown us all.

"It was a hell of a job," I say. "Remember your history, okay? When the Creepers first arrived in the system, most all of the scientists thought it was a cluster of comets . . . until it was too late. And when they set up station in LEO and started their attacks, about a half-dozen nations who had the capability returned fire, from ground-based missiles, submarine-based missiles, aircraft borne, and a few classified satellite killers in orbit . . . and none of them even got near."

"Yeah," Lileks says. "I don't think none of us skipped school that day. Melendez is right . . . you talked to an Air Force colonel who was part of the attack, right?"

That bright memory comes to me, of spending a few precious moments alone with Colonel Victor Minh, back at the Red House in Albany, as he told me the still-secret tale of how the attack took place.

I say, "It took years of planning. Years. Couriers and ground communications with other countries . . . Russia, China, Japan, to set up a time for a diversionary attack. Then Air Force crews managed to salvage some solid-fuel rocket boosters from a factory in . . . Nevada, I think."

"Utah," Balantic says. "Morton-Thiokol. They made rocket engines. That makes sense . . . Sarge."

"So it does," I say. "They dragged those solid-fuel rocket boosters to some site, and they started making one-person crew capsules for them, using wood, plastic, anything that would help slip by whatever sensors the Creepers were using. Each capsule also had a warhead . . . and when it came to launch, it was light the rocket and step back. Once those solid-fuel rockets were torched, up they went . . . and minutes before the launch, those countries all launched some of their surviving ICBMs or satellite killers to the orbital battle station . . . so the Creepers thought they were under attack from the usual hardware us poor earthlings still had."

My little trio here is part of my battered platoon that belongs to K Company, 1st Battalion, 14th Army Regiment, also known as Kara's Killers, and none of them are more than fifteen years old.

"They sure had the element of surprise," I say. "Eight missiles went up. One blew up right after takeoff, scattering the missile and the poor pilot over the desert. So you've got seven going up . . . and one is the squadron leader. The only capsule that has a heat shield and a possibility of reentry, so he can report back on what happened. The other six . . . they're on a one-way suicide mission. They all knew it, they all volunteered, and they all went in and destroyed the Creepers' orbital station."

Silence at that. The open air feels nice. It also feels nice to be goofing off without any duty to perform. I say, "So I'm sure the Air Force is planning how to get up there again and repeat the success, but a lot is going to depend on who wants to suicide him or herself in the process."

Balantic says, "I heard that colonel got the Medal of Honor."

"That's right," I say. "Colonel Victor Minh. I was there, at the Red House, when he got it."

Lileks says, "I hear you got the Silver Star at the same time."

Any evasion or answer on my part is interrupted when a Navy gal comes over, short blonde hair, black-rimmed glasses, wearing the weird blue/gray-patterned fatigues that the Navy uses. She has chevrons that I can't puzzle out, but it's obvious from the way she moves and asks that she's an NCO of some sort.

"You Knox?" she asks me.

"That's what my nametag says."

"Well, the rest of your skinny ass better say the same thing," she replies. She juts a thumb behind her. "My CO wants to see you. Now."

"Good for him," I say. "Or her. What's the deal?"

"There's no deal," she says. "Commander Morong wants you, pal. So get to it."

"Sorry," I say. "He's not in my chain of command. I kinda like it here on the grass. Tell me, you folks really mow the grass? For real?"

The rest of my squad snickers and smiles, and then the Navy NCO smiles, too. "Yeah, I heard you could be a pain in the ass. Captain Wallace, she's there, too. And she told me to get you moving."

I wake up Thor and he instantly snaps-to, but since things are calm and there isn't any Creeper sign in the vicinity, he relaxes. I rub his shoulders and get up, and I say, "Lead on, ma'am."

"Outstanding," she says, and I note her nametag says RESPERS.

We start walking to one of the low-slung buildings marking this Navy outpost in this part of rural New York State, and after a few steps I ask, "Any idea what this is about?"

"Sure," she says, and she keeps her mouth shut.

I give her that. I was being a pain in the ass. Part of who I am, and my age, of course.

"Ma'am, sorry I gave you grief back there," I say. "It's been a long few days. I was just letting off steam."

"Fair enough, Sergeant Knox," she says. "It seems Commander Morong wants to talk to you about something."

"Like what?"

"Like you shooting a member of the United States intelligence services last night."

At the guard station inside the building, access is being controlled by two young Shore Patrol NCOs, who wave in Respers and check my identification. The chairs and tables are all back where they belong, unlike last night, where I followed in Captain Kara Wallace and the rest of our platoon when we barged in here and took control of the facility.

There are no Army personnel in sight.

It looks like the Navy has control of its base back again.

The SP guy on the right, who's plump under his odd-colored

fatigues, passes over my Armed Services ID and says, "The dog can't go in."

"Sure he can," I say. "I'll even hold the door open for him."

The other Shore Patrol guy holds a hand in front of his face, maybe to hide a smile, but his partner says, "Bud, I got my orders. No animals in the building."

"He's not an animal, you moron," I say, probably sharper than I should have. "He's a member of the N.H. National Guard, with his own pay and quarters, and he's fought against more Creepers in a month than you've probably seen your entire life. So we both go in, or none of us do."

Thor senses the stress in my voice and lets out a low growl, and even though I've heard it scores of times, the sound can still make me shiver. Both Shore Patrol guys step back and Respers says, "Banson, give it a rest. C'mon."

A glass door is unlocked and opened for us, and we walk down a clean hallway, lit by gas lanterns. There's a door marked COMMANDING OFFICER and Respers knocks, and a muffled voice from inside calls out "Enter!" and, in doing so, my whole life gets changed and upended.

There are two people in the large office, Captain Kara Wallace, whose unit I've been with during the past several days, and a Navy officer in a khaki shirt and trousers. I nod to Captain Wallace but don't salute—occasionally we've gotten a chance to watch prewar movies, and I can't believe how many times those old directors had their actors salute indoors or without the personnel having their covers on—but she doesn't acknowledge my presence. She just looks at the Navy commander with a placid face, her short red hair looking recently washed, even her facial burn scars looking clean.

"Have a seat, Sergeant Knox," he says. "I'm Commander Ben Morong."

"Sir," I say, deciding to be polite.

Commander Morong is old, in his thirties, I'd guess, with once-black hair that's almost been entirely overtaken by white. His face is puffy and leathery, and his nose looks like it's been broken a couple of times. His office is tidy with the usual bookshelves, filing cabinets, and "look at me" plaques and photos, but I instantly note something wrong: He's in none of the photos.

"Sergeant Knox, you're not permanently assigned to Captain Wallace's platoon, am I correct?"

"That's right, sir. I'm in Second Recon Rangers, 'Avenger' Company, First Battalion, New Hampshire Army National Guard."

He rubs at his face with both hands. "Which division?"

"The Yankee Division," I say. "The 26th." Then I add, "My duty station is in Ft. St. Paul, in Concord."

He lowers his hands. "Long way from home."

"Yes, sir."

Morong picks up a typewritten sheet of paper. "Mind telling me how it was that you broke into a Navy facility last night and nearly fatally shot one . . . Hoyt Cranston."

I look to Wallace and she's ignoring my glance.

All up to me, I guess.

I say, "Sir, he started it."

Morong's eyes widen. "He started it? What the hell do you think this is, a school playground?"

"I don't know what a school playground is, sir, but I do know this," I say. "Mister Cranston and his deceptive activities caused the death of numerous members of Captain Wallace's company. He also illegally seized and took prisoner two Army personnel, Corporal Serena Coulson and her brother, Buddy, and forces under his command shot and killed their father, also an active duty Army officer."

I pause, take a breath, go on. "While at this facility last night, he threatened me with a pistol. I shot in self-defense. General Scopes, the officer in command, said in the presence of witnesses that I did act in self-defense. Sir."

Morong slowly nods, slides a sheet of paper to one side. "Not a bad recitation, young man."

"Thank you, sir."

"Plus the fact that Mister Cranston was arrested on other charges a few hours ago will no doubt overshadow . . . your circumstances."

"Sir?"

He glances at the sheet again. "Mister Cranston was arrested by the FBI on charges of domestic terrorism. It seems he and a small group managed to secure a Creeper arthropod and use its weapons for a few terrorist attacks . . . including one on a train in western Massachusetts several days ago."

I was on that train. I saw the attack, and I also saw how Thor didn't respond to the nearby arthropod, and it makes sense. There was no bug inside, controlling it. Nope, some human attempting to kill Serena Coulson's brother Buddy, one of the only humans I know who can communicate with the Creepers.

But I keep my mouth shut.

Morong says, "I understand you've been on active duty for four years."

"Yes, sir, since I was twelve."

He leans back in his chair a bit. "Just to update you, Sergeant, General Scopes is not the officer in command here. I have been now for . . ." He checks his watch. "For at least the last eight hours. Somehow the CNO found out what the hell was going on over here at Saratoga and told me to come in and clean shop. I've debriefed Captain Wallace and others, and the shop has been cleaned. Your little adventure last night is now also concluded to the Navy's satisfaction."

He turns in his chair and says, "Captain Wallace?"

"Commander."

"I've ordered the motor pool to prepare transportation for you and the other members of your troop. How long will you need to prepare?"

She shrugs, and I note a slight smile on her face. She and the rest of Kara's Killers that are here are going home, with me and Thor in tow. I suddenly feel loose limbed and relaxed, even with everything that's gone on for the past several days, even knowing my dad is out there somewhere at a medical facility, being treated for losing his leg in a Creeper attack yesterday.

"Commander, I'd say within an hour."

Morong says, "Make it three. I want your folks to get another meal at the mess hall, with full rations for your trip back to . . . where the hell are you located?"

My captain says, "We're a mobile strike force that used to be at Ft. Drum before it got smoked. Now we're semibased in Rome."

"I see. With luck, reasonable roads, and no Creeper attention, you should get back home by the end of the day."

Wallace stands up and says, "Thank you, Commander. You've been very gracious."

"Hah," Morong says. "Gracious, hell, I'm just trying to keep on top of things." He glances out the window and in a reflective tone says,

"Look at me, commanding a desk hundreds of miles away from the ocean. Before the war I was stationed aboard a cruiser, the USS *Bunker Hill*. Sweet ship, fine crew. I was away on leave when the Creepers struck. She's still there, from what I hear. One of these days I intend to get back there . . . they say when it's low tide, you can still make out her overturned hull."

He stares out the window and Wallace and I leave.

Outside in the hallway she softly closes the door and Wallace whispers, "Whew, that was too close by far. I was sure with our little mission last night, breaking and entering, and you shooting the man from Langley, that we'd all be in the brig tonight."

We start walking and Thor ambles along, sniffing here and there, no doubt because he's not used to being in strange buildings, and I say, "Me, too, Captain. I'm looking forward to the trip."

Wallace stops, right under a gas lamp that does odd things with shadows on her worn face. "Oh, Randy."

Her using my first name really gets my attention. "Captain?"

"Randy," she says, "you're not coming with us."

CHAPTER TWO

Outside of the administration building, the sun is still up in the sky, but I don't feel particularly warm. We take our time along the clean sidewalk and she says, "You were temporarily assigned to us, to provide intelligence when we went after that Creeper Dome."

"Domes."

"Sure, there were two Domes, but that mission is over. It's time for you to go back to your own unit, in New Hampshire."

For some reason my throat is choked up. I can't speak.

Wallace says, "Sergeant, don't you want to go back to Ft. St. Paul?"

"Sure I do, Captain."

"Then what's the problem?"

"Well . . . ma'am, I've sort of gotten used to being with you and the company."

"And your platoon," she says.

"That, too," I say. "Then there's my dad, ma'am. I'd like to find out where he is, maybe visit him. But . . ."

My voice dribbles off. Wallace's voice, though, gets stronger. "I'm surprised you haven't learned this, in your four years of service, Sergeant Knox. The requirements of the service supersede your own personal needs. I'm sure that your unit back in Concord will welcome you back. They must be shorthanded with you and your K-9 unit deployed elsewhere, especially with your experience."

"Yes, ma'am," I say, feeling like a dopy recruit.

Then her voice softens. "There's a convoy heading through here

15

tomorrow. They're going to Connecticut and then Massachusetts, and they'll be passing by a bus station at their end destination. I'll make sure you have a travel chit ready for you and your dog, and you'll be on your way home."

"Yes, ma'am," I repeat.

She says, "And you'll have full rations and kit before you leave. Anything else?"

"No, ma'am."

Wallace surprises me by giving me a gentle tap on my shoulder. "Before I leave, I also promise to find out where your dad is and how he's doing. Fair enough?"

That lightens my mood. "That'd be great . . . Captain."

"Good," she says. "Now, if you'll excuse me, I've got a hell of a lot of work to do. Feel free to join us at the mess."

"Yes, Captain," I say.

But I choose to skip the mess and the food and the fun chattering among my squad and the other troopers, and I mope around until I see Corporal Serena Coulson, standing at the edge of a paved lot, with a knapsack at her feet, with her quiet and very scary younger brother Buddy standing next to her.

Serena is one year younger than me, with a pretty, flawless face and long blonde hair, and she's wearing clean Army fatigues and turns and smiles at my approach. It's against regulations but we hug and she kisses my cheek and says, "Buddy and I are going back with Captain Wallace."

"Oh," I say, and my gut feels heavy. Serena and I have a relationship of sorts, with some hand-holding, kissing, and affection, but things have changed a lot in the past few days. I had been hoping that she might be going back with me to New Hampshire, and now, well . . .

She doesn't seem to note my disappointment. "We're going back to that hidden Air Force installation in Stratton. Captain Wallace thinks me and"—she turns to her brother—"Buddy belong there. Isn't that right, Buddy?"

Her brother, out on medical leave from the Army, just stares out, his face blank, wearing blue jeans rolled up at the legs and a too-large old sweatshirt that says NAVY. He stands still, not even moving when Thor comes up to him, whining and pushing his muzzle up against his still hands.

"Buddy?" I ask. "Thor wants some attention."

The twelve-year-old boy doesn't move, doesn't say a word. Thor keeps on nuzzling him. Serena slips her sweet arm into mine. "Poor Buddy. He's been like that since . . . last night."

"When we saw the replacement battle station up there in the sky."

"That's right."

I like the sensation of her arm through mine, and I don't want to disturb her, but I also need to know something. "Last night, Buddy said something about the battle station. He said, 'Please don't send me up there again.' Serena . . . what does that mean?"

Serena slowly withdraws her arm from mine, and I feel a slight tingle of defeat. But she doesn't move, doesn't break away.

"Serena?"

She says, "Last year . . . some men came to our station, up near Bar Harbor. At Jackson Labs. A woman was with them as well. They met with Dad, and Buddy. I wasn't allowed in. They . . . took him away for a couple of weeks. Then he was gone, about a month."

I kept quiet.

"I should have done more," she says. "I was his older sister. It was my responsibility. When he came back . . . it was worse. He had suffered when he was with the Observation Corps, all that standing around at night, looking up at the sky with telescopes, trying to track the killer stealth satellites. But he changed."

"He learned some of the Creeper language."

"Yes."

"The battle station . . . he must have gotten up there somehow."

"I . . . I only found that out last night, same as you."

"How did he get up there? And how did he get back?"

Serena says, "I don't know."

"Serena . . ."

She snaps at me, "Randy, I don't know! Why don't you ask him yourself?"

Not a bad suggestion. I step closer to Buddy and gently take his arm. "Buddy, it's me. Randy. And Thor. You like Thor. C'mon, tell me, what happened up there? How did you get there? Who took you?"

Buddy doesn't say a word.

And neither do I.

I let loose of his arm, and I now see closer, what's going on.

His whole body is trembling, like he's seized with a fear so strong that he just might faint.

I step back. "It's okay, pal. Sorry."

Horns honk from the other side of the building, and I help Serena with her gear, as we head to the sound of grumbling engines. She takes Buddy's hand and she says, "Time to go," and he walks with her with no resistance.

As we go along, Thor sticking close to Buddy, tail wagging, Serena says, "How about you? Are you coming back with us?"

"No."

Now she takes my hand. "Going back to Ft. St. Paul?"

I say, "That's where I belong . . . but it feels different, now. So many days away from the base, so much that's gone on . . ."

"How's your dad?"

"Not sure," I say. "Captain Wallace says she's going to find out what she can. Last she heard, though, is that he's doing okay, even with one leg gone."

We turn a corner and three vehicles are lined up, with the members of First Platoon, Kara's Killers, gathered around. Serena sighs. "My dad . . . nobody knows where he's buried. Or if they do know, they're not telling. I . . . you're lucky, Randy. Even with your dad hurt like that, you've got him still. My dad . . . last I saw, he was shot, helping me and Buddy escape. And nobody knows where his body is."

"I'll try to find out."

She squeezes my hand, and we move forward, and First Sergeant Hesketh comes to us, an old guy with leathery skin and a leathery attitude, and he says, "Corporal Coulson, if you and your brother will follow me."

I follow as well, and I look on with amazement now at the three vehicles that will be taking Kara's Killers home. They're prewar pickup trucks, with double cabs and a bed in the back, and they're painted dark blue with yellow letters on the side of the doors: U.S. NAVY OFFICIAL BUSINESS ONLY.

Balantic says, "Look at that, will you? Traveling in style. Up front and in real cushioned seats."

"Looks great," I say, my words empty. I should be looking forward to going back home to Ft. St. Paul, but I've fought with these guys, and have eaten and drunk with them, and have served with them in rain and sunshine, night and day.

I realize how much I'm going to miss them.

There's laughter and a few shouts, and gear is passed up and put in the rear of the trucks, and then Commander Morong comes out, and confabs with Captain Wallace. One by one the members of First Platoon come forward and shake my hand, and there's murmured words of thanks, and good wishes, and the ever popular "keep in touch."

But they don't stick around. They want to get moving, and I don't blame them. Doors open up and each pickup truck has a Navy driver, and from the sound of the engines, I note they're all diesel. Not electric, not steam, not coal or wood powered. Diesel. The Navy is sure going all out to help their fellow service members.

For a moment I lose track of Serena, and then I see her blonde hair from inside of the second truck, and I go over, and she rolls down the window, extends a hand, and I squeeze it. I so want to give her a kiss, but in the midst of all these troopers, I see how it won't work.

Serena holds my hand with two of hers. "Randy . . . you know where I'm going. Write to me, all right? And I promise, I swear, I'll write you back."

"Deal," I say, and then I say, "Buddy, be a good guy. Don't fight."

He just stares straight ahead.

Thor jumps up, puts both of his paws on the side of the door, and he whines.

Buddy turns his head.

Thor yelps with pleasure.

Buddy looks to my K-9 buddy, and for the very briefest of moments, so quick I wonder if I'm imagining it, he slightly nods, moves his mouth in what could be the beginning of a smile, and then he turns back.

I decide that's good enough, and I say, "Be safe, Serena."

"You too, Sergeant," she says, and she rolls up the window.

"Sergeant Knox!" comes a voice, and at the head of the three-vehicle convoy is Captain Wallace, and since the both of us are wearing our covers, I salute her as I approach and she salutes right back.

She's smiling. "I just got a telegraph from the Red Cross about your dad. He's in stable condition, and he's being transferred to the VA center in Northampton, Massachusetts."

My feet and hands suddenly feel light and airy, like they're made of paper. "Captain . . . that's great news. Thanks, thanks so very much."

Wallace steps over to me. "Glad I could pass it along. When you visit him, give him my best, will you?"

I have a brief memory, of seeing her and my dad kissing and in an embrace a couple of days ago. At the time, it bothered the hell out of me, thinking Dad was somehow betraying the memory of Mom. But now . . . it's been ten years since Mom and my older sister Melissa died, in the first attacks. Who was I to tell my dad what or what not to do?

"Captain, I'll make sure I do that."

"Good." Her face changes, as she looks up and down at me and says, "Knox, why are you out of uniform?"

I'm puzzled. "Ma'am?"

She smiles wider, reaches into a pocket, pulls out something that she presses in my right hand. I open up my hand, see that I'm now in possession of a set of single silver bars.

"Fix that, Lieutenant, will you?"

"Captain . . ."

She reaches up, removes the metal chevrons of a sergeant from my collar tabs, replaces them with the lieutenant bars. "It's a battlefield commission, and it might be reversed, but I doubt it. The first sergeant and I can write one hell of a recommendation."

"Ma'am . . ."

"There," she says, stepping back. "Lieutenant, safe travels, and good luck back at Ft. St. Paul. If you care to drop a line to me at some point, to let me know how your dad is doing, and you, and that mutt . . . well, that would be a delight."

"I'll make sure."

One of the Navy drivers honks a horn. "Time to leave," she says.

Damn it, tears are in my eyes. She turns and I call out, "Captain?"

"Yes, Lieutenant Knox?"

Lieutenant Knox. It's going to take a long while to get used to that.

I salute. "Ma'am, it was an honor and privilege to serve with you, and your troops."

She returns the salute. "Very well, Randy."

Then she surprises me, and everyone else who's looking, when she comes to me, gives me an embrace and a kiss on the cheek, and then goes to the lead pickup truck. With a roar of engines and honking horns, they soon leave, and I'm by myself with Thor and no one else.

I touch the side of my cheek.

I guess I got my kiss after all.

CHAPTER THREE

The next morning it's overcast, and I'm standing outside again in the parking area, and Thor is lying on the grass, content and breathing softly after scarfing down sausage at this morning's breakfast. My battle pack is stuffed with supplies and rations, and over my shoulder is my M-10 Colt, freshly cleaned, and I have a bandolier of six shells around my shoulder. I'm wearing a MOLLE vest with the usual stuff hanging off that, and my helmet is dangling from the side. My 9 mm Beretta is holstered at my waist, and I wait.

I should feel pretty good, happy, content. I'm now a lieutenant, I'm well fed, I took a shower last night and one this morning, and I'm safe, relatively secure, and I'm heading home.

But I don't feel good, happy, or much of anything else. In between eating, sleeping, showering, and getting ready to go home, I've talked to a number of Navy personnel and a few civilians at this base, and none of them can tell me anything about the shooting death of Major Thomas Coulson, the father of Serena and Buddy. I get grunts, denials, and shrugs. That's it.

"Lieutenant Knox."

Coming up the concrete pathway is Commander Morong, looking fresh and crisp in his Navy khakis. In the short time I've been here, I have to admire the Navy: Their uniforms are nice and freshly washed, and they have pretty good chow.

"Good morning, Commander," I say.

He looks up at the clouds and says, "Rain coming."

"Yep."

He says, "Those asteroid strikes in the oceans, not only did they wash away cities and most of the world's navies, they pretty much screwed up our weather for the next couple of centuries."

"That's what I hear, sir."

Morong crosses his arms. "Sorry you ran into brick walls last night."

"Sir?"

He says, "Lieutenant . . . for a while this little out-of-the-way naval installation was taken over by Mister Cranston and his . . . associates. Decades ago they did things in chasing terrorists that were highly controversial. Now? They're doing what they can to kill aliens, and worry about history later."

"They shot and killed the father of a friend of mine."

"I'm sure they did," he says. He lets his arms drop and says, "Those who did that ran for the hills once you and Captain Wallace got here. The ones that are here . . . they don't want to think about it anymore. You looking for whatever justice last night was a good effort. But don't let it chew at you. There's so much more to worry about."

"I'm not looking for justice," I say, lying slightly to the Navy officer. "I'm looking for a body to bury."

The sound of engines comes to us. Thor slowly gets up, stretches, yawns. Morong turns, offers a hand. I give it a shake. Morong says, "I'll see what I can do. But don't count on it."

"Thanks, sir," I say.

Then he turns, and the convoy rolls in, and I grab my gear.

There's an up-armored Humvee in the lead, and one in the rear. In between are two old steam-powered M35 transport trucks, an oil tanker, and a battered New York MTA bus. The door to the bus slides open and a tough-looking Asian woman comes out, wearing oil- and dirt-stained fatigues, and chevron pins marking a staff sergeant and a name tag denoting NAKAMURA. She has two pistols holstered at her belt, and is carrying a sawed-off pump-action shotgun in her dirty hands.

"You Knox?" she asks.

"I am," I say, wondering if I should push the point of her having to salute me, but no, I've been a lieutenant less than a full day, and I'm still learning. Besides, I'm a passenger on this trip, not an officer.

She juts a thumb to the open door of the bus. "Then let's haul it. All right?" She gets back into the bus and I follow her in.

About half of the seats are taken by soldiers, a few dozing with their arms crossed, mouths open. There are overhead bins, doors removed, and they are stuffed with duffel bags, knapsacks, and a few weapons, none of them M-10s. I find two empty seats near the front, by the driver's seat—occupied by a chubby African-American female driver who's tapping a dial on the bus's instrument panel—and take one, trying my best to store my gear, and Thor sniffs the seat, jumps in, and takes up his and most of mine.

"Nice job, bud," I say.

He just grins at me.

Nakamura comes back and says to the driver. "Let's go, Diller. Time's a wastin'."

"Yes, ma'am," she says.

Diller closes the door, honks the horn, and the convoy starts moving out, and within a couple of minutes, we've left the Saratoga Naval Station.

Nakamura is sitting across from me, looking through a clipboard, and then checks me out and says, "Just the M-10, Lieutenant?"

"And a pistol."

She laughs, flips through some pages. "Won't be any good against a Coastie ambush."

I don't like her tone. "No, but if a Creeper comes trotting after us, I'd rather have my M-10 than an M-4."

"Won't see no Creepers," she says.

"That a guarantee?"

Nakamura looks up from the clipboard. "I've been running this express for three years. We even get a couple of miles close to a Creeper Dome in Connecticut. But I've never seen a Creeper out in the open. You know why?"

"Do tell, Sergeant."

She says, "We move fast, we move on the most remote roads, and we don't keep to a set pattern . . . and we don't make any threatening moves, like heading fast to that Creeper Dome. Haven't seen a Creeper in all those times."

"Nice to be safe," I say.

"Oh, we're not that safe," she says. "We've been hit three times, and each time by a Coastie gang. Looking for food, fuel . . . women. Each time we fought them off. Each time we didn't manage to take any prisoners. Fortunes of war."

I nod. "Good job."

"Yeah, well, they should have stayed in their refugee camps."

"Those camps have been up for ten years. I guess some get tired of the camps."

"Well, better than to get tired from a 5.56 mm round through your skull."

She goes back to her paperwork and there's a tap on my shoulder. I swivel in my seat and there are two soldiers back there, about a year younger than me, and with each of them wearing name tags saying POWERS, I make a good guess that they're brothers.

"Yeah?"

"Sorry to bother you, Lieutenant . . . but you've fought Creepers, for real?" asks the one on the left.

They've got rough complexions, black hair trimmed back real short, and are wearing specialist tags in the center of their BDUs.

"That's right," I say.

The one on the right says, "Lots?"

"Enough."

"What's it like?"

I say, "What's your MOS?"

"Tommy and me," the left one says, "We're mechanics. I mean, we wanted to get into infantry but—"

"Ross and me," his brother says, almost apologetically, "we grew up on a big farm, north of Albany. Started working with tools almost as soon as we could walk . . . could repair much of everything that had an engine or wheels. Like Ross says, you know, when we enlisted, we wanted to get into infantry . . ."

I say, "Guys, don't feel bad. If it weren't for wrench pullers like you, we'd still be running around on horses."

They smile and Ross says, "That your dog?"

Technically, it was the Army's dog, but I say, "You better believe it."

"He hunt Creepers?"

"The best."

Shyly, his brother Tommy says, "You kill many Creepers?"

I'm tired now, and just say, "Not enough," and I turn back, rub Thor's head. He shifts around on the seat so he can drop his leg on my lap, and I let him. I rub his back, past the burnt fur and the scar tissue, and he settles in, legs draped over the aisle. The smooth rocking motion of the old MTA bus makes me drowsy and I fall asleep.

I wake up when there's a horn honk, and we pull over to the side of the road. Despite ten years having gone for most road and bridge repair, this stretch is relatively smooth, with few potholes and cracks in the pavement. We're in an old shopping center, something called a strip mall, and it looks like there had once been five stores here, all in a row, but the windows are smashed and the roofs have collapsed. There's also about a dozen prewar cars, on flattened tires, windshields milky white, paint faded. I get out with Thor and stretch my legs, and he trots over to an old Saab and lifts his leg, peeing against a flat tire.

Funny thing, I see that all of the little doors on the side of the cars, marking where the fuel caps were located, are still open. Some enterprising soul or two no doubt drained these dead cars—dead because the NUDETs fried the electronics—of their precious fuel.

Other soldiers come out of the bus, yawning and talking, a few sharing a cigarette or half-smoked cigar. The armored-up Humvees take covering positions on either end of the lot, and from a wide dirt road in the trees, two horse-drawn wagons appear, riding up to Sergeant Nakamura. It seems she knows the drivers for each wagon, for there's laughter, handshakes, and papers exchanged, and then the wagons go up to the side of the two transport trucks. Canvas tarps are pulled away and in a few minutes, bushels of corn are being unloaded from the wagon and brought into the trucks.

I wander around, M-10 slung over my back. I'm enjoying being out in the fresh air, and I'm just letting random thoughts roll by, of being back in Ft. St. Paul eventually, seeing Abby Monroe, a combat courier that I've been dating, wondering if I'll ever tell her about Serena, thinking I didn't have to decide that now, and I just kick at the dead leaves, look around again.

Other soldiers are now sitting on the ground, legs stretched out, chatting it up. The Humvees are still there, but the doors are open, and troopers are hanging around the open doors. Each gunner is leaning over his 50-caliber machine gun.

I suddenly don't like it.

They're too relaxed, too unaware.

I pause.

I'm just a freshly made lieutenant, heading home, and this wasn't my unit. It was Sergeant Nakamura's, and she knows the turf, she knows the routine.

I don't.

So it wouldn't do for me to override her, start issuing orders, and being a pain in the ass. Besides, for a few days earlier, I had been running a platoon for the first time in my life, and I was tired of being in charge. I'm a Recon Ranger, assigned with Thor to go out and hunt Creepers, and that's the job I was trained for, and one I loved.

The wagons are nearly all unloaded. I check my watch. Not even 10 a.m. yet. I wonder where and how this convoy was going to get lunch. I had rations and other stuff squirreled away in my battlepack, but I didn't want to start dipping in there yet, unless it was a snack for Thor—

Thor.

Where is he?

I yell, "Thor, come!"

I spin around, checking my 360.

No Thor.

Oh boy, I really don't like it now.

Where's my guy?

The last I saw he was relieving himself over by that dead Saab, but right now there's just a drying puddle of dog pee to mark where he'd been.

"Thor!"

The two Powers brothers, sharing a cigarette, point to the far end of the crumbling buildings and one says, "Loo, I think I saw him over there."

I start to trot over to that last crumbled building, which looks like it had been a bank, and lots of not-so-good thoughts tumble along in my mind, including that even in some of the more rural stretches, dogs are at risk from hunters for obvious and stomach-churning reasons.

"Thor!"

And just like that, my big boy runs around the corner of the broken-down bank, running straight at me, and I'm filled with so much relief that it takes me a long number of seconds to hear my boy.

He's barking.

Barking loud.

And not because he's happy to see me.

I stop in my tracks, put both hands up around my mouth and yell back to the convoy:

"Creepers!"

CHAPTER FOUR

I tug my bulky and heavy Colt M-10 from my back, pull a round from my bandolier, and I arm the round by spinning the base from SAFE to arm it, setting it in the middle range—twenty-five meters—and loading it into the Colt's breech as I run back to the parked vehicles of the convoy.

"Creepers!" I yell again, and the soldiers just freeze for a moment, most looking to Nakamura for guidance, and she looks equally pissed and confused, and she says, "Lieutenant, how in hell do you know there's Creepers out there?"

Thor is barking, barking, fur bristling, and I yell, "My K-9 is keying on an approaching Creeper! Get this convoy out of here!"

Nakamura says, "How do you know it's not a dead Creeper out there—"

"Sergeant, get these vehicles moving!"

And bless the old sergeant, her training kicks in, and she goes to one truck, and I go to the other, and I slap the door and tell the driver, "Go, go, go! We got Creeper sign!"

The drivers don't wait, and with a belch and a bellow, they start grinding their way out of the parking lot, and it sounds cold and cruel, but it's so very true, that in this interstellar war, trucks and gear are more important to save than bodies.

The farmers are also speeding away, the drivers standing up, working the reins, yelling at their horses to get moving. Bushels of corn bounce off the rear of the open wagons, tumbling to the ground. The armored Humvees button up and back away, even though their powerful machine guns are a waste against aliens. At the MTA bus there's a frenzy of soldiers climbing in, others getting out, weapons and gear being tossed, and that engine starts up as well.

Nakamura runs to the bus, yelling, "Off! Off! Everybody off that bus!"

Diller yells back, "It's my bus goddamn it, my bus!"

She starts driving out of the parking lot, two troopers tumbling out, and the tractor trailer unit hauling the fuel tanker grinds and grinds. I've got the M-10 up now, looking, seeking, and hating the fact that I'm the only damn soldier here with a weapon that can kill a Creeper. Each cartridge has a binary nerve gas in it, and when the round explodes at the set distance, the cloud—if you're good and the wind isn't blowing too hard—will come up against the Creeper and be brought into its breathing membrane, killing it in its buggy tracks.

I'm scoping left, scoping right, wondering if the Creeper is going to come from one side of the building or the other. Thor is still barking frantically but he's at my side, and then there's the whiff of cinnamon, and then—

Click-click.

Click-click.

Click-click.

Creeper approaching, coming in quick, coming in now, and I'm still looking left, still looking right, when the damn thing comes at us over the roof of the strip mall.

It's a Battle Creeper, segmented arthropod, eight legs moving quick, its two weapons pincers up and ready for attack, and there's yells and some of the M-4s start firing, and from the corner of my eye, I see two soldiers running down the road. The right segmented Creeper arm snaps into their direction and with a quick *flick, flick,* laser bursts take them down at the base of their skulls.

But the Creeper made a mistake. It ignored the threat in front of it. Me.

The M-10 is tight up against my shoulder, I get the Creeper square in the center of my Colt's open iron sights, and—

BLAM!

I'm so very used to it but the recoil still hammers me, and I work the big bolt, eject the spent cartridge, get another round from my bandolier.

So much happens in the next few seconds.

So very much.

There's a satisfying and loud *pop!* as the M-10 round explodes right in front of the Creeper's center arthropod, but the Creeper is still moving, and its other weaponized arm sends out a rolling tongue of flame that laps up against the end of the moving MTA bus. The bus catches fire at its end, wavers, and then hits one, and then two old utility poles before coming to a grinding halt.

But just as that's happening, the gas cloud I've sent down range is enveloping the Creeper, and it skitters back, back, like it's trying to get away, but my shot was too good and for once the wind is in my favor, and the alien is enveloped. It starts to shudder, move to the side, only one set of legs now working, and then it crashes through a weak section of the strip mall's roof, its tail flickering again and then stopping.

There's smoke and the bus is on fire, and a few soldiers get out, dragging their gear, and Diller the driver is the last one off, and she's got a small red fire extinguisher in her hands and she goes to the rear, screaming, "It's my girl, it's my girl!" and she starts spraying at the roiling flames and smoke with small spurts of CO_2, not making a difference at all.

The Humvees are out on the road, their soldiers still looking over their twin 50-caliber machine guns, and I'm maneuvering away, trying to find some cover, and the fuel truck is still grinding and grinding its engine.

Nakamura is in front of me, yelling something and there's movement, and another Creeper emerges from the wooded path where the farmers had escaped. I push her aside, hammer off another shot, and this time, damn it, I've fired too soon. My elevation is off, and the round screams over the Creeper and explodes against a tree, its gas cloud useless.

I yell, "Sergeant, take cover!" as I move with Thor—still barking away—and get behind a black suburban with a bundle of rags and bones in the front seat, and Nakamura says, "Lieutenant, I think—"

A flash of light that hurts my eyes, and Nakamura falls against me, her head lolling on her shoulders, the smell of burnt and scorched flesh, and then her head falls off and her torso hits the cracked pavement.

The Creeper takes its time coming at us, and one Humvee does the right thing and gets the hell out of this bloody and burned mess, but the other Humvee stays put, the twin 50-calibers chattering, and I know that the guy running the Humvee and the gunner are hoping for that magical "golden BB," the one uranium-depleted round that can punch through a crack in the arthropod's segmented body, but there's no magic today.

The Creeper's right arm rolls out another stream of flame and the Humvee is swallowed up so quick and fast there's no time for any screams, and when the arm stops flaming, the Humvee is on fire, the charred gunner up top slumped against her machine guns.

"Thor, silence!" I yell—bless him, but I think we're beyond being warned at this point—and I quickly put in a new cartridge, just as a combination of laser and flames strike the fuel tanker, which goes up in one hell of an impressive ball of fire and smoke that warms my hands and face, even though I'm scores of meters away.

I wait for the smoke to clear some and then I take my time, and in a few seconds, my shoulder and ears are aching again, there's a second dead Creeper in this old parking lot, and three burning vehicles, and a score or so dead troopers.

The live ones are scattered around the lot, crouched behind cars, some carrying their M-4s or other gear, and I step out and yell, "Troopers, rally here! Come on, move your ass!"

By ones and twos, they emerge, and I put another fresh shell in my M-10, and damn it, Thor begins barking again, and I hear that damn noise once more.

Click-click.

Click-click.

Click-click.

Another attack? A third Creeper? For a damn convoy?

"Move it!" I yell out, and with six soldiers coming after me—including the two Powers brothers—we run across the road, into a small drainage ditch, and into the treeline.

I give the ambush area one last glance.

A third and—sweet Jesus—a fourth Creeper are coming around the building, going up and over the old parked cars, moving in our direction, and the last thing I see is the doomed driver of the MTA bus—Diller—desperately tossing handfuls of dirt into the inferno of her burning bus.

Another second later, a Creeper opens fire, and the inferno at the bus expands to take her down.

We run, we run, and run some more. I hold up my arm, chest heaving and hurting. Only three of my crew are armed—two guys and a gal—and the two Powers brothers aren't among them.

I take a deep breath, try to ease my hammering heart. Thor is a couple of meters away, fur bristling, growling, his body tense.

The soldiers are clustered around me. Too tight, they need to scatter, but I don't have time to do things the right away.

"Out of you six, who are the best with the M-4s, hands up, right now."

A brief pause, and the Powers brothers, and an older guy and a young woman join them. The other two boys stand tight, M-4s in their hands. I say to the woman, "You're coming with me. You two . . . give the brothers your M-4s. Now."

They move with some grumbling and whispering, but in a few seconds, the woman—PFC Stella Martin—along with Ross and Tommy Powers, are the only ones armed. I say to the other three, "Scatter. Run. Find your way to a unit or installation, tell them what happened here."

Two of the fortunate three don't have to be told any more than that, including one young boy and the older guy. They bail out, crashing and running through the woods like a fat deer smelling gunmetal.

One of the boys stays behind. He says, "Stella . . ."

"Donny . . ." she says.

Donny is fourteen or fifteen, and he looks behind him, where the ambush took place, and then at Stella, and he says, "Stella . . ."

"Shut up," I say, realizing what's going on. "Stay or go, make up your damn mind. We don't have time to waste."

"Sorry," he whispers, and he turns and he's gone, too.

When the war began, ten years ago, there were lots of horrific stories of fathers abandoning their families, parents abandoning their children, loved ones breaking up, all in a desperate attempt to survive.

Still hard to see, ten years later.

I wince as I hear another boom off in the direction of the shopping center. Maybe one of those vehicles was carrying something explosive, because any remaining gasoline back there would just be sludge by now.

But it means the Creepers are still there, lasing and flaming.

Stella wipes at her eyes and says, "What do we do now, sir?"

For a moment I feel like shaking her hand, for this is the first time in my Army career that anyone in uniform has called me *sir*. Instead I say, "We stretch out in a skirmish line, you with me, Tommy and Ross at my right, and we start moving, as fast and as quiet as we can."

Tommy's face is red, either with fear or excitement. "We gonna fight the Creepers, Lieutenant?"

I call out, "Thor! Pace!" and to the rest of my crew, I say, "Hell, no. We're going to get moving and survive. Let's go."

I don't have a compass, I don't have my battlepack, I don't have a lot, but I'm doing the best I can. From where the sun is setting I can tell we're moving west, but I have no idea where in hell we are. My squad doesn't know either, and the only thing we're certain of is that we've left New York State and we're either in Massachusetts or Connecticut.

It's mostly brush and trees we push through, and I keep our breaks as quick as possible, stopping for a breath and to take sips from the two canteens that PFC Martin managed to carry with her. And that's about it for supplies, save a couple of food bars that Ross Powers was carrying in his trousers.

At one break we're in a rocky area, and there's stream nearby, and Martin fills up her canteen, and the Powers brothers take a moment, bringing up water in their cupped hands. I'm glad for the water. We can go days without food, but water . . . that's another story.

But I'm hoping it won't come to that. I'm hoping that at some point, we'll hit a road, or a farmhouse, or something that will lead us to an Army unit, somewhere we can report the ambush and get hooked up with the nearest installation.

Hope.

Thor should be lapping at the water, refreshing himself, but he's not. He's about two meters away, staring at where we've come from, and he's on full alert. Martin comes up to me with a canteen, I take a cold and refreshing swig, and she says, "Your K-9 . . . what's going on?"

"Creepers are following us."

Her eyes are puffy and red rimmed, either from the smoke earlier on, from seeing her boyfriend run away. "But . . . in basic, they told us that Creepers usually stick around their Domes, only come out for raids or to hit military targets. There are only four of us here! Why should they be following us?"

Ross comes up from the stream, wiping his wet hands on his fatigue jacket, his M-4 slung over his shoulder. "Because they're aliens. We can't understand 'em, we never will."

Tommy joins him, carrying the M-4 at port arms. "I don't hear anything. Or smell anything. Aren't you supposed to hear or smell 'em?"

"My dog does," I say, "and that's all that counts. Let's get going."

It looks like we have a couple of hours of daylight left, and I'm confident we'll run into something marking civilization, but we don't. It's hard making way without a compass without going in circles, but I do my best by trying to aim in the direction of one landmark—like a stand of birch trees—and checking off another landmark—like a fallen pine tree trunk—and proceeding that way. It's awkward, difficult and slow, but I sure as hell don't want to circle back to our alien pursuers.

After our third rest break, Tommy Powers comes to me, face lit with excitement, and he says, "I see light reflecting from something, Lieutenant. Like a window."

"Show me," I say, and he leads me to a clump of boulders, and climbing up, I see where he points. Sure enough, the setting sun is reflecting off something. I slap him on the back. "Good eyes. Let's see what it is."

We start to move in that direction—a bit to the southwest, it looks like—and for a few minutes, we lose track of the light, but the woods are definitely thinning out. Maybe a farmhouse, maybe some sort of outlying community, I don't know, but a reflection like that means glass, and glass doesn't come up naturally.

Now we're on a slope, and it's rough going and I see open areas, and then there's metal in the distance, and Martin says, "Looks like something, Loo, it looks like—"

We all break into a run, get up to the top of the slope, and look around us.

Damn.

Ross swears and wipes at his sweaty forehead. "A crash site. That's all. A goddamn crash site."

We move slowly through the old burnt tree trunks and the scattered chunks of metal, plastic, and wire. I kick at what looks to be a piece of a wing. Further on is a huge airliner engine, resting up against a shattered pine that's gone gray for the years that have passed. There are also rows of seats here and there, the plastic still there, bits of clothing, but no apparent bones, thank God.

"Look at this," Martin whispers. "The poor folks. Imagine what it must have been like."

I really don't want to, but it can't be helped. I was told in class years back that on any given day, there could be up to five thousand airplanes in the air, carrying hundreds of thousands of people . . . until the time the Creepers let loose the NUDETs in our upper atmosphere that fried everything electronic on the globe, from cell phones to computers to power plants and cars and trucks, and airplanes. All those airplanes . . . and to think of being safe and secure in such a comfortable jet airliner, and to feel the engines shudder and cut out, the lights go off, and you fall, and fall, and fall, for long minutes, all that screaming, yelling, shouted prayers . . .

"Come on," I say. "Let's get out of here."

And just as we manage to clear the crash area, the trees overhead burst into flames.

CHAPTER FIVE

"Move, move, move!" I yell, as I lead my squad away from the burning trees, the heat warming me up, the light throwing everything into stark relief, and one of the brothers yell, "How do they know we're here!"

And I yell back as I try to run to some sort of safety, "They don't! They're just burning the woods to flush us out!"

We scramble down a hillside, the flames and smoke behind us, and Thor is anxious, and he's trembling, but he's not barking with the sense that the Creepers are close behind us.

So they're torching these woods from a distance.

To flush us out.

Why?

I'm cold now, right at the base of my neck. I know why.

We keep moving, running, smoke and flames billowing out back there, and then we come to a slow-moving river. We skid to a halt, and one of the brothers says, "If we had a boat . . . if we had a boat. Creepers won't cross a river this wide."

Something catches my attention downstream, and I motion them to follow me. The riverbank is a tangled mess of weeds, grass, and low bushes, and a couple of times we have to slog through up past our ankles.

But it's worth it.

An old wooden bridge, broken, battered, and with most of the center gone, but enough there to get us to the other side.

"Move it," I say. "Ross, go."

He looks to me with wide fear in his eyes. "Why me?"

"Because you're the heaviest," I say. "You fall in, we'll need to do something else. Go!"

He slings the M-4 over his shoulder, gets up at the start of the bridge, stays to the left, where most of the framework and lumber is still there. It looks like the bridge over the years has been battered and torn by the river freezing and refreezing, or maybe some locals tearing away the planks for firewood and repairs.

Ross is about halfway across when he yelps, flails his arms, and Tommy whispers, "Don't fall, don't fall," and by God he doesn't, and he races across with a shout, turns in triumph, and I push his brother.

"You're next," I say. "Haul ass."

Behind me, Thor is whimpering, dark fur bristling up and down his neck and back.

The wind comes our way.

Smoke, soot, and cinnamon.

Thor starts barking.

I take my Colt M-10, remove the live round, spin the dial down to ten meters.

A shout.

The other brother has made it.

Martin says, "Lieutenant?"

"Make it snappy," I say, looking up and down the riverbank, looking for little flashes of light, bursts of flame, tree branches moving and falling, all the signs of approaching Creepers.

She says, "Thanks for sending me over last."

"Hunh?"

A quick grin as she scampers up the broken timbers. "It means you think I weigh less than the other two."

Martin moves across the bowed and cracked wood, above the moving river, and Thor is still barking, and I'm still eyeing the riverbank, and up there, tall pines are swaying, like a heavy wind is pushing them, but there is no wind.

She's almost at the other end and I tug on Thor's collar. "Move, let's go."

He whines as he gets up on the bridge, and I push his butt. "I don't like it either, Thor. C'mon!"

He jumps, he moves, he skitters, sometimes a paw here or there scrabbling, and he's doing all right, and I think he's going to make it, and then—

A plank falls free and my boy tumbles into the river.

"Thor!"

I jump over the gap and my heart is damn near still, and the three troopers on the other side have seen what happened, and they race down to the side of the river, but my strong boy, he's swimming hard, swimming fast, his proud and handsome head out of the water, and by the time the three of the soldiers get to him, he's already on the bank, shaking himself dry, looking back at up me with a disgusted look, like I had done this on purpose.

Click-click.

Click-click.

Click-click.

Move, I think, you're so damn exposed here, get your ass in gear.

M-10 in hand, I resume running as best as I can across the bridge, and I'm about six meters from the end, three meters, and then another plank slides free and I yell a very naughty series of words, and fall flat on my belly, the M-10 nearly slipping away, and I'm looking down into the river.

At a rusted car, on its side, two doors open, frozen in place. There's something pink in the rear, around . . . a seat, a small seat, it looks like, designed for a child or infant.

I get up on my hands and knees, start working my way, and then I'm on the ground.

I roll over and Thor is there, barking, and the two brothers and Martin are there as well, and I get up and say, "You three. Break out now. Run. Separate. Keep low. I'm sticking here for the moment."

Ross says, "Lieutenant, we don't want to leave you. We'll stay and fight."

Tommy and Stella nod in agreement. I get up on my knees, give the opposite side of the riverbank and a quick glance. More movement. "It's a goddamn order," I say. "Your M-4s won't do shit against the Creepers . . . now get!"

I move back toward a tumble of rocks and a fallen oak tree, and the three of them come with me, and Tommy says, "Lieutenant, I—"

A flicker of light illuminates our surroundings. Stella screams. Ross hits the ground and Tommy is still standing there, looking stunned as he holds up his right hand.

All four fingers have been lased off, leaving tiny black stumps.

I grab him by his collar, pull him behind me and then Ross is holding his brother and Stella is looking through her jacket for some sort of medical gear, and I shout, "Move! Or do you want all to get crisped here! Go!"

They go.

They rush past me, into the woods, and then Tommy starts keening in pain as he moves further into the trees, and I kneel down, take off my bandolier, stretch it out. One round in the chamber, two more left. Thor stands next to me, gently panting, his fur sopping wet. I rub his head and say, "Just like old times, eh? You and me. Against the aliens."

He licks my hand, usually a symbol of *Hey, you got a treat handy*, and I scratch his ears and say, "We get clear, and we get some chow our way, you're first up. I promise."

My heart has eased some and despite the situation, I feel reasonable. Creepers hate the water, although they're fascinated by it. They'll move along the side of a river or a creek, and look at the water, and circle a lake, but they hardly ever cross a wide stream or river, unless they find a bridge.

Click-click.

Click-click.

Click-click.

Which counted for a lot of bridges being blown that first year of the war, when it was learned that this was one of their very few weaknesses. This bridge wasn't much of a bridge, and I wished I had a grenade or two, or some thermite, or something to knock it over, since that would increase my odds of living until the next sunrise.

Trees whipping back and forth.

Still, it doesn't look like it could hold a Creeper, which I'm counting on.

Thor growls.

"I hate to bring this up at a time like this, but when you get wet, boy, your fur really stinks," I say, trying to lighten my mood.

He growls again. I don't think he was amused.

Then a couple of trees crash into the river, and a Battle Creeper emerges. I hunker down, wait. The smell of cinnamon is pretty strong. The Creeper goes up one side of the riverbank, and then the other, its legs sinking into the mud some, slowing it down. It hesitates at the bridge, lifting its center arthropod up, like it's surveying the area.

I rub the back of Thor's head. "Quiet, buddy, stay quiet."

He settles in next to me, whining just a bit, and then staying still, but with his fur still bristling.

The Battle Creeper starts moving across the bridge, gingerly placing its eight legs here and there to stay upright and out of the water.

"Well, I'll be damned," I whisper, and then I aim my Colt M-10, and just when the bug is halfway across the bridge is when I let it have it. The *BLAM!* is loud and my shoulder smarts, but the round flies out in a perfect arc, explodes right in front of the alien's breathing membrane, and within a second or two, the Battle Creeper is enveloped in the gas, and it starts to shake, quiver. Its claws rise up and fire off a burst of flame, a weak laser blast, and the claws fall to its side. The trembling in the legs increase, until the Creeper collapses, its legs falling through the open planking and timber, until it rests on its side, dead.

I say, "Correction . . . you'll be damned."

I eject the spent cartridge, take one of the remaining two, snap it into the breech and slam it shut, and—

Two more Creepers emerge.

I'm suddenly frightened so much that I have an urge to pee.

They're not Battle Creepers. One is a Transport Creeper, which has a wide and deep trough at the rear of its main arthropod, which is used to haul stuff around. It can be human bones, old computer equipment, books, chunks of plastic, bloody pieces of vivisected humans, or whatever else the Creeper decide needs to be moved. The other Creeper is a Research Creeper. It looks like a Battle Creeper but the end claws—besides being weaponized—also have ancillary claws that are used to pick up and examine things. The Battle Creeper doesn't care about examining things, just burning and lasing them to soot.

But the current theory is that the Research Creeper is lead among the three variants.

And this Research Creeper is lifting up its main arthropod, and using one of its arms, reaches into the rear of the Transport Creeper and pulls out—

A long, wooden plank.

It drops it to the ground.

A long pipe comes out. Another long pipe.

One more wooden plank.

The Research Creeper goes onto the bridge, and it works behind the dead Battle Creeper, and pushes it into the river, where it hits with a gentle splash and then rolls over, and sinks some, leaving six of eight legs up in the air. The moving water makes little V-shaped eddies around each exposed leg.

And then the Research Creeper starts working.

It starts repairing the bridge.

That's why I'm so scared.

I know what's going on now for certain.

They're after me.

I move down some, Colt M-10 in one hand, bandolier in the other, and I take cover, and with another successful shot, I kill the Research Creeper dead in its tracks, holding a plank.

The plank drops into the water first, followed by the Research Creeper. The Research Creeper doesn't sink, though. It just gets tangled up in the first Creeper I killed.

My breathing quickens. My shoulder is hurting something awful.

I'm down to the last round for my M-10.

What next?

The Transport Creeper moves up to the bridge.

I fire and the round is either a dud or my shaking hands knocked my aim off, for the round arcs over the Transport Creeper and rattles around as it hits the trees.

The Transport Creeper waits.

Another tree crashes to the ground, and then another.

A Research Creeper emerges, fires six or seven laser bursts in my direction, scorching tree bark, leaves, and dropping two burning branches. I hold my breath, move again, tumble into the dirt.

I lift my head.

The Research Creeper is halfway across the bridge, making it secure. More movement in the woods.

Two more Battle Creepers emerge.

They pause at the water's edge, waiting.

Very patiently waiting.

Not me.

Grabbing the empty bandolier and my now-useless M-10, I start running, and God, do I start running.

CHAPTER SIX

Thor is loping right next to me as I race through the woods, occasionally whining and letting off a high-pitched bark, and I know why he's reacting this way, because he's sensing my fear, and my trying very hard to push back the panic that's about to cripple me.

Since I was six, all I've known has been war, war, and more war. I've learned about the Creepers, how they attack, how they move, and in the past several weeks, I've also learned part of the reason why they're here, on some sort of quasi-religious mission to kill us and injure us and do all of this for some unknown reason.

I've also learned about the history of war, conflict, tactics and strategy, but never, ever have I seen Creepers act this way, coming in groups of four or five or even larger, attacking a remote and barely armed convoy, and then chasing after a squad, and then chasing after one freshly minted Lieutenant Randy Knox, of the New Hampshire National Guard. In the past several days I've encountered Creepers both close and far—once killing one with knife and luck, and another time yelling at one being kept prisoner at an underground Air Force base—but to be chased like this . . .

Either they're smelling me, or sensing me, or something, but the damn things are on my track and I've got to lose them.

The woods start to thin out, branches whipping at my face, Thor dodging around the trunks of the pines and the hardwoods, and I keep up a pace, the ineffective M-10 in my hands, the empty bandolier thumping along my back, my 9 mm Beretta holstered at my side.

Think, I yell at myself, think!

I can't outrun the Creepers. With eight mechanized legs, it's impossible.

Terror is really tugging at my heels as well, and the stories come back to me, told around campfires, during break times in basic, tales of how even the most experienced and hardened military forces from around the world—from ours to the Brits to the Russian to the Chinese—how so many dropped their weapons and ran when the Creepers first attacked.

Stories that will never appear in print.

I flip my head back, see there's a glow back there. Creepers setting the trees ablaze, like they're pushing me, propelling me . . .

I need to get someplace safe, and fast.

Thor is still with me, and then the woods suddenly end, to a wooden fence. I climb over and Thor squiggles underneath, and we're in a farmer's field. Off to the left, up on the top of a rise, is a barn, an outbuilding, and a home. Smoke is coming up from two chimneys and there's lights on. It's getting dark and rain is starting to come down.

"Come along, bud," I say. "Looks like we might have a way out of here."

I run across the field, filled with stubble from corn, and now we're on a dirt road, I'm running more, legs pumping better without the trees and brush tugging at me.

Run, don't ever stop running.

I smell manure, I hear the lowing sounds of cows, and this is one fine-looking farm, and I skitter around, find another fence, a wooden gate, and I undo the gate, and there's even a flagstone path leading up to the front door.

And sweet God, I can't believe it, but there's a wooden garage attached to the left, there are lights on in there, and there's a truck, with a man standing next to it.

A truck!

I go up, bang on the door, bang on the door, gasping for breath, and from the garage, a side door opens up and a flashlight beam hits me.

"Who's there?" comes a man's voice.

I gasp again. "Sergeant, I mean, Lieutenant Randy Knox, U.S. Army . . . I need your help. Can you help me and my dog?"

The front door to the house flies open and two more men come out, and then I step back, for these two have shotguns, pointing right at me, and the guy from the garage has come over, flashlight in hand, revolver in the other.

I step back again. "Sir, Lieutenant Randy Knox . . . I, there was an ambush, back over there by the river. Creepers attacked . . . and they've crossed the river, and they're coming this way."

One of the guys says, "Dad, he's right. Look over there. Woods are burning."

Dad was the man who had been in the garage, tending to his truck. "Shit. You're right."

I say, "Please, can you give me a ride. In your truck. Get me and my dog out of here."

Nobody says anything, and I see a woman peek from the side of the open door, who talks to the duo. "Kelly? Mike? Stay right there with your father. Don't move."

Dad comes closer. "You alone?"

"Yes, my squad has dispersed."

"What happened?"

"Creeper ambush," I say. "Look, sir, I know I'm asking a lot. Give me a ride, I'll make sure you get a fuel chit to replace whatever's been used."

"Dad," one of his sons says. "The fires are coming closer."

The older man says, "Yeah, I see that." He gestures with the revolver. "Get the hell off my property, and take the Creepers with you."

My mouth is so damn dry. "Sir . . ."

"You hear me? Get moving. Get the hell out or I'll tell my boys to shoot you dead, and I'll drag your body to the edge of my property. Then the goddamn Creepers can have a barbecue over your corpse for all I care."

"Sir, I—"

"Now, or we'll shoot your dog, too. And I'll sell his body to my neighbors the Quaids. They're not as queasy as we are when it comes to meat."

My eyes are swollen and I'm crying, damn it.

"Why? Why?"

The man with the flashlight and revolver says, "Why? Look at what

I've got here. I'm one lucky son of a bitch I am . . . I used to be an investment banker in the city, before the war started. Ate at the finest restaurants, could fly anywhere in the world where I wanted. I thought food came from supermarkets, wrapped in plastic. Farms were a place where I could take my boys on a tour when they were kids."

I can't think of anything to say.

He goes on. "We starved, I stole, I . . . killed, all to keep my family together. All to keep my family alive."

"Dad . . . the fires are getting closer."

"Now we're safe, we've built something, we're not going to starve. And son, I'm sorry, I'm not going to let a soldier like you get everything crisped. I don't care about the war, I don't care about you, I don't care about the country no more. Now, move."

"Derek!" the woman yells out, and he goes up to the front of the house, and there's a brief conversation, and he comes back, bearing something for me.

"Here," he says. "Now get going."

What he's offering is an apple, and my mouth waters and my stomach grumbles. I take it, look at it, and then toss it back at him. One of his boys catches it.

"Go to hell," I say.

He shakes his head. "Already been there and back. Go."

I find a roughly paved road, and my running has slowed to a trot. No other farms, buildings, or places of safety in sight. My feet hurt and all of the running is causing stabbing pains in my lungs.

I take a break, sitting on a broken piece of stone wall, as Thor comes to me, looks back at where we've run.

He growls.

I rub his head, the tears coming back.

"Yeah," I say. "They're still chasing our respective asses."

Thor, my boy, named after a Norse God, and one of the Norse realms is a mythical place called Asgard.

Asgard.

Could I say that word aloud?

I rub my dog's head again.

A glow of light from down the road.

I will if I have to.

"Come along," I say.

More running, more resting, and now I'm hearing the familiar and deadly sounds.

Click-click.

Click-click.

Click-click.

Fear and exhaustion, dueling inside of me, each trying to take control, take command. I can even sense Thor is running out of steam. The road is fairly straight and I try to keep a pace of running, and then walking, and running some more.

But the glow back there grows brighter.

Click-click.

Click-click.

Click-click.

This isn't right. This is so wrong.

Creepers don't act like this, or move, or attack.

There must be four or five back there, and they're chasing . . .

Me?

A single soldier?

I rest, bend over, try to catch my breath.

But not just a single soldier. There have been incidents, experiences, where I forced a Creeper Dome to surrender to me, when I later came face-to-face with an imprisoned Creeper back at a hidden base in Stratton, where we even managed to communicate through the skills of young Buddy Coulson, and when I saw two Creepers examine pieces of bloody clothing and bandages, like they were seeking a single soldier . . .

Me.

Click-click.

Click-click.

Click-click.

I wipe at the drool running down my chin. My sides ache so very, very much.

I get up and keep on running.

And I keep on being chased.

Another few minutes later and I'm on my hands and knees,

panting. Thor is whining, poking his nose into my side. I wipe at my face again and glance back, and now I'm smelling cinnamon.

So close, so very close. More flames and smoke. I think I can even hear their damn claws skittering on the road.

Rain is coming down hard.

I've been alone in my fights with the Creepers over the years, but never this alone. I've had the rest of my platoon out in the woods, I've had my girlfriend Abby Monroe, combat dispatcher, ready to seek help. I've had a variety of colored flares to send up to mark my position and request assistance.

Now . . . it's just the empty bandolier, my M-10, and a 9 mm Beretta holstered at my waist.

Not even a water bottle.

I slowly get up, realizing what a fool I've been, what a mistake I've made.

Fool.

The road has been good for running, but it's also been even better for chasing.

"Time to go cross-country," I say. "See if we can get some distance."

Thor pants, and the tears come to me, as I rub and rub his brave head.

"Let's go."

I thrash through the woods and saplings, and then I start running, and then—

The land quickly drops away.

I fall.

Fall.

Tumble and roll, dirt in my mouth and eyes, and I land flat on my back.

Stunned.

I try to catch my breath.

What the hell?

I'm soaked through, and I get up.

A stream, with steep, loose embankments going up on both sides. Thor splashes through the stream, barking.

Click-click.

Click-click.

Click-click.

I climb up the dirt and mud, and the glow from the near fires lights up everything.

Two Creepers before me, the center arthropods swaying back and forth.

Thor is nearly howling he's barking so hard, and I spin and there's a Battle Creeper, right behind me, not more than ten meters away. Even though it's useless I tear my Beretta out, hammer off three shots, as flames roar over my head, nearly scorching my helmet and shoulders.

I drop down.

Panting.

I've fired off three rounds. Nine left.

Thor's growling, whining, running back and forth along this stretch of the stream.

I climb up again, slowly this time. The Creepers have boxed me in, four of them.

Four!

Thor whines some more.

I drop back down.

Tears are suddenly coming down my face so hard it surprises me.

This is it.

This . . . is . . . it.

Stories, always the tales.

When the time comes, I'm never going to surrender, never . . .

I've heard that dozens and dozens of times.

Tales of squads, isolated on a hilltop, all of them suicided.

A line of troops being led into a Creeper Dome, one of the soldiers taking out a grenade, the troops hugging him so they're all killed when the grenade goes off.

Bodies found after a skirmish, self-inflicted gunshot wounds into the mouth or at the side of the head.

I'll never surrender.

Thor comes to me, licking my face and hands.

But Thor has a chance.

A slim chance, but a chance . . . better than me.

All that training in K-9, getting used to working with a dog, and one cold day, being told . . . *"All of you are pretty useless, compared to your dogs. They're smarter, tougher, and braver than you. And if the time comes when all hope is lost, when the Creepers are coming at you . . . do one last thing. Send your dog home. Save your dog . . . for his or her next partner."*

"Thor!"

His ears stand straight up, he looks at me with hope, trust, and love. I'm his partner, his Alpha leader, the one who heads the pack. Thor knows we're in trouble, knows the Creepers are right out there, and he's trusting me to make it all right, to find a miracle, to find a solution.

I rub and rub his head.

"Thor . . ." And I manage to choke out the word I've never wanted to utter in front of him.

"Asgard, Thor, Asgard!"

He hesitates, looks confused.

"Asgard! Now!"

He trots, stops, turns like he wants me to run along with him, and he whines again.

Asgard. The command to send him back home to Ft. St. Paul in Concord, to go back to his home turf. A long distance away but if any K-9 unit can make it, it's my Thor.

Who will someday be somebody else's partner.

I rub my sleeve across my eyes and nose. I'm bawling like a baby, and I hate myself.

"Asgard, you damn fool! Move!"

He stands there.

Frozen.

Tail wagging, like maybe I'm joking with him, playing with him, slightly panting.

I toss a rock at him, nearly hitting him. I toss another rock and it strikes his hip, and the surprised and hurt yelp makes me sick to my stomach.

"Asgard, get the hell out! Move!"

He whines.

I fire a shot over his head, and he yelps again and finally disappears, and I'm bawling even more, and I climb up the side of the embankment, a Creeper is leaning over, right down at me, and I hold my Beretta in my hands, fire off six rounds, yelling all the time, and then I drop back, pistol in my hand, and one more yell:

"You're not getting me, you bastards!"

I fire off one more shot, and move my hand, and a bright flare of light and darkness.

CHAPTER SEVEN

The darkness doesn't last long. I'm on my hands and knees, my right hand throbbing, hurting. I look up into a nightmare, two Battle Creepers peering over the edge of opposite embankments, their weaponized arms pointing right at me. My right hand is throbbing something awful but I rub the crumbly dirt and find a piece of metal, and it's my Beretta.

"Assholes," I mutter, and I pick up the Beretta and instantly drop it. The pistol is hot.

From the flickering lights at the end of the Creepers' arms, I see that the damn thing has been turned into a lump of melted metal.

A flick of light, striking behind me.

I get the message.

I stand up, hold up my arms.

"Knox, Randall, lieutenant, United States Army, Service Number—"

Two more flicks of laser light, pushing me to climb up the embankment.

I go.

Up on the wooded surface I feel a quiet panic coursing through me, and I can't help it, I giggle. Well, you screwed up in suiciding, I think, another in a long line of screw-ups. Let's have the Creepers finish us off.

So I break out and start running, thinking, hoping it will be quick, a roaring ball of flame, a laser beam taking off my head, anything besides becoming a prisoner.

I get about two meters when a flickering hail of laser fire comes my way, skimming my feet, my hands, my shoulders. I scream and dance and fall to the ground, crying.

They won't let me run away.

And they won't kill me.

I struggle to get up, look at the four of them, two Battle Creepers and two Research Creepers.

I say, "Swear to God—if there is one—I'll find a way to kill you all."

A laser burst that nearly blinds me.

I get the message.

Get walking.

It becomes a parade out of nightmares, it does, with me being in the middle with two Battle Creepers leading, and two Research Creepers following. In my history lessons back at Ft. St. Paul, I've heard of marches like this, the famed retreat from Moscow by Napoleon's battered and freezing army in 1813, losing hundreds of thousands of troops, all the way up to the Bataan Death March in 1942, where my long-ago predecessors were shot, beaten, and starved by Japanese soldiers as they marched into a prisoner of war camp.

But if I live through this one, I can't see this trek not going into a history book, if such a book ever gets written. A single soldier, sixteen years old, being pushed along and escorted by four Creepers, when more often than not, I would have been left behind as a smoldering pile of crisped flesh and burnt bone.

Not much time to think of it, as I just move along, trying to keep on my feet. I'm exhausted, hungry and thirsty, and the longer we go, the more I stumble and fall, tripping over my feet, rocks, or branches.

A number of hours pass, and then I slip again, and find myself in a muddy ditch. I push my face into the mud and slop, try to drink as much as I can, until one of the Creeper's legs snaps out and catches me in my right side, rolling me over, crying out.

I slowly get up.

Keep on moving.

This parade of horrors goes on and on, and at one merciful point, the Creepers stop and huddle and there's some sort of communication going on among them. There's hisses, snaps, whines, and a crackling noise that sounds like paper crunching up. Something else going on there attacks my ears, even the left one, which is twenty percent deaf, and I hold my muddy and worn hands to my ears and hold them tight.

In this brief period I think of my dad, in a hospital somewhere in Massachusetts. Thor, I hope, running back to safety. Serena and her brother. My girl Abby, back in New Hampshire. And Captain Kara Wallace, Kara's Killers, and I have a brief thought, a fantasy, about Kara's Killers roaring through the tree line, blasting away at my captors.

One Creeper seems to spit at another, and they break apart, and a Research Creeper behind me lowers an arm and makes a gesture, and I don't know if it's sympathy on her part, or if she's tired of pushing me along with a laser blast, but I take the hint and start moving.

Trudge, trudge, trudge.
Fall.
Get up.
Trudge some more.
There's a Rudyard Kipling poem I learned in school at Ft. St. Paul, and only the first stanza remains in my tired memory:

WE'RE foot—slog—slog—slog—sloggin' over Africa!
Foot—foot—foot—foot—sloggin' over Africa—
(Boots—boots—boots—boots—movin' up and down again!)
There's no discharge in the war!

Good ol' Rudyard and his Tommy Atkins, at least they were marching with humans, though we do share something similar, for there's no discharge in this war, unless you're wounded or scorched.

Trudge, trudge, trudge.
Skitter, skitter, skitter.
And, as dawn starts to break, a dog barks.
My feet and spirit and heart just fill up, like an observation balloon with helium.
Thor!
The dog barks again, and I think, you fool, you damn order-ignoring furry fool, you didn't run back at all, did you.

You've gotten help.

We're trudging along a field, and there's a slight hill to the right, and I see a dog bounding up and down, tail wagging, and even though my eyes are tired and worn from crying so much, I have no problem seeing the dog halfway down the hill.

It's not Thor.

No mistake.

Thor is a dark colored Belgian Malinois.

This pup is a yellow Labrador.

Poor guy.

Then I drop to the ground again, as gunfire erupts from woods on the hill.

It barely slows down the Creepers, but it sure as hell gets my attention. There's at least a dozen folks up there, shooting at the Creepers, and damn near hitting me, and after just a few minutes, I can tell it's not a National Guard, Army, or Marine unit. The firepower is pistols and long rifles, with not a mortar round or Colt M-10 among them.

Militia unit, then, belonging to the county, organized to provide common defense for the civilians against gangs or Coasties, and to act as a warning system to the regular, stretched-out and exhausted military. No heavy weapons, no real armament, most of them riding in pickup trucks or horseback.

So why open fire here?

Either because they're stupid and brave, or they're trying to slow down these four until a regular unit approaches.

The Creepers barely take notice at the bullets ricocheting off their armor, but I sure as hell do, crawling in the muddy field, yelling up at them, "Cease fire, you idiots! You'll kill me instead!"

More gunfire comes my way.

Idiots!

And if they were just trying to slow down the Creepers, by now they'd be shooting off flares in the morning light, to let the military know where they are and what they're fighting, but the only thing drifting up in the air are the faint tendrils of gun smoke.

I crawl and crawl, and eventually one of the Battle Creepers figures out what's going on, and it turns and skitters its way up the hill, firing off long lances of fire, and soon that tree line is burning from one end to another, and except for a brief scream, all I hear then is the frantic barking of the now abandoned dog, and it's funny, I feel a taste of betrayal.

I had hoped that Thor would once again disobey my commands, and go get the cavalry, and as a child, I start weeping again, disappointed that it hasn't happened.

The day turns out to be sunny as this march continues. At one point we cross a paved road and I spot a horse-drawn wagon at one end quickly make a U-turn and race away, and the thirst is getting to me. No more muddy ditches or streams, just burnt and shattered woods, once a suburban housing development with the pricey homes of yesteryear stripped and robbed, and more empty fields. My mouth is so very dry. I chew on my tongue, grab a pebble and toss it in my mouth, try to get saliva moving, but it doesn't work.

Starvation I've gone through plenty of times, but I know from rough experience what happens when you don't get hydration.

As the sun nears the noon time phase, I stop and yell at them, "I need something to drink, all right?" I motion to my mouth. "Got it? I need some water!"

The Creepers behind me try to get me to move.

I sit down.

Point to my mouth.

"Water!"

They chitter among themselves again.

"Water!"

The Research Creeper near to me crawls right up, lifts its center arthropod so it shadows me, and the two weaponized arms lower down, like they're ready to cut me in half or pick me up.

I don't budge.

"Water!"

Laser light flashes to my left and right.

I don't move.

"Water!"

Then its right arm rotates some, spins, and I think, all right, here it comes, we're—

A liquid sprays out from a joint within the upper reaches of its right arm. It gushes over me and with my mouth open, I can't help it, but I swallow it.

It seems to be water.

It seems to be.

It's metallic tasting and has the heavy odor of cinnamon about it, and for all I know it could be lubrication for its limbs or the Creeper version of urine, but I'm so thirsty I don't care. I swallow, cough, and choke, and then when the liquid stops, another laser flash.

I get up.

My stomach is growling and grumbling, and I'm doing my best to ignore it, for I'm afraid what I might get for a meal if I sit down and beg for food.

My eyesight is foggy and I'm just trudging and falling, and then I trip over a chunk of metal.

I get up, walk another meter or so, and fall again.

More metal.

I rub at my eyes, keep walking with my alien terrors before and after me.

Wrecked vehicles.

An Abrams tank, split apart by laser fire, small saplings growing through.

Treads.

Wheels.

Artillery pieces, broken and shattered, like they were plastic toys and some angry giant child has stomped them. Burnt transport trucks. Flapping pieces of old canvas. Decaying boots. Crumpled and faded clothing. Human bones, here and there. Torn up dirt that's covered by grass, trying and failing to heal this, an old battle site. Tree trunks on the ground, bark falling away. And even through my exhaustion, thirst and hunger, something that briefly cheers me up, seeing a Creeper exoskeleton curled up on its side, no grass or trees growing nearby.

I manage to croak out, "Sure hope that was a relative of yours, assholes."

No surprise, they don't reply and don't seem to take notice.

The land clears away to even more scorched earth, and what I see before me should scare me, should send me running away in terror, should do lots of things, but I see what's before me and just shrug my shoulders.

A Creeper Base Dome, sitting by itself, which means we're somewhere in western Connecticut, according to the latest intelligence reports I received, way back when I was just a relatively safe and relatively dumb Recon Ranger in New Hampshire.

But the Dome doesn't scare me anymore. When I get there, I won't be walking anymore. That's a given. I might be tortured, burnt, lased, be autopsied alive but what the hell.

I won't be walking anymore.

I stumble ahead across the dead land, the Creepers *click-clicking* their way in front of me and behind me, and we get closer, and closer, and this is the closest I've ever been to a Creeper base. The Domes are impervious to everything save a nuclear device, and since most electronics were fried ten years ago, getting a workable nuclear device up and running has always been a challenge, and with no airborne assets to use against a Dome, it's usually a suicide mission, with someone driving a heavily armored vehicle right up against it, or like the Russians do with their *Spetsnaz* special forces, take a month or so to crawl up against it, carrying the components, and then putting the components together at the last second and flicking the switch.

Whatever.

All I have is my increasingly heavy helmet, wet and smelly clothes, my MOLLE vest, and the near certainty I'll be dead within a very short time.

No matter.

I won't be walking anymore.

A section of the Dome dilates open, and my four escorting Creepers move away, leaving the way open for me.

A licking line of flame comes out, hitting the ground behind me.

I get the message.

I walk forward, get right to the edge of the entrance. I slowly turn around, raise up my arms once more, and say, "Knox, Randall, lieutenant, United States Army, Service Number 020 45 6882."

Then I extend my middle finger to all four of them.

"Later, bugs."

I turn and take a breath, square away my sore shoulders, and march into the darkness.

CHAPTER EIGHT

There's a wide and smooth ramp before me that I take, and the ramp goes down, down, and then gently banks to the left, and then banks again. The rock and dirt are smooth and I'm sure the side of the Creeper base has dilated shut, but the way is still illuminated, though I don't know how. It was dark when I started and as my eyes adjust, I begin to see more clearly.

The ever-present scent of cinnamon washes over me, and I can hear thumps, distant rumbles, and whining and grinding noises.

I'm in a Creeper base.

No one who has ever gone into a Creeper base since the war began has ever come out.

Ever.

I touch the near wall and it's warmer than I expect, and I recall all the theories and ideas about how the damn bugs have built the Domes over the years. It's not that ferrycraft come down from orbit and spend a week or so building the damn things. No, one night there's an empty field, and during the night, a line of hard light coming down from low Earth orbit, and in the morning, there's the base, and in the base, are lots and lots of Creepers.

But so far—thank God—I haven't seen a single one, and I know that's an empty appreciation, because I'm sure I'm going to run into one, real soon now. Those four Creepers have brought me here for a reason, and if I live, well, it's going to be real interesting to see what that reason is.

The ramp curves once more, and then flattens out, widens, like a wide and empty room, ceiling about five or so meters high, and that's it.

No door.

No hatchway.

No Creeper welcoming committee.

I look around, check out the ramp leading back up to the outside, and I have a brief thought of running back up, maybe getting to the outer wall, and then sneaking out the next time there's an opening that dilates open to let Creepers in or out, and as I'm thinking that, well, the ramp is gone.

There's a wall there.

"What the—"

I swivel my head, thinking that maybe I've gotten turned around, but no, I'm in a large and empty rectangular room, nothing to be seen, nothing—

Then an entrance is there, opposite from the ramp, and I go to it. There's light, noises, and scents, and I get to the edge of the square opening and peek in, and what I see convinces me that I must be dead, that the last long hours of walking with the Creepers has just been one long, last nightmare.

There are ghosts staring at me.

Starved, skeletal creatures wearing scraps of clothing, uniforms, holding sticks in their hands, knives, a few weapons like a spear or a crossbow and—

The smell just hits me, of decay, sewage, sweat, burnt things, and then something happens to the floor, it lifts me up and drops me in front of the line, and the horror before me starts toward me, talking, pressing, and now I wish I was dead, I wish this was all a dream on the way to my afterlife, as the figures begin chattering at me.

". . . food, you got any food . . ."

". . . you armed, got a pistol, hand grenade, anything mobile . . ."

". . . where are you from . . ."

". . . what year is it . . ."

". . . who's the President, can you tell us that . . ."

". . . is New York still abandoned, is it . . ."

". . . you got any smokes . . ."

Fingers poke and probe and touch at me, and I back up until I hit the wall, and the faces are of starved men, faces unshaven, eyes protruding, some in bare feet, and a whistle blows, and a man pushes his way through, waving a metal staff, knocking them back, opening up some space. He's not as skinny as the others but he's skinny enough, and he's wearing fatigues and handwritten over the right pocket is PITMAN, there are captain's bars on his frayed collars, and he's got a trimmed beard and he says, "Who are you?"

"Lieutenant Randy Knox, Second Recon Rangers, from Ft. St. Paul."

A voice: "Where the hell is Ft. St. Paul?"

"New Hampshire," I say. "Concord."

Captain Pitman says, "Far from home, Lieutenant."

"Long story," I say.

Pitman coughs. "You got any food? Medical supplies? Water?"

"No," I say.

"Better tell me now," he says. "Tell me now and give it up . . . I find you're lying, Knox, it's a week in the stockade."

Another, weaker voice. "Better do what he says, Lieutenant. Give it up. It's share and share alike here . . ."

The smell is so strong I find I'm breathing through my mouth. Beyond this crowd of beaten-down and starved soldiers, I'm seeing . . . a sand dune? A small hill? What the hell is going on here?

I say, "No, no food, water, or medical supplies. I wish I did."

Pitman looks me up and down. "Weapons?"

"Nothing."

"Shit," he says. "That'd be nice . . ."

"What . . . who are you?" I ask.

Pitman laughs, a high-pitched sound that reminds me of Thor when he whines at night, having a nightmare. "Us?" He gestures to the dozen or so men who are around him. "We're . . . what, Second or First Platoon, I forget."

"Second Platoon, Mark," a man says. "After the General reshuffled things last week."

"Yeah," Pitman says. "Second Platoon, Company A, Lost Army of the United States." He coughs again. "Sometimes known as the Dome Boys . . . or the Doomsday Boys, depending on how we're feeling."

A horn starts blaring, louder and louder, and the men wince and a couple—including me—put hands up against their ears. The horns get louder and louder, and then drift off, and two men start weeping, others start cursing, and the guy near me—a sergeant, it seems—starts saying, "It's not fair! It's not fair! It's not fair!"

Pitman spits on the ground, which appears to be dirt. "Fair or not, we've got to go . . . Second Platoon, let's move! And . . . Sergeant Snook, give the new guy something to fight with."

The men move and start trotting past the sand dune, and I stand there, still trying to figure out where I am, and what's going on, and another gaunt man bumps into me, gives me something to hold.

"There you go, Lieutenant. Best we can do."

I look at what I have.

A length of metal pipe, about half the size of my arm.

Then I'm alone, and Pitman shouts, "Knox! Move it!"

I'm still frozen.

Pitman shouts again: "Knox, if you don't move, then it's desertion! And in here, deserters are executed!"

I start moving.

I'm tail-end Charlie, which is fine, and I try to slow my pace, because even with my earlier forced march, I'm still in better shape than my new platoon members. The landscape . . . its flat rock, sometimes flat dirt, and other times, rolling sand dunes. No grass, no brush, no trees, nothing growing.

I glance up. There's a dim illumination but I can't see anything above me, just a gray-blue color that makes me think that I'm looking at an overhead roof that can be ten meters high, or a hundred. It's a dead-looking sky.

We bunch up some as we go up a hill, the sand slippery and moist, and I'm next to Snook, the guy who just armed me, and I say, "Where . . . what the hell is going on here?"

Snook says, "Didn't you hear the horns?"

"I'm not deaf," I say. "Yet."

"Yeah, well, those horns are the warning. Prepare to be attacked. We're gonna be in the middle of it pretty soon."

Now we're at the bottom of the dune, and we're moving again, and Pitman shouts, "Okay, guys, we're almost there. Almost there . . . the marker's coming up!"

I don't know what the marker is, or what it looks like, but there's a soft groan from some of the guys, like they're returning to a place of nightmares, of fighting, of death.

And then I spot a pillar, about three meters tall, that stands in the middle of this stretch of sand and dunes that looks like an old Egyptian obelisk, or photos of the Washington Monument before the war started, and half the line of gaunt men goes to the left of the pillar, and half go to the right.

Pitman says, "Good job, guys. We made good time. We might even have some rest before it starts. Everybody, take a break. Ah, Knox. Stick with me."

I get up to Pitman and another soldier approaches him, holding something in a blanket. The object is put on the ground and the blanket is gently unrolled, like some religious artifact is being exposed, and after three unrolls, I see what's revealed:

An M-4.

Battered and cracked and discolored, but an M-4.

"Haley," Pitman says. "If you please."

The soldier named Haley holds forth a magazine, and Pitman says, "How many rounds?"

"Six, sir."

"You positive?"

"Yes, sir, I am."

"And if I were to strip this magazine, right now, how many rounds would I find?"

"You would find six, Captain Pitman."

"All right, then," Pitman says, and he slides in the magazine with a satisfying click, works the action, and stands up.

I feel like a childish fool, next to him, with a length of pipe in my hand.

My legs are shaking.

We're going to be attacked and this is all we have?

"Captain . . ."

"Hold on, Lieutenant." He climbs up a small rise near the monolith, looks around and says, "Dress up the line, some. Remember who you are. And when the battle is over . . . we'll see if luck is with us this time."

A few soldiers cheer. Most don't.

He comes back down and says, "Where were you captured?"

"I'm not sure," I say. "In southern Massachusetts, I think. I was on a convoy, heading back to my duty station."

"What's your job?"

"Recon Ranger."

Pitman says, "What's a Recon Ranger? Must be a new specialty. I've never heard of it."

That little sentence right there scares the crap out of me. "Sir . . . how long have you been . . . a prisoner?"

Pitman's voice grows cold. "Forever, kid."

Usually I get real pissed when someone calls me kid, but I'm giving the captain a pass. He says, "What does Ranger Recon do?"

"Hunts for Creepers. Spots them. Kills them or calls for reinforcements."

"Well, Knox, you're in luck. You don't have to hunt for Creepers, because there's scores of them, all over the place."

One of the soldiers says, "Hey, Mac. Ask the new guy about who the President is?"

Pitman says, "What the hell difference does it make, hunh?"

"I'm a curious fellow."

"Aim your curiosity to the front line, Corporal."

An ear-splitting horn starts sounding, over and over again. I wince and I put my hands up to my ears. The horns are so damn loud that they even make my bones and eyes ache.

Then the horns stop, and there are echoes.

Pitman yells, "All right, last warning. Get ready! Hold the line! Whatever happens, hold the line!"

I grip the pipe even harder and whisper, "This is insane."

Pitman says, "Good for you, kid. You've only been here an hour and you've figured it out."

I say louder, "Sir . . . how the hell are we going to fight?"

"With what we got," he says.

"But the Creepers . . . we don't have a single M-10. The only real weapon we've got is your M-4, and with all due respect, sir, unless you're very, very lucky and those rounds are uranium-depleted, the Creepers are going to kill all of us in about thirty seconds."

A couple of the soldiers start laughing, and there's whispers, and I feel like I'm at school and I've been called up to do an oral report, and I've forgotten every word and every line.

Pitman says, "Jesus Christ, kid, whatever gave you the idea that we're fighting the Creepers?"

"Uh . . . I, we're in a Creeper Dome, and I just got captured by Creepers, and—"

An area about fifty or so meters starts to lighten up, revealing a smooth wall.

"Here they come! Get ready!"

Pitman says, "Kid, we're not fighting the Creepers."

The wall over there . . . it just blinks away.

Forms start running toward us.

The Captain says, "We're fighting the Russians."

CHAPTER NINE

They roll up at us, a long line, holding spears or lances or whatever the hell these medieval weapons are called, and they're yelling, "Ooh rah! Ooh rah! Ooh rah!" Their uniforms are as ragged as ours, but are a different style and cut, and my hands are very tight on the length of pipe as they come closer. A line of lights appear up on the overhead roof, and one of the Russians in the center is carrying a long pole with a red square of cloth attached to it.

"Ooh raah!"

"Ooh raah!"

I've fought my fellow soldiers in training, have fought and killed a number of Creepers, and have caused harm to refugee gangs, the Coasties, who rob convoys and murder civilians. But this . . . a cold, rational part of me thinks this is not a battle, I have no quarrel with these starved men running at me, and I quickly put that cold part away as one Russian comes at me with a lance.

I swing the length of metal, knock the lance away. The Russian, face grimacing, dirty and bearded, rears back and tries again. I swing again, connect with the lance, and I sense it's loose in his hands, and in a gamble, I drop the pipe and grab the shaft of the lance, hold it tight and pull it toward me. It pops out of his hands and for a frozen moment, we stare at each other, and I want this guy to run away, I don't want to hurt him, but he grabs a knife or a shiv from his pants, comes screaming at me, and in a sharp reflex, I shove the base of the lance at him.

I catch him in his open mouth.

He flips back, moaning, and I rotate the lance and as he tries to get up, shiv in his hand, I press forward and stab him in the chest.

An awful sensation.

The lance vibrates in my hand, and it feels like the blade is hitting a rib until it slips through the ribcage, and he's stunned, drops the shiv, tries to grab onto the lance, his hands pawing at it, and I'm crying and I'm tugging but the damn thing is stuck.

It's stuck.

Then he's dead.

The lance is still stuck.

I look around.

The battle looks to be over.

I give one more sharp tug, the lance comes out, and I step back, and I heave and heave as I try to throw up, but nothing comes out but bile and spit.

The Russians are still there, on the opposite side of this rocky and dune-covered field. The lance with the bloody blade at the end seems to vibrate in my hands. I'm with a couple of soldiers and one says, "Hey, kid, don't forget your other weapon."

I have no idea what he's talking about and then I remember, oh yeah, the other weapon. I pick up the length of pipe and manage to secure it by pushing it through my belt.

Two of our guys are on the ground, dead, it looks like, and two others are being bandaged by a female soldier—the first I've noted—who has a hand-painted Red Cross on a white piece of cloth pinned to the back of her fatigue blouse.

Pitman is standing there, holding the M-4, and a lieutenant is standing next to him. COLLIER, says his handwritten nametag. He's missing a hand but his good one is holding a length of wood with spikes at the end.

"Colly," Pitman says, "it looks like the Reds are regrouping. What do you think?"

"Could be, Captain," he says. "They might think the Creepers aren't happy. But it looks like they took three hits."

I take "three hits" means three of the Russians are dead. In the final equation, I guess, it means a victory of sorts, with three of their dead compared to two of ours.

Some victory.

Pitman looks around and sighs. "What I wouldn't give for a quality pair of binoculars. Or field glasses. Or even one of those cheap telescopes you found at Kmart, back in the day."

He says to me, "Good job, kid. And you got a lance in exchange."

Earlier the lance seemed as light as a feather. Now I need two hands to hold it.

"I don't know if I want it," I say.

Pitman says, "Don't be a fool. It's a weapon. You earned it, fair and square."

"I killed a starving kid."

Lieutenant Collier says, "Better you than him."

The Russians have lined up again. More shouts. The red banner is waved back and forth, back and forth.

"Looks like they're lining up again," Pitman says. "Shit, okay—"

The horns return, as loud as before. I can't help it. I drop the lance, put my hands over my ears. The sound of the horns seems to split right through my skull and down my gullet. On and on, and then they stop, echoing and echoing.

Pitman looks satisfied. "All right, then. The bugs seem happy. Doctor Kendall!"

The tired woman with the Red Cross pinned on her back says, "Yeah, Mac."

"Can the wounded move?"

"Yeah, if we help."

"They gonna make it?"

"Probably," she says.

"All right, we'll help. Snook!"

"Sir," he says, sitting on the ground.

"Paul, you and . . . the new lieutenant here, prep our dead. Make it snappy. I don't want to wait for the bugs to change their minds."

I pick up my lance and say, "What do you mean, sir, prep?"

"Just follow Sergeant Snook, he'll show you what to do." Then he grins and examines the M-4. "Fought them off, won, and didn't even fire a shot. The General will be pleased."

Snook gets up and says, "Big frickin' deal. Come along, Lieutenant."

The two dead soldiers are old, thin, with scraggly beards. They're stretched out on the dirt and thankfully, their eyes are closed. One is dead from a throat wound that gushed blood all over the front of his jacket, and the other has a crushed skull at the rear—hair, bone, blood, brain a mushy mess—but at least it's not as bad as the first.

Snook kneels down, starts unbuttoning the jacket of the dead guy with the gashed throat, and I say, "We're stripping the dead?"

"They don't need the clothes no more, do they?"

"But it's . . ."

He opens the jacket, starts working one arm out. "Get over it, Lieutenant. We're trapped in here, there's no escape, never an escape, and we've got to make do with what we can. Terry and Gus here, they might be a couple of shitheads, but they'd do the same to you and me."

I just stand and look, and he says, "Hurry up, Lieutenant. You don't want the Creepers to change their mind and have us mix it up again."

I keep on standing.

Snook gets one arm out. "Look, it's your first time, I'll give you a break. Get their boots, okay?"

I get down on the dirt and get to work.

A few minutes later we're finished and I can't look at them anymore, and I say, "Do we bury them?"

"No," Snook says, rolling up the clothes and boots into a bundle. "Learned that years ago. Damn Creepers are still interested in what makes us breathe and fart. So we have to leave the bodies behind so they can slice and dice 'em, and maybe put 'em in a Creeper museum or something."

I offer my lance to him and he nods in thanks, putting the butt end through a knot of sleeves. "Let's get a move on," he says, and my pipe drops on the ground, and Snook picks it up. "We don't want to be left behind."

We walk at a brisk pace to catch up with the column, and I'm tail-end Charlie again, but this time, I'm not by myself, which is an improvement. He's carrying my pipe and his own weapon, a length of wood with a bloody piece of sharp metal at the end. The lance is balanced on my shoulder, the bundle of clothing and boots dangling at the end.

Snook says, "Hell of a thing, hunh?"

"Sure is," I say.

"That's what becomes of property."

I say, "Property?"

"Yeah, that's my theory," he says. "Everybody's got their theory, why not mine? You ever hear of a guy named Charles Fort?"

"Nope."

Snook says, "My dad was a real nut about conspiracies, weird stuff, flying saucers and things like that."

"He wasn't too off about the flying saucers."

"Maybe," he says. "But he was about this British writer and researcher, hundreds of years ago, who collected all these oddball stories. Fish dropping out of the sky. Farmers falling into holes that closed up behind them. Diplomats walking around a horse carriage and disappearing. All these weird stories would add up, and one day, Fort said, 'I think we're property.' Why the hell not?"

The line of soldiers ahead of me trudges along, going up and around sand dunes and rocks, and then there's other sounds, smells.

Snook says, "What do you do with property? You can look at it, and sell it, or play with it and break it. That's what the Creepers do. For some reason they like to watch us fight. Why? Who the frig knows. The Creepers are smart about some things, pretty dumb about others. But somehow, along the way, they found out that for more than a century, there was a rivalry between us and the Russians. So they arrange fights. Like dog fights. Whaddya think?"

"I miss my dog," I say, my voice choking up.

"You got a dog? For real?"

"Yes," I say. "He was a K-9, my partner. I . . . I just miss him."

"Well, lucky you, he didn't come in here with you. Or he'd be tonight's dinner."

My stomach flip-flops at that thought, and at the moment I hate Snook, and I hate him even more in knowing that he was right.

We're within a few meters of our camp, or outpost, or fort, and Snook whispers, "You watch out for Captain Hudson . . . he's in charge of First Platoon, and he's a real suck-up when it comes to the General. Hell, Captain Pitman's a suck-up, too, but at least he keeps it somewhat under control."

There's a low fence of rocks and timbers, and some wooden stakes jutting out, and a wooden gate is dragged open, allowing us in, and the next few minutes pass in a ghastly blur, of thin men and a few women, our bag of clothes and boots being taken by someone who claims to be a quartermaster, and there's a couple of wooden huts, and some tents made of cloth or canvas. One hut is set about ten meters away from the rest, and is in better shape, better built.

Pitman looks out to the darkness, leans on his staff. "Now we wait."

"For what?" I ask.

Some laughter, and one soldier starts to speak, and Pitman cuts him off. "Nope, let the lieutenant find out for himself. Snook . . . take the lieutenant and set up quarters for him, will you?"

"Yes, sir," and with a sad smile, he says, "This way, Lieutenant."

Quarters means one of the canvas shelters, and one of the dead soldiers was rooming with other soldiers, and I can tell from their sharp glances that they're not interested in having a new barracks mate. The shelter for the second dead soldier is a single one set into the side of a dune, with a canvas top protecting it, and there's another soldier there, on his knees, going through the meager belongings when we get there.

"Kent, get the hell out of here," Snook says. "Bloomberg belonged to Second Platoon, not First. You don't have any right to be here."

The soldier named Kent doesn't move. "Captain Hudson told me to come here. Captain Hudson said that Terry owed him a shirt from last week's poker game. So that's why I'm here. Bug off."

Snook kicks Kent in the boots, and he steps up and Snook says, "Stand at attention, Specialist."

"Up yours," Kent says.

"You want to fight for Terry's shirt?"

Kent grins. He's about six inches taller than Snook and looks in better shape. "Sounds good."

Snook says, "Then you'll have to fight the new lieutenant," nudging me with his elbow. "Lieutenant Knox just came from up top. He's fresh meat. In great shape. You think you can take him?"

Kent ponders that and Snook says, "And you know the regs. The lieutenant beats you in a fair fight, he gets to take whatever he wants from your stash. You up for that, Kent? You know, I hear from some of your buds that you have an old *Maxim* girlie magazine. You charge 'em to borrow it for a day. What might happen if you were to lose that magazine?"

Kent eyes us both and I keep my mouth shut, which is a struggle. But I don't know this place, I don't know the setup, and I sure as hell don't know the regulations.

"Fine," Kent says, stepping away. "But Captain Hudson won't like it."

Snook says, "Dave will get over it. Now, Specialist, get off Second Platoon turf."

He moves across the dirt and sand, up and over a dune, and then he's gone. Snook sighs and says, "All right, Lieutenant. Here's your quarters. Not much, but it's your few square meters of paradise."

"Thanks," I say, and I take in what's now mine. A plastic sheet on the ground, two thin blankets, a couple of trinkets, and a ditty bag with spare clothes. Carved out in the dirt is a drawing on a dirty piece of paper, about the size of my hand. It shows a young woman. I pick up the drawing and hand it over to Snook.

"Who's this?"

"Terry's wife, Cheryl," he says. "We had a major here, woman named Curtiss, man, could she draw. She drew this for Terry, just based on what he told her. Damn fine artist. Russkies killed her a year ago . . . or maybe two, I don't know."

He tries to hand it back to me and I say, "No, I don't want it. Throw it away."

Snook shakes his head. "Lieutenant, you got a lot to learn here . . . and here's lesson number one."

He slips the paper into a coat pocket. "The Lost Army of the United States never throws anything away, ever. Remember that."

"I'll try," I say.

"No offense, Lieutenant, you better do more than try."

I sit on the two filthy and smelly blankets, try to think of just how hungry and thirsty I am, when I hear something above the background noise, and some of the talk from my fellow platoon members nearby.

I stand up.

What is it?

I cock my head, letting my good ear try to do its work.

The noise gets louder.

Louder.

Click-click.

Click-click.

Click-click.

I yell, "Creepers!" and run to find Captain Pitman.

CHAPTER TEN

The next few minutes pass like one of those nightmares where you know you're in incredible danger, and nobody pays you any attention. Or you're trying to run and your legs are stuck in sand. Or a Creeper rolls up on you and you have no weapon, or if you do have a Colt M-10, there's no ammo. But if you do have a Colt M-10 with ammo, it misfires, as the Creeper gets closer.

What is terrifying is that I can see a Creeper approaching from one side of the encampment, and as much as I yell and point out what's going on, I'm ignored.

Except for one moment, when I tug at Snook and yell a Creeper is approaching, and a soldier I don't know looks in puzzlement to Snook, and he shrugs and says, "New guy."

Then I get it.

Feel the burning sensation in my face and the sweat on my back.

We were all prisoners in the depths of a Creeper base.

Of course there will be Creepers around.

Snook says, "Come on, Lieutenant, let's see what Oprah's bringing us today."

I join up with Snook and a few others, and Captain Pitman leads us over to a wide and flat spot in the dirt. Another group of soldiers is across from us, and a very tall and angry looking soldier with captain's bars on his shirt collars looks to Pitman, and cold nods of acknowledgment are exchanged.

I ask Snook, "That Captain Hudson?"

"It is," Snook says. "See, you're learning already."

The Creeper moves slowly and deliberately to us, and my legs are shaking so hard with fear I'm afraid the members of my new platoon will notice. But everyone is looking up at the approaching Creeper—a transport model that has a storage bin built into its main arthropod—and I hear a soldier whisper, "God, please, food this time . . . please . . . please let it be food . . ."

Pitman says, "Colly, I think that's Oprah. What do you think?"

Collier says, "From here, Captain, I think its Ellen."

"What makes you so sure?"

"The scorch marks on the left front leg," Collier says. "I don't think Oprah has that."

"Bet you a meal ration I'm right," Pitman says.

Collier says, "Sir, that's I bet I'm not prepared to make."

The shaking in my legs eases just a bit. They name them, I think. They've been here so long that they name the damn things.

The Transport Creeper—either Oprah or Ellen, I don't care—swings around and waits, and then a soldier from the other platoon goes forward, cups his mouth with his hands, and starts talking to the Creeper, in its own language! Hisses, clicks, snaps.

Snook says, "That's Moran over there. Thinks he's so smart. He's been learning Creeper language for a couple of years, or so he says."

"Does it work?"

"Sometimes, but who really knows."

The Creeper's head ducks down twice, and Moran yells back, "See? See? She understands me!"

A voice: "If you tell her to go away, I swear to God I'll have your liver for breakfast!"

A couple of jeers and shouts, and then everyone quiets down as the Creeper lowers its legs on one side, raises its legs on the other, and the open section of the main arthropod tips over, and junk and packages and other stuff tumbles to the ground. Then the Creeper gets back up, and within seconds, skitters away.

No one moves.

I say, "What's going on?"

Snook says tiredly, "We fought the Russians. We did as we were told. The Creepers then reward us . . . like we're goddamn dogs or something."

"Why are we still waiting?"

"Because we don't get first dibs, that's why."

The door to the better-looking shack opens up and two men emerge. Even at a distance I can tell they're better dressed, not as gaunt, and each has a weapon holstered at their sides, one being a revolver, the other being a black semiautomatic pistol. They slowly walk to the pile of dumped stuff, laughing between themselves, and Pitman whispers, "Hurry it up, you jerks, hurry it up."

They get to the pile, look in, and move stuff around, and in a couple of minutes, they return to the hut, a stretched blanket between them, about a dozen or so cans of food between them.

"The General's staff," Snook explains to me. "They get to go first."

"Why?"

Snook looks to me like I now have four legs. "Because they're the General's staff, that's why."

With the two men gone, the two captains—Pitman and Hudson— step forward, and start divvying up the pile, with Hudson going first.

Snook explains, "The way it goes, First Platoon goes first, and then we go second. A month ago, though, we were First Platoon . . . you wouldn't think that would make much of a difference, but it sure as hell can."

"How can the platoons change like that, going from First to Second? Aren't they permanent?"

"The General's orders," Snook says. "If he thinks one platoon is goofing off or not following . . . orders, then the General will switch around so the other platoon goes first."

"That's not right," I say.

Snook just gives me a look, like he's saying, *Yeah, tell me something else I don't know.*

The two captains move quickly but not in any cooperation or friendship, just quickly taking what they can for their own platoon.

I clench my fists.

In my years in the National Guard and when I've been attached to the regular Army, I've never seen such despicable behavior. Platoons being set up against each other like this ruins unit cohesion, hurts teamwork, hurts readiness and performance.

But when Pitman says, "Second Platoon, come on over and load up," I join the rest of my fellow troopers.

⊕ ⊕ ⊕

Back at our encampment, there's a survey of what we've got: a roll of plastic sheeting, three planks of wood, a dozen or so cans of who knows what (the labels having fallen off years back), a fishing rod, a half-dozen items of girl's clothing, blouses and skirts, a number of shoes and sneakers—all for the left foot—and maybe a bushel or two of corn.

Captain Pitman surveys our loot and says, "Not much, and definitely not worth the lives of two troopers . . . but it's not a bad haul. Quartermaster, get it secure, and get evening chow going."

Dinner seems to be something brown and meaty in gravy—about four bites worth—an ear of corn, and a metal cup of water. I've had much, much better and much, much worse, but I don't like having the Creepers being in charge of our supplies, and as I try to make this meager meal stretch, I hear stories that make me even more scared.

Collier says, "Remember last year? Three of the supply dumps . . . nothing but wood, wood, and wood. Nice to build shelter, and maybe the damn bugs are like termites and eat cellulose, but damn, that was a rough time."

"Moran saved the day, don't you remember?" another trooper says. "Went out and raised hell with Ellen, until we got food the next day."

In the voice of a child remembering Christmas, Snook says, "Cow day . . . as long as I live, I'll never forget cow day."

Murmurs and nods and I say, "What was cow day?"

A trooper wearing an eye patch and at the edge of the group says, "One day Oprah—"

"It was Ellen," someone interrupts.

"Whatever, Oprah, Ellen, Noah . . . this Transport Creeper comes out after we fought the Russkies, and we were feeling down because the sons of bitches had two AK-47s on their side, we took a beating, but the Creeper, she dumped three scorched cows. Three! God, we didn't even have to cook that first day, the meat was already cooked . . . shit, we made those three cows last months . . ."

"Why are the Russians here?" I ask, nibbling as best I can the raw ear of corn.

Pitman says, "To fight us, kid. To entertain the bugs."

"No, I know that . . . now. I mean, how did the Russians get here? Were they part of an expeditionary force to North America, got captured?"

"Nope," Pitman says. "They were transported."

Now I'm really confused. "Transported how? In the Transport Creepers? All the way from Russia?"

The rest of the platoon stops eating, stares at me. Pitman says, "You really don't know?"

"No, I don't."

The captain says, "For real? I mean . . . could information like this be so top secret that you don't know?"

"Depends on the information," I say. "What's the big deal?"

There's a pause, and then Pitman says, "The folks out there, up top, they ever figure out how the Dome bases get set up so quickly? Without anyone seeing them being built?"

"My dad, he's in Intelligence," I say, trying so very hard not to think of the last time I saw him, in a crowded medical room, being worked over after having a leg burnt off by a Creeper. How was he doing, I thought, in the VA hospital, and there's a thud of guilt in my belly, thinking of Dad getting that telegram about my current status, *The Department of Defense regrets to inform you . . .*

I say, "There's been reports of long lines of light, beaming down from the orbital battle station. Not the killer stealth satellites. The theory is that those beams of light represent some sort of system that can transport prebuilt Dome structures, Creepers, other things to the surface. And maybe retrieve them up to the orbital base."

Pitman says, "Well, whoop-tee-do, military intelligence gets one right. Yeah, it's a transport system, called the *Grantztch*. It's based on their orbital battle station and they can transfer bugs, Domes, and . . . people, within seconds. Not sure how it works. Not as fancy as that transporter beam they used in *Star Wars*."

"*Star Trek*," a soldier corrects.

"Whatever," Pitman says.

"So it can transport people from one part of the planet to another?"

"Sure," Pitman says. "I was captured in California, same as Snook. Collier, he was . . . Oregon?"

"Washington State," comes the reply.

"Yeah, that's it," Pitman says. "The Creepers, they can use the *Grantztch* to move things around, instead of hauling crap across the continent. Boom. One second you're in a Dome, next second you're someplace else, floating somewhere—probably in their orbital base—and boom again. Back on the ground, in a different Dome. That's how the Russians got here, same as us. Transported from the Motherland to the States, to fight us poor Yankees."

"Why fight?" I ask.

"Hunh?"

"Why fight? What's the point of it? What would happen if you and the Russians, shit, I don't know, go on strike?"

Some low laughs and I realize I've stepped in it, and the answer comes to me before anybody else says it, so I say it aloud.

"You don't fight, you don't eat," I say.

"That's right, kid," Pitman says.

"Well, lucky for any of you that you weren't in the orbital battle station last month," I say, looking around. "This place sucks, but at least you weren't up in orbit."

Snook says, "Why's that?"

"Because the Air Force destroyed it last month."

Somebody drops something and in a moment, everyone's standing around me.

"... when did it happen ..."

"... how do you know ..."

"... how the hell did they do that ..."

Pitman's voice cuts through with a "Stand down, stand down, let the lieutenant speak!"

I guess I just got promoted in Pitman's eyes from a kid to a lieutenant.

"I was lucky enough to talk to the Air Force officer who led the raid last month, in Albany," I say.

"Why Albany?" Collier asks.

"Albany's the capital," I say.

"I thought Harrisburg was the capital," a very young soldier says.

"It was . . . then the Creepers scorched it two years back. But it's Albany, and I met the guy who was in charge of it. A Colonel Minh. The planning had been going on for years, right after the invasion. The

Air Force recovered some old solid-fuel rocket boosters, adapted them for manned flight, made the capsules as primitive as possible so the Creepers wouldn't sense them . . ."

"The boys in blue," a solider whispers. "The boys in Air Force blue . . . bless those pampered bastards."

"Not that pampered," I say. "It was a kamikaze mission. Six of them went up with warheads built into their capsules, blew the orbital battle station to pieces."

"Captain," Collier says. "That . . . well, remember last month? Oprah dropped off those MREs . . . and we didn't have to fight the Russians that week? Maybe . . . well, maybe that wasn't a coincidence. Maybe the Creepers were confused. Scared of us . . . maybe, well, I think there's a connection. Like what the Japs did when World War II ended. They were scared of how they'd be treated once the POWs were released."

"Maybe so," the captain says. "But they've gone back to their old ways. Why's that?"

I have the answer but I realize with horror that I shouldn't have said anything. I had given them something important I can't possibly follow up with. Hope. I had given them the taste of hope, and I feel like a fool, and keep my mouth shut.

But Pitman sees the expression on my face before I duck down, and he says, "Spill it, Lieutenant. What's going on out there?"

I speak quickly and to the point. "We thought we had the Creepers beat. We destroyed their orbital battle station. Some of their killer stealth satellites were malfunctioning, burning up in orbit . . . and then another orbital battle station showed up. The Creepers had a spare . . . maybe hidden behind the Moon. It's been on station now for nearly a week."

Someone throws a rock at me. I duck.

Pitman says, "Kid, you should have kept that flapping mouth of yours shut."

I guess my promotion only lasted for a minute or two.

I rub up the rest of the brown sauce on my plate with my fingers, lick them clean, and desperate to change the subject, say, "Where did the General come from?"

Nobody says a word. It's like the place has suddenly dropped a few degrees in temperature. All eyes are on their food or their little tasks, this depleted platoon of the Army of the United States.

"Nobody knows?" I ask. "And what's the General's name anyway?"

Pitman stares at me. "It's just the General. And we try not to talk about the General."

I press on. "Why?"

Pitman says, "Shut up, kid," and there's so much dark menace in those three words that I do just that.

I volunteer for KP duty and find out that KP duty is considered light and privileged duty, so I work with a young soldier named Boone, who's missing a few fingers and has burn scar tissue on his chin, on another, more disgusting task. A few sand dunes away there's a latrine, and with a piece of wood and a broken spade, we're supposed to dig another latrine, about three meters away from the old one. The stench is so bad I tie a soiled handkerchief around my face, and Boone takes the spade and gives me the piece of wood. I don't feel like pulling rank so I dig and he digs and when we're about done, I say, "Private, you haven't said one word to me since we started. Why's that?"

He stares at me and tries to clean his hands by slapping them together and rubbing them on his soiled jeans.

"Private, nothing to say?"

He motions to his ears, motions to his mouth, and in the dirt, writes a two-word obscenity in my direction, the second word being *you.*

"Sorry, Private Boone," I say. "I didn't know."

With a violent motion, he points to the dirt words once more, and then kicks them away with a foot, and goes back to camp.

I follow him, feeling so out of time and place that I'm praying this is all one long and disgusting nightmare, but no surprise, my prayer goes unanswered.

There's a small fire and four of the soldiers are playing poker, and two others are working to repair tears in their clothing, and I just sit there and Pitman says, "All right, guys and gals, lights out. Hit your bunks. Have a quiet night."

I say, "Any guard postings?"

"Why?" Collier says. "We're already in a goddamn prison. What's the point?"

"Don't the Russians . . . couldn't they raid our camp?"

Pitman says, "No, the Creepers don't play like that. For some reason, they like us out in the open. Easier to watch, maybe, or maybe that's how they think we humans fight. Who the hell knows."

And in a practiced chorus, about a half-dozen voices say, "Because they're aliens!"

I leave it at that and head to my new quarters.

Even with the campfire doused and no other means of light, there's still some sort of ambient light from the Dome that makes it look like dusk or predawn. I hadn't even noticed the dulling of the overhead lighting system. I shuffle around in my new home, trying to ignore the chill-cold feeling in my gut, wondering how long this will be my home, how will I fit in here, and how many starving Russian boys and men out there will I need to kill to keep on living?

I take off my helmet and MOLLE vest, unfold one blanket, slide in on top of the other one. Both blankets reek of the previous soldier—Terry—and I try not to let that bother me as I stretch out. I take a deep breath, fold my arms, try not to think of anything at all, and I surprise myself by falling asleep.

I don't sleep long.

There's a touch on my shoulder and I roll over, metal pipe in hand, and a voice says, "Lieutenant, calm down, calm down."

"Who is it?"

"You don't need to know. I just gotta ask you this . . . you got any smokes on you?"

"No."

"You sure? I got stuff to trade . . ."

"No, I don't have any smokes. Leave me alone."

"C'mon, Lieutenant, candy? Crackers?"

"Bud, not interested. Go . . . or I'll report you."

He snickers. "Report me where?"

"You know what I mean."

"Like . . . report me to a senior officer, the whole chain of command nonsense?"

"Go away."

He moves back into the darkness, but not before leaving me with this:

"Lieutenant, we ain't no Army unit. Just a gang playing make-believe. You'll find out, soon enough."

CHAPTER ELEVEN

I don't sleep well—thinking of what my nameless visitor had told me last night—and when I roll over and wake up, with the Dome interior lighting increasing, it looks like he or a friend came back to visit me during the darkness.

My helmet and MOLLE vest are gone.

I get up and look around one more time, and then straighten myself out as best as I can, and then go to look for Captain Pitman. I find him supervising whatever our meager breakfast is going to be, and he sees me approaching and says, "Good to see you, kid. You did such a great job digging yesterday afternoon I'm going to send you out to do it again."

"Captain," I say. "Two pieces of my gear were stolen last night. My helmet and my vest."

Pitman lowers his head over a dirty pot that's hung over a fire by a pipe and a twisted piece of wire. To the young soldier stirring he says, "Don't let it stick to the bottom, all right? Or you'll be the one eating the scorched oatmeal."

The cook nods. "Absolutely, sir."

"Captain Pitman."

He looks up. "Yeah?"

"Sir, someone—"

"Yeah, yeah," he says. "I heard you the first time. What do you want?"

"I want you to find out who stole my gear. And get it back."

"Go away," he says. "I'm busy."

"Captain Pitman—"

"Away, kid. Now."

I turn and walk away.

Over the next half hour I don't make any new friends as I go from platoon member to platoon member, talking to each soldier, and I get a few grunts, a couple of "go *bleep* yourself" and Snook, trying to repair a broken shoelace, says, "It wasn't us, Lieutenant. That's not good for the platoon, having guys nick stuff from the others."

He nods in the direction of a line of dunes, where there's a slight haze of morning smoke. "I'd say it was somebody from First Platoon."

"Thanks for the advice," I say, and I start heading over there, and Snook says, "Word of advice, sir?"

"Sure."

"Have some breakfast first," he says. "If you're going to look for trouble, have something in your belly."

I hesitate, and realize he's right.

I eat my morning ration of very thin oatmeal—more of a gray liquid with flakes of oatmeal floating through—and I line up and give my plate and spoon to the lucky trio on KP duty, and Pitman pulls me aside and says, "Kid, time to get digging."

"Begging the captain's pardon, I'm going over to First Platoon."

"Why?"

"To get my gear back."

Pitman says, "You'll be wasting your time."

"Then it's my time, isn't it, sir."

He says, "Second Platoon's time."

I say, "No offense, sir, but I'm here by accident. And if you were my platoon leader, you'd be assisting me. Not the other way around."

Pitman, "Kid, you—"

"It's Lieutenant Knox," I say. "Not kid."

I leave before he says anything else.

I just head in the direction of the smoke and after going up and down two sets of dunes, I come into First Platoon territory. There's just something different about the setup, and it feels like this platoon is tougher and meaner than the one I belong to. Heads turn as I approach and someone calls out, "Hey, we got a visitor!"

"Who is it?" someone replies.

"I don't know . . . looks like the USO."

Laughter and a sergeant gets in front of me, and I say, "I'm looking for Captain Hudson."

The sergeant says, "You got an appointment, Ell-Tee?"

Laughter and the sergeant looks back to his fellow troopers. I say, "No, I don't."

"Captain Hudson is otherwise engaged," the sergeant says.

I say, "I'm sure."

"Go back to your own platoon. Go back to Pitman."

"Not until I see Captain Hudson."

The sergeant says something but I'm looking over his thin shoulder, and Captain Hudson is coming over from a hut, wiping his hands. His eyes are sunken, dark, and he has thick eyebrows, thick black hair slicked back.

"Well, good morning to you, Lieutenant," he says, face flat, showing no emotion. "What seems to be the problem?"

"No problem, sir," I say. "I'm looking for some missing gear of mine. A helmet and a MOLLE vest. It was removed from my quarters last night."

Hudson says, "Then go back to your unit and give it a look-see."

"I've already done that, sir. My gear isn't with Second Platoon. And the bugs didn't take it. And it didn't walk away."

Hudson's dark eyes seem to get darker. "Are you saying somebody from my platoon stole it?"

"I'm saying I'd like to take a look around, see if it's here."

"Sorry, not allowed," Hudson says. "Go back."

"Captain . . . if I may, where did you go to basic?"

He laughs. "What, you want my bio?"

"My dad's a lifer," I say, which was a lie. "I'm thinking the two of you might have joined up about the same time, sir."

"Hah," he says. "Out west."

"Where?"

"Fort Carson," he says. "We done here?"

"No, sir, I'm afraid we're not," I say. "I'm sorry, I must insist. I need my gear back."

"DeMint!" he calls out. "Front and center!"

A soldier comes from a huddle around their cooking fire, and he's laughing, and he's carrying something in his hands.

My helmet and my vest.

Hudson takes the vest and helmet in his hand, and says, "This yours?"

"I believe so, sir."

He laughs and tosses it back to DeMint.

"Go away, kid," he says. "Your platoon leader, Pitman, he should do a better job taking care of his troops."

"Sir, with all due respect, that's my gear, and I want it back."

Hudson says, "With all due respect, you're not getting it back."

I nod, walk forward, and punch him as hard as I can, right in the center of his chest.

He lets out an impressive "oomph!", falls back, and then I approach DeMint, who looks scared, and drops my helmet and vest on the ground. I pick it up.

"This is mine," I say. "And I'll beat the crap out of anyone who tries to take it."

Hudson is on his hands and knees, trying to catch his breath, and before he does that, I move quickly and rapidly away from First Platoon, and as I do so, there's a creaking noise, and off a ways the door opens to the General's cabin, and one of his staff members looks out.

Back at Second Platoon, my captain sees me approaching, and shakes his head. "Damn it, there's going to be hell to pay," he says, and he's very correct. In about ten minutes Hudson is at our camp, face red, accompanied by two tough-looking soldiers, and he meets up with Pitman and says, "I'm placing your lieutenant under arrest."

Pitman says, "For what?"

He points his finger at me. "Assaulting a superior officer. And I have witnesses."

Pitman says, "Sorry, he's Second Platoon, my responsibility. Whatever punishment the lieutenant receives will be my job."

Hudson shakes his head. "No. That's not going to happen."

"Afraid it is, David," Pitman says.

"Afraid you're wrong," Hudson says. "I've spoken to the General. Your kid's up for a court-martial, within the hour. Assaulting a superior officer. And just to remind the both of you, under the current martial law, that's a capital offense."

He looks at me with emphasis. "That's execution, kid. Death penalty."

It goes fast, very fast. Pitman walks with me to the General's hut, and I'm hoping for some words of advice, or encouragement, but Pitman keeps quiet. As we get closer I say, "What's the General like?"

"You'll see, soon enough."

"And there's no other senior officers? Just you and Captain Hudson?"

"Just the two of us, that's all."

"Captain Pitman—"

"Lieutenant, save it for the court-martial."

At the hut the door is open, and Captain Hudson is standing there, smiling, and with him is DeMint, the soldier who had apparently taken my gear.

Hudson says, "All right, let's get this over with."

Pitman says, "After you, Hudson."

He smiles. "First Platoon, leading the way."

Inside the hut it's dimly lit, and when my eyes adjust, I take in the General's quarters. There's a real bed to the right, a chair before me, with two other folding metal chairs, and there's some sort of kitchen off to the left. There are rows of canned food on three wooden shelves. My mouth waters. The two men who are supposedly the General's staff sit in the metal chairs, arms folded, looking amused, wearing BDUs that while being mended and patched, look in pretty good shape. They have dark hair, fair skin, and from where I stand, they look like brothers, and they keep on smiling and smiling.

Sure, I think. A court-martial. Something nice to break up the routine.

Behind the chair is a curtain that is drawn back, and a heavy-set woman comes out, wearing BDUs.

The General?

Even though we are in a structure and nobody is wearing a cover,

Pitman, DeMint, and Hudson all salute the General, and she makes a halfhearted gesture with her right hand, sitting down, breathing hard. There's no name badge on her BDUs but on the shoulders are straps that have four stars on each strap.

Four stars?

She breathes heavily, "All right, let's get this over with. What's the charge?"

Hudson says, "Assaulting a superior officer during time of war."

The General nods. "A serious charge. Which soldier?"

"Me," I say. "Lieutenant Randy Knox."

"Who's your commanding officer?"

"Captain Pitman," I say. "Second Platoon."

"Interesting," she says. "But Captain Hudson is from First Platoon. How did this come about?"

I say, "I was attempting to retrieve gear that had been stolen from me . . . ma'am. In the process, I had an altercation with Captain Hudson."

She nods again. "I see. How do you plead?"

"Not guilty, ma'am," I say. If coming into this Creeper Dome had turned my world upside down, being in this stuffy cabin with these people was sending my world out into space. Nothing was right, nothing made sense. The soldiers, the setup, the set matches with the starving Russians on the other side of this part of the Dome . . . even naming a damn Transport Creeper.

The General says, "Captain Hudson? What happened?"

He says, "This young man came over to my platoon. He was upset that his helmet and vest were missing. He accused someone in my platoon with having stolen them. I told him to return to his unit. He then punched me, took the helmet and vest, and that's when I made the complaint. Ma'am."

"I see. Captain Pitman, do you have anything to add?"

"No, ma'am."

She wipes at her lips. "Yet you say you're not guilty. Why's that? Did you in fact strike a superior officer?"

"No, ma'am," I say. Even the two men who are supposedly her staff look confused.

"Hold on," she says. "Did you or did you not strike Captain Hudson?"

"I did," I say. "Right in the chest. I thought about kicking him in the head when I left, but I thought that would be too much."

Hudson says, "General, please, this is ridiculous."

"I agree," she says. "Lieutenant . . . Knox?"

"Yes, ma'am."

"You're being confusing," she says.

"Probably," I say. "I'll make it clear. I did in fact strike this man over here. But he's not my superior officer."

"The hell I'm not!" Hudson says, stepping closer to me, like he wants to return the favor.

"But it's true," I say. "Sorry to embarrass you in front of your friends, but you're not in the Army. You're not a soldier, not a captain. My guess is, he's a Coastie who grabbed a uniform at one time, and decided to play pretend."

Lots of talking breaks out and everyone tries to get a word in, except for Captain Pitman, who stands there, glum and looking down at his feet. I keep quiet and when the talking finally dribbles away, I ask, "General, if I may?"

"Go on."

"This . . . man told me earlier he had done basic training at Fort Carson, in Colorado. That's impossible. I don't know if it exists anymore, but it was a big base, lots of armored units and Special Forces headquartered there. But never basic training. Never."

Hudson says, "The hell you say."

"The hell I do," I reply. "One of my instructors at Ft. St. Paul had spent time there. Talked it up a lot. And there was no basic training at Ft. Carson."

Now it's really quiet in the little cabin. "And you, ma'am. Your shoulder epaulets have four stars. Begging your pardon, ma'am, I really don't think you're a four-star general."

She purses her lips. "None of your business, now, is it."

"Considering I'm supposedly under your command, it most certainly is my business."

She rubs at her lips again. "Perhaps, but not for long. Lieutenant . . ."

"Knox."

"Yes, Lieutenant Knox. Stand at attention, please."

I don't.

"Very well," she says. "I find you guilty of assault. The sentence is death. To be carried out forthwith."

A big cold hammer comes out of nowhere and slams right into my chest.

"I request an appeal."

"Certainly," she says. "If you can find some way to contact any military forces on the surface, do file your appeal. In the meantime . . . Captain Hudson?"

"Ma'am," he says, sounding relieved and happy.

"Sergeants Glenn and Corsi of my staff will assist you. Carry out the sentence immediately."

I decide not to wait.

I punch Hudson in the side of his head, and bail out of the General's hut.

But I don't get far. Two First Platoon members are hanging outside of the hut, and seeing me burst out and start running, they figure something is amiss and wrestle me to the ground, pushing my face into the dirt.

I cough, spit out the dirt, and I'm dragged back in, the two soldiers holding me still, twisting my arms behind me. The General looks to me and says, "As I was saying, the sentence will be carried out immediately. Sergeants Glenn and Corsi, please proceed."

A length of chain is wrapped around my wrists, the links biting deep, and I'm dragged outside, with the General staying behind. I guess immediately means immediately. Captain Pitman stays at my side, which I guess is a nice gesture on his part, and I'm led away by the two staff members.

I spit out more dirt from my mouth and say, "Captain Pitman?"

"Yes?"

"You a fake like Hudson?"

He keeps quiet for three or four steps. The chains are cold against my wrists. The rest of the First Platoon slowly stand up and start following us. I wonder if any of my temporary fellow troopers from Second Platoon are coming over to see the show.

He says, "How old where you when the invasion came?"

"I was six."

"I was twenty," Pitman says. "Was going to community college. Studying to be a medical records technician."

"A what?"

"Never mind. Then the war started. We practically lost it in the first day . . . one thing though, was some senator, on the radio, saying all men and women who could resist, should join up or join a militia. I tried that. I really did . . . and . . . ah, hell. I was a guy in a uniform with a gun, trying to survive. Was that any different from any other soldier out there?"

I didn't feel like answering. I tugged at my chains. Tight and biting. The two sergeants did a good job.

"The General? Her staff?"

"Nobody's too sure . . . the guys are her nephews. They talk a lot about missing their motorcycles. We guess it was a gang from around Las Vegas."

We go up a slope and down a slope. A thick piece of wood, stuck in the dirt and at an angle, is waiting for me. Chains dangle from the side of the wood, along with a stained piece of canvas with a hole cut in the middle.

"Are there any real military here?"

"Some, scattered here and there. Pope, he's in the Army for real, so's Snook. A couple of others."

Okay, then. I pull at the chains. Still damn tight.

I'm taken to the wooden pole, which is also stained, and I'm equally part terrified and curious on how this is going to be done, and Captain Hudson comes over, carrying the stained canvas with the hole in the center. He drapes the canvas over me, and my head pokes out, and it's like I'm wearing a very stained and stiff poncho.

He smiles. "We used to strip the prisoners, get their clothes off so they wouldn't get stained, but that got bad for morale. Thing I learned is, you got any morale at all, you try to preserve it."

I want to tell him off, like saying drop dead or go to hell, but those words seem very childish. I'm chained to the post and Hudson returns, with a bayonet and I yell out, "I'm Lieutenant Randy Knox, a duly-sworn officer of the United States Army! Any military personnel present, I'm your commanding officer. Disarm this man and the others, and—"

Hudson slaps me hard. "Shut up, kid. You're hurting morale." He grabs my hair and turns my head, and says in a calm voice, "Sentence having been duly passed by the General, I thereby—"

I have a brief but vivid memory of old Western movies, when the cavalry arrives to save the day in the nick of time.

And by God, the cavalry comes to save me.

With eight legs, not four.

Click-click.

Click-click.

Click-click.

CHAPTER TWELVE

It's a Research Creeper, not a Transport Creeper, and this bug moves fast. Lots of times I've seen Creepers in action, moving slow and deliberate, like they have all the time in the world to burn us and lase us, but this guy appeared in the distant haze of the far Dome, and raced across the dunes, and now I think I know why the bugs built this place for the humans, with the dunes and little ravines: It must be what it's like on their home world, wherever the hell that damnable place might be.

This Creeper races up and then comes to a halt, its eight legs kicking up dirt and dust onto the onlookers here, its two weaponized arms swiveling and moving around, the lead part of the arthropod—where the bug sits and controls its exoskeleton—moving up and down.

I'm even more scared than I was a minute ago—when it looked like my throat was going to be slit, but at least by a human—but I give these guys credit. They look up with curiosity, or interest, or little fear.

My heart, though, is thudding so hard that a desperate part of me wishes it could break the chains.

Hudson yells, "Moran! Get over here."

Moran emerges from the small group, gets over to Hudson, and Hudson says, "Ask the bug why it's here."

"Sir?"

Hudson kicks his left leg. "You think you know the Creeper language so well, ask him why he's here!"

Moran licks his lips and glances around, like he's seeking support or someone to come forward to volunteer, but Hudson is looking like he's going to kick him again, and Moran steps forward, puts his hands around his mouth, and starts clicking, chattering, and snapping to the Research Creeper.

The lead arthropod whips around and then down, like it's examining this strange two-legged creature that's learned its language, and the Creeper spits back in its own words. Moran hesitates, tries again.

More spitting, chattering, clicking.

Moran shakes his head, tries one more time.

The Creeper spits out one little phrase, and even with my ignorance of the language, I can tell that the bug repeats it twice.

Moran turns and says, "Captain . . . best I can tell, it's saying 'stop.'"

"Stop what?"

"I . . . I'm not too sure, sir. She keeps on saying 'stop,' and there's other words and phrases I can't really make out, but I think she wants us to stop and not um, kill, er, execute the prisoner."

"What?" Hudson strides forward and says to Moran, "No, no, we're not going to do that. There's . . . an agreement, a treaty, or something. The General's told me. We keep our own order, we do everything on our own, except when we have to fight. Tell the bug no, no way."

Moran says, "Captain, no, I really can't—"

Hudson grabs his shoulder. "Do it, do it now, soldier!"

Moran pulls away, starts running. "Do it yourself! I ain't doing it! Do it yourself!"

Hudson turns back to the bug, fists clenched, face red. The Creeper repeats the phrase.

"Whaddya gonna do, Cap?" someone calls out.

"Yeah, David." It's Snook this time. "You're the big man. Tell the bug to go screw."

Command is many things, and one of them is not backing down. I think I know what's going on in Hudson's mind: If he backs down before this bug, by the end of the "day" here in the Dome, he won't be First Platoon leader anymore.

He steps forward, yells up at the Creeper, "Look, we're in charge here, not you! That's the agreement!"

The Creeper repeats the last phrase, slower this time, like he's hoping speaking slower will help the two-legged beast better understand.

"No!" Hudson says, his voice wavering. "We're not going to—"

A flicker of light that dazzles my eyes for a moment, and then Hudson falls to the ground, his trunk and legs going one way, his upper torso, arms, and head going another.

Nobody moves. The Creeper repeats its phrase. A couple of soldiers at the edge of the group slip away. I can't blame them. The Creeper comes closer to me—to me!—and lowers its claws, its center arthropod, looking, examining, maybe even sniffing. I'm so close the stench of cinnamon makes me gag, and I can hear things whirring and wheezing from inside the exoskeleton.

Then it rears back, lowers one of its weaponized arms, *flick-flicks* a laser beam, and something smokes and falls to the ground.

One of the chains holding me to the execution post.

The Creeper repeats the same phrase again, slower. Moran yells out, "I think I know what the bug is saying! It wants the lieutenant off the post!"

Two soldiers don't wait for orders. They race over to me, start working the chains binding me to the post, free me, and then they get the canvas poncho off, and I say, "My wrists, free my wrists." That's not part of what the Creeper apparently wants, but the two guys don't hesitate.

My wrists are free.

I bring them forward, rub them. They're both bleeding some. Based on what was about to happen sixty seconds ago, I'm not complaining.

The Creeper comes to me again, motioning with its arms.

I don't want to do anything.

The same movement, more pronounced.

I keep still.

A burst of flame spears out, hitting the ground behind me, about a half meter away, close enough for me to feel.

Shit.

I start moving and the Research Creeper skitters behind me, shoots off another little tongue of fire, and I can't pretend to be stupid anymore, and I start moving away from the execution site and the encampments of both the Second and First Platoon.

I walk as slow as I can, and turn my head. "Mr. Pitman!" I call out.

"Right here," he says, breaking away from the onlooking soldiers.

"Raise your right hand and repeat after me," I call out, and he looks puzzled, and then nods in recognition, and I start off, "I, state your name. . ."

"I, Mark Pitman . . ."

"Do solemnly swear . . ."

"Do solemnly swear . . ."

"That I will support and defend the Constitution of the United States against all enemies, foreign and domestic . . ."

We manage to get through the oath of enlistment before I'm too far away to be heard, and at the end, Pitman yells out, "But I don't believe in God!"

"Not my problem!" I yell back. "Under Martial Law and the State of Emergency acts, you're assigned a battlefield promotion of captain! You're legal! Take command of these forces . . ."

He yells back but I can't make out the words, but it seems like he wasn't swearing at me, so maybe it was all legal after all.

Not that it mattered much, but it mattered to me.

Another little tickle of flame.

I turn back, give the Research Creeper the two-fingered salute. "All right, all right, I get it. Don't waste your fuel."

My second long march begins.

It turns out pretty dull. Unlike the last one, there's not much to break up the monotony, just the march up and down, up and down across the sand dunes, and after what may be an hour, or two, we come across a pile of bug machinery. There's piping and flickering lights that hurt my eyes, and a deep hum that rattles me, and my escort pushes me to give it a wide, wide berth, like there's something in there that might jump out and kill me.

That makes me giggle for a while, at the absurdity of it all, and then we top another dune and walk into a scene of horror that makes my earlier experiences seem as horrible as a platoon picnic.

It takes me a few minutes to comprehend what I'm seeing as I get closer. There's a Creeper ahead of us, but it's on a pile of rocks and timbers. It looks dead, a Battle model. Figures are around the base of rocks and timber lying down. There are a few shelters of scrap wood and cloth, and a small, smoldering fire. One figure stands up, and then another, and another.

My bug escort and I get even closer, and I whisper, "Oh, God," at seeing the figures stumble toward us. If the so-called soldiers I had met looked hungry and gaunt, these are walking skeletons with flesh stretched over them, wearing bits of cloth.

Two or three seem stronger, start toward me, waving long sticks. One is bearded, wearing a hat—a top hat!—and he yells, "Our prayers . . . they've been answered! Pray to God and we are rewarded. Meat! Meat!"

A chant starts up, weak voices that get stronger. "Meat! Meat!"

Others kneel and bow before the dead Creeper, and two things strike me hard and with despair: one is that these starved humans are worshipping the Creepers, and with their yells of "Meat! Meat!" they're staring right at me.

I start running, moving away from them, at an angle, and the Creeper doesn't give me any trouble, just sending off a little laser flash to the right, to make sure I don't go too far afield. Driven by desperation and hunger, though, the little mob is keeping up with me.

The man with the top hat swings his club over his head and says, "See? See? I told you not to despair! Not to give up! Our God will provide! Our God will take care of us!"

I keep up a good pace but the mob is closing in, and I'm not looking forward to the fight. I'm sure I can take the lead guy down but all it would take is one lucky blow to stun me, and then . . .

I don't want to think about it.

The Research Creeper crackles out some sort of sentence, but the mob presses in, still chanting, "Meat! Meat! Thank you God!" and then I think the Creeper is either tired or amused, and with a little spurt of flame, takes down the two near skeletal men chasing me—just missing the leader with the top hat—and the forms stand and then slowly collapse, burning in greasy flames and a thick cloud of smoke.

There are shouts and whoops from the others, and some start to throw dirt on the burning forms, and when the smoke and flames clear, it looks like one of those old static-filled and scratchy *Mutual of Omaha's Wild Kingdom* programs shown for entertainment back home, with the huddled figures of the predators tearing at the fresh kill.

I move along and maybe the Creeper is showing mercy— doubtful—or it's distracted, because I fall to my knees and try to throw up whatever's left in my belly, and then I get up, wipe at my face, and keep on moving.

At some point the dunes drift away and then thin out, and now we're moving on wide and smooth stone. I don't know if it's bedrock or construction or whatever, but it just feels good to be walking on something firm.

From the indirect lighting I can see scratch marks and gouges on the stone, as if hundreds, if not thousands, of Creepers had moved around here, and keeping it all together with one Creeper at my back is challenge enough. I can't stand the thought of seeing more.

Up ahead a shape comes into view. A dome, big enough but small enough so that it doesn't overwhelm the scenery. A dome within the Dome. I stand still and my escort back there flickers laser beams behind me, *flick-flick-flick*, and I get the message. I start toward the dome, thinking that it will dilate open like the larger Dome did earlier.

I'm about three meters away when the dome starts lifting up. I don't see any cables or support mechanisms. Just the damn thing lifting up like some sort of magician's trick.

The area underneath the dome is illuminated, again, from recessed lighting I can't make out. There's a round metal platform revealed that has a lip of about a third of a meter high around all around.

The Research Creeper talks to me, the usual mix of hisses and crackles. I turn and look up and say, "Sorry, asshole, I can't make out what you said. Terribly thick accent you've got there."

It moves an arm and a ball of flame spurts out, and I run under the lifted dome, jumping up over the lip.

I turn and the Creeper seems to be staring at me.

Then, the damnedest thing happens.

The Creeper lowers both arms, and then its forward legs, and the center arthropod, like it's bowing in thanks, or acknowledgement, or some sort of supplication. I don't understand it.

For some reason I remember a number of old movies shown back at the mess hall, most from the World War II era, showing enemies on a battlefield, recognizing each one's honor, maybe saluting in respect to a foe on the other side of a conflict.

As the dome overhead starts to descend, I give my own salute back to the Creeper, lifting up both middle fingers.

My little moment of defiance only lasts a few seconds, as the Dome comes down over me, snapping into place on the very wide metal circle, and putting me into complete and utter darkness.

Darkness.

It's rare anyone is in complete darkness, because there's always some ambient light leaking in somewhere from a fire, a gas lamp, the moon, the flares of light from space debris burning up minute after minute through the upper atmosphere.

But this is complete darkness, like being in a deep, deep cave or bunker, with no lights on at all.

I bring my hand up to my face, and don't see a thing. I even touch my face and I still can't see a damn thing.

I decide it's time to wander some, to get to the edge of the dome and see if I can hear anything, or note a crack of light.

I can't move.

I try again.

Motionless.

Not like a bug caught in a spider web. At least that little bug can squirm and wiggle around. I can't move. My legs won't shift, and my arms are now being pushed to the side.

I'm standing straight at attention, like a first day inductee at boot camp.

I yell out, "I'm not having much fun in here!"

Then the world explodes in light and my chest is crushed.

I try to scream and I can't. Nothing is going on in my chest, mouth, lips. The light is so bright it hurts my eyes, and even when I close my eyes, the glare hurts and hurts so much.

The pressure against my chest spreads to my arms and trunk and legs, and I can't even open my mouth, and it even seems like my nose is pushing down against my sinuses, and the glare and the pressure and now there's noise, and it goes on for long miserable eternal seconds.

Then it stops.

Just like that.

And I'm falling.

Falling.

Now I'm screaming.

I'm falling, flailing, and a reptile part of my mind says I'll hit the metal, I've got to hit something solid, and I'm thinking of the hundreds of thousands who died on the first day of the war, jumping from their burning, drowning, or crumbling skyscrapers.

I hit the ground.

I yelp.

I bounce.

Bounce!

Then I come to rest again.

On my butt.

I run my hands across the surface. It feels like where I was standing.

A thumping noise makes the surface vibrate, and then a crack of light extends all around in me in a perfect circle, and the dome starts to rise up, up, up.

I stand up, woozy, aching, sick to my stomach.

The dome lifts higher and higher.

I blink my eyes.

It's all wrong.

I'm not in the Base Dome, back in Connecticut.

Before me is rough-hewn rock, with cables and boxes and odd protrusions about ten or so meters off the ground, and tunnels going off in every direction, at least six I can see, carved or melted or drilled into the rock.

The air is thin. I take a few deep breaths, and yes, there's a strong smell of cinnamon.

I know where I am.

Oh God, now I know where I am.

I'm on the Creepers' orbital battle station.

I'm in space.

I'm frozen, unable to move, unable much to think.

Then comes a noise.

Click-click.

Click-click.

Click-click.

Creepers on the move.

I get off the round stone pad, down to the stone surface, nearly slip and fall. I windmill my arms.

Something's not right with the gravity.
I feel much lighter.
Click-click.
Click-click.
Click-click.
Closer and louder.
So what.
Time to run.
So I run.

CHAPTER THIRTEEN

With six tunnels I have six choices to take, and I go to the one that seems further away from the clicking sound of the approaching Creepers, which also happens to be the nearest.

Run, run, run, and I slide and skip and fall due to the damn change in gravity.

The tunnel is wide, tall, and burrowed out of smooth rock. Above me are conduits, cables, tubing, and oddly shaped objects that look like crystals of some sort, growing out of the rock. As I run I'm desperately looking for a hidey-hole, a smaller tunnel, some sort of door or opening, but there's nothing, no escape.

Deep in my marrow I know that I have no chance, that there's no escape up here in this orbiting nest of Creepers, but I'm also in no mood to give up and surrender. I've already done that once in my Army career and I'm going to delay this surrender ceremony as long as possible.

Perhaps because I'm young and stupid.

Or just stupid.

The tunnel curves to the right and the clicking noise sounds like the damn bugs are on my tail, and I keep on running until I run out of room.

Damn it!

The tunnel ends in a round hatch, blocking my escape. Huge. It looks like those big doors blocking bank vaults that I've seen in old movies shown back at the mess hall at Ft. St. Paul. There are more boxes and lights and cables around one side of the door, but there's no way to puzzle out how it controls the door.

And who knows what's on the other side.

I whip around.

The clicking sound gets louder.

What now?

I look up and there's another mass of conduits and cables, and I can't reach it, no matter how hard I try.

The stench of cinnamon nearly makes me gag.

I jump.

Yeah, I jump.

And hard to believe, with the lower gravity, I make it.

I grab two thick cables and haul myself up, and there's a stone shelf behind the cables that I roll onto.

Light illuminates this part of the tunnel.

The clicking stops.

I sense a large object is now below me.

I should stay put and hidden, but that would be the smart and reasonable approach.

I edge out and peer over, and I have to force myself to stay still, because I want to shove myself back in, deep in the stone, and stay there until I die from starvation or thirst.

Below me is a Creeper. I've seen lots of Creepers over the years, and even had a hand in killing some. Each time I see a Creeper, something cold and twisted squirms at the base of my chest, seeing the armored center arthropod, the segmented legs, and the two weaponized arms. A couple of times I've read confidential reports that Dad had left out in the open back at home, how Army psychs determined that the reason so many troopers and civilians ran at the first sight of the Creepers was some innate fear of bugs, especially bugs the size of small school buses.

But if anything, this is worse, because the bug below isn't wearing its armor. It's wearing some sort of transparent hood or large bag about its head and center arthropod, with tubes and canisters, and I guess it's a breathing apparatus to wander around in this part of the orbital battle station that has been converted to human use.

So unlike the many, many other times, instead of just seeing smooth and jagged armor, I can see the damn bug in the clear. It has dark segmented legs with fine hairs, and the center arthropod is also the same dark color, and there are things that look moist or wet, and the head is a jagged horror of open incisors and jaws, and two eyes on segmented stalks.

The upper arms are examining the door, skittering around, and then it backs away, and moves back down the tunnel.

My chest is tight and it's hard to breathe, and I roll back into the stone and curl in a ball and try not to think anymore. I'm hurting as well, my ribs, my arms and legs, the top of my skull. It feels like I've been caught up in a squeezing vice that somehow has just let go.

God.

I wake up because my bladder tells me to. Damn it.

I roll out and move down some along the way of the cables, find a smaller opening, drop my trousers and let loose.

I feel pretty good afterward, pissing on Creeper property.

Not much of a victory but I'll take it.

I look over the lip of the stone and the cables, see the empty tunnel. Now what?

I have a flashback to cartoons shown back at the barracks, some more than a century old, of a cat and mouse chasing and fighting each other in a house. I'm definitely the mouse in this environment, and I plan to keep on avoiding those buggy cats as long as possible.

Again, I know what's going to happen.

It's inevitable.

But I'm staying free as long as I can.

I push myself over the edge, hold onto the nearest cable, let go.

I drop slowly in this weird gravity, and I hit the ground and roll. No problem.

I get up and start down the tunnel, keeping close to the side, hugging it as if I were a little mouse.

I should be scared out of my wits—and yes, part of me is that scared—but the Recon part of my job is begging to be let out, and I'm glad to be doing something instead of just hiding.

I slip my way down the tunnel and come out into the main . . . chamber? Concourse? Central terminal?

I rest at the tunnel's opening, try to take everything in. Huge stone dome in front of me that obviously is part of the transport system, what is called the *Grantztch*. The other five tunnels. Big overhead curved roof that can't be made out.

All right, I think. Let's Recon the shit out of this.

For some reason, back down in the Base Dome, I was rescued from being murdered by my fellow humans and then was brought up here, to low Earth orbit, in the belly of the second orbital battle station. It looked like there was a greeting party waiting for me when I arrived, but either it was too late or I was too quick to get off the *Grantztch's* surface and hide out.

All right.

What does this mean, Recon boy?

It means I was taken up here for a reason. I don't think they'd go to this time, effort, and using energy to transport one teenager soldier up here to be interrogated or to have my brain removed for later study.

So why?

I recall the odd things that happened to me in the past several days, when I was first detached from my duty station at Ft. St. Paul and was tasked to escort Serena Coulson and her brother Buddy to Albany, the capital. Along the way there was an ambush, fighting, me and Thor getting injured, and weirdness of all weirdness, me being awarded a Silver Star for bravery. I even got to meet and shake the hand of the President.

Not bad for a guy my age.

But there were other things as well . . . me forcing Buddy Coulson to talk Creeper talk, and get the Creepers in a Base Dome to surrender. A dark country road in New York State, where it looked like Creepers were examining bloody bandages and other battle debris, like they were hunting for someone. And a time later, in a buried and secret Air Force base, coming face-to-face—or bug—and seeing a live Creeper, kept prisoner and shorn of its armor, and how it seemed to react to my approach.

Reason.

I was certainly brought up here for a reason.

My bones and organs are aching, and although I'm hungry and thirsty, I'm still tired. I take one last look around and whisper, "Well, dang, it'd be nice to see a big lever with a sign that says, 'Tug this way to get back to Earth,' but we do what we can."

And what I do is to crawl back into my hidey-hole, and try to relax.

There's a vibration in the stone, from Creeper machinery at work somewhere deeper in their station, and a distant *click click click*, and before I fall asleep, I'm almost convinced I'm hearing human voices, whispering frantically, but I must be hearing things, and then I fall asleep.

A loud horn bursts out and scares the crap out of me, and I bang my head against the stone.

Damn it!

I'm really hungry and thirsty now, and then the horn repeats itself, louder and louder.

I should stay in my hiding place.

I've grown accustomed to it.

But the battered taxpayers of the United States are paying me to do a job, so I get to work, tossing myself out again from the crevasse, and get back down on the tunnel floor, and work my way back to the center terminal.

There's something different with the large stone dome. Its color has changed, and it looks like it's vibrating. Hard to explain, seeing something so big and so solid vibrating, but it's vibrating so much that it seems to shimmer, like a desert mirage, though I've never been on a desert in my life.

The horns grow louder, such that I don't hear the *click click click* of the approaching Creepers, but two of them roll in, and surprise, surprise, they're in full arthropod armor, like they were back on Earth, spoiling for a fight.

My hands ache, wishing for a Colt M-10, because these two bugs are situated in a perfect firing solution, and I'm sure I could kill them both—to what end, well, okay—but I keep plastered to the side of the wall, curious what's going to happen next.

The horns grow in volume and pitch, and then stop. The stone floor is vibrating, like it's matching the vibrations from the dome. The two Creepers—Battle versions, of course—move like they're flanking the dome, and then a bright light glares out from the base of the dome, nearly blinding me.

Then the damn thing is lifting itself up, with no apparent wires and cables.

One damn spooky scene, that's about to get spookier.

The dome lifts higher and higher, and then there's figures standing there . . . about five, maybe six.

Dressed in uniforms.

Soldiers.

Humans.

My throat seizes up and I want to cheer them, thinking maybe they're a raiding or invading force, but no, they stand still, bewildered, in a small group, like a small herd of cattle gathering together, smelling or hearing wild dogs or wolves in the distance.

The Creepers approach, a weaponized arm from each setting off a burst of flame, and I know exactly what they're doing: They're herding those poor guys off the stone platform.

One by one they get off, and they start talking, and I don't understand their language. I can also see them better from my vantage point and all six are small, smaller than me, but they look muscular and compact, and their skin is dark and their eyes are—

"Gurkhas," I whisper. "I'll be damned."

Some of the toughest fighters on the planet, known as such for centuries, and here they are, up with me in LEO. Their uniforms are stained and tattered, some are carrying rucksacks, and I wonder where they were captured. Their home turf is in Nepal, of course, but the Creepers usually stay away from mountainous terrain, which is one of the very few things that has worked in our favor during the past decade.

But they also have long and storied history with the British Army, and that makes sense, that they—

One, and then two of the Gurkhas scream and race right to the Creepers, holding long curved knives in their hands, and in the *blink-blink-blink* of an eye, they're both cut down by laser fire.

The other four huddle and shout, and one soldier's voice is louder than the others, and maybe he's an officer, maybe he's an NCO, but he gets them in order. They line up in perfect parade formation, and with one Creeper leading and the other following, the four survivors march away, keeping eyes front, and they go down a tunnel I've not yet explored.

I exhale, shudder.

The two dead Gurkhas are about thirty meters away.

The lasers have taken off their heads.

Their rucksacks are still on their bodies.

Their rucksacks are still there.

No time to think it through, or to have a moral debate, or anything else than thinking what might be in those canvas strapped knapsacks, and I run out in the open and make a good sprint to the two dead soldiers. I skid to a halt on the stone and kneel down, and one knapsack is easy to remove, but the other one is harder. The straps are all tangled up and there's a heavy stench of burnt meat, and I breathe through my mouth and work, and work at it, and damn it, the straps won't cooperate.

Click.

Click.

Click.

Bugs coming back. Maybe a clean-up squad.

Damn it!

Then I see one of the curved knives next to the first body, and in a few seconds, the other knapsack is free.

I grab them both and the knife and run back to the tunnel that I'm now calling "mine," saying prayers along the way, one's for me, and others for the two dead, brave and foolish men back there.

But they were warriors.

Maybe they were foolish, but they were warriors.

Into the dark tunnel I go.

Back up in my hidey-hole, and by touch I push the knife into a near crack, get the knapsacks squared away, and I let my eyes adjust to the semidarkness before I take an inventory. I unzip each rucksack and first take out some clothing, trousers and shirts that just might fit me There are also paper-wrapped and plastic-wrapped packages, some with English notations, others with squiggles and lines that must be Nepali words. From the dim light I unwrap one of the packages, and there's some kind of dried chicken mixed with cold rice and spices. I offer thanks to the dead soldiers back there and chew and swallow. My mouth and throat starts burning, and I'm lucky to grab a plastic bottle of water. I open the cap and take a slow swallow, and then another. The label is faded and peeling but says HIGHLAND SPRINGS. I'm not sure where Highland Springs is but they bottle some fine water.

After I've eaten and taken another swig of water—I'm not sure if I'll be able to find a water source on this giant hunk of rock anytime soon—I drag the two knapsacks closer to the light and do a more thorough examination.

There's a crinkly foil blanket that will be good to keep me warm tonight, and additional bits and pieces of clothing, socks and such. In one pocket of the second knapsack there are some folded papers and photographs. I pull them out and spread them out on the stone. Letters, and written in the same script as the food packages.

There's also a color photograph, faded, of a woman dressed in what I guess was Nepalese clothing, smiling, and her arms around two young boys. On the reverse is some more writing.

The soldier's wife, and children.

Kept at his side, all this time, and brought up into space.

I carefully fold the letters back and slip the photo into place. I'll bring them back, I think. I'll bring them back and somehow contact the British army liaison in the United States, and somehow—

I shake my head.

Idiot.

I put the papers and photo back into the knapsack.

Who am I trying to fool?

I'm never leaving this rock. I'm free for the moment, as free as a condemned prisoner wandering around in his large cell, but at some point, I'll be discovered and killed, or I'll be recaptured and killed, or recaptured and tortured, interrogated, or dissected.

I take one more sip of water and unfold another foil package, and there are two squares of chocolate. I break off one and slowly chew it, trying to make it last as long as possible. My stomach rumbles but I try to be a good boy, and I rewrap the remaining square and put it away.

I take some of the clothing out and make a nest of my own, and try to get to sleep. The clothes smell of sweat, smoke, and odd spices and scents. In any other place it would have caused me to toss them aside, but not in this place.

It smells of humans, and I find that incredibly comforting, and I manage to sleep.

CHAPTER FOURTEEN

I sleep and dream of running in a field, chasing after Thor, and no matter how much I call to him, he either can't or won't hear me. My voice should be strong, shouting, but is only coming out in a strangled whisper, and I slowly wake up, realizing where I am.

A dream.

A damn dream, that's all.

I rub at my face and the whispers continue.

Hunh?

I slowly roll over and make my way to the edge of the stone, look down.

Shapes.

Three of them.

And not Creepers.

Humans?

I can't believe it.

I call down, "Hey!"

And the shapes run away.

Damn it!

Without thinking of grabbing anything to take along with me, I jump down, hit the stone floor, and start running as well. I make a good start but as I near the end of the tunnel, I trip and fall, rolling and rolling, and stop rolling with something sharp jabbing into my side.

I'm held down with hands on each of my arm, and a male voice whispers, "Jesus, shut the hell up. You want the bugs to jump us?"

119

"Let me go," I whisper back.

"You gonna fight?"

"Not unless I have to," I say.

A woman's voice says, "Slit his throat and leave him be."

Another woman says, "Joanie, you're overreacting you are. Shut your mouth."

"He'll get us killed, that's what."

"No," the male's voice says. "I think he's new. Smells too good. We'll bring him down and talk to him, find out what we can."

Then he talks to me. "Buddy, I'm gonna let you up, and you're gonna follow us, and not give us any trouble. Okay? You come with us, we'll give you somethin' to eat. Fair? But I tell you . . . you give me any grief, I won't kill you. I'll just abandon you somewhere in the dark, and later you'll wish I'd'a killed you."

Not particularly fair, but I want to know who these people are, how and why they're here, and what's going on. Once again, back to my Recon job.

"Sure," I say. "I'll cooperate."

My arms are let loose and I sit up, and in the semidarkness of the tunnel, it's hard to make out who's before me, and all I can tell is that there's a man and two women. The man comes up to me and he says, "Grab a hold of my belt. I'll lead you."

I do that and we shuffle forward, and then he says, "Gonna crawl. Get down now. Hold onto my boot, and hold tight . . . you let go, you'll get lost, and trust me . . . there's a bunch of bones deep in here from other guys who got lost."

The crawling starts and I grab the boot tight, and then we move along, and then I feel like we're entering a crack or fissure, and I lift my head for a moment, and get a nasty scrape, and we're squirming into a large crack, moving along, my breathing sharp and harsh, feeling the rock close in on me.

Crawl, crawl, and once I lose grasp of the boot—which terrifies me in the darkness—and the boot snaps out and catches me in the jaw.

The pain doesn't matter, because I get a hold of the boot again. This little dark parade continues, and I hear one of the women up ahead muttering, and I shift my head and see that she's counting off where we're going.

It's a long haul.

And I hope they're not taking me somewhere for a meal, with me the main course, because there's no way I can find my way back.

"Hold on," the man whispers, and we go forward, and I take a tumble.

But it's a short drop, and I feel like we're in a room or a chamber. Then the man says, "Watch your eyes," and there's a *snap* as a lighter is lit off, and with the sudden flare of light, the chamber—which seemed as huge as a barracks—shrinks into its real size.

I ignore the chamber for a moment, and take in the three humans before me. Man, woman, and another woman.

They are the palest human beings I've ever seen, and it's hard to determine their ages. They could be thirty, they could be sixty. I don't know. The guy has a full beard and all three have long hair, pulled back and tied off. The women . . . it seems like they are mother and daughter. Their clothes are a mix of military and civilian gear, and they are thin, but unlike lots of civilians I've seen over the years, they're relatively clean. The man lights off little bowls that have wicks and grease in them, and when four of the little bowls are lit, he snaps the lighter shut.

"My name's George Cooper," he says, and gestures to the two women, who have sat down on a collection of torn pillows and blankets. "My wife Gwen, and our daughter Joanie."

Joanie frowns. "You're my stepdad. You forget to say that, all the time."

George says, "Knock it off, Joanie. God's sake, it's been a long time, okay?"

But Joanie presses on. "And you and Ma never got really married. So I don't know how legal it is."

Gwen puts a hand on her daughter's hand. As I said, both are quite pale, but they have dark brown eyes, and black hair, although Gwen's is streaked with white and gray. They look at me with fascination and wide eyes, and George starts.

"That an Army uniform?"

"Yes."

"You in the Army, or you scrounge it somewhere off a dead guy?"

"I'm in the Army," I say. "New Hampshire National Guard, attached to the 26th Division. My name is Randy Knox."

Gwen says, "They're still fighting going on down there?"

"Yes," I say, "There's still fighting going on. Where are you folks from?"

George looks to the two women. "I'm from New Mexico. My girls here, they're from Iowa."

"I'm not your girl," Joanie says.

Gwen says, "Stow it, honey. Please. Sorry, you guys go on."

I say, "I've been here about two days. How long have you folks been here?"

Joanie looks down at the stone floor, and Gwen wipes at her eyes. George takes a deep breath, slowly lets it out. "Long. Way too long. Years, at least . . . what year is it, anyway?"

I tell them and they all just shake their heads, and Joanie turns and starts sniffling against her mother's shoulder. George says, "Damn . . . didn't know it was that long. I guess I shouldn't have asked. Damn . . ."

I say, "Were you captured together?"

George shakes his head. "No . . . I was a civvy volunteer, right after the bugs came. Set up a line supporting the National Guard near Roswell, got slaughtered. Me and about thirty or forty or so was captured. They . . . I still don't know what they call it, but they beamed us up to one asteroid rock, and then this one."

"Orbital battle station," I say. "I bet that was the first place you went."

Gwen is rubbing the back of Joanie's head. "What's that?"

"After the war started, a big object was seen in orbit. It's where the Creepers ran the war, and where they were able to transport stuff up and down from the surface. It's called an orbital battle station. This must be the second one."

George says, "You mean we're in orbit, around Earth?"

"Yes," I say. "There was another battle station that was destroyed about a month ago. This must be the backup."

I thought the news that their captors had taken a serious hit from humanity last month might have cheered them up or caused them a bit of happiness, but it didn't happen. Gwen turned to her husband and said, "You . . . you said we was traveling. That was the plan! That we was traveling."

George's pale face is flushed. "It stands to reason, all the farm stuff we've seen here."

"What farm stuff?"

Gwen is looking away from the two of us. George runs his hands through his hair, like a guy who's just found out he's lost a close friend. "This place . . . a battle station?"

"That's right."

George shakes his head. "Nah, that can't be right. I mean, there's lots of Creepers here, but . . . it's always seemed to be a supply place. A floating warehouse, maybe. Or repair shop. They do a lot of work repairing their armor, you know what I mean?"

"If you say so," I say. "But you three . . . how did you escape up here? Or get free?"

Gwen says, "We were in a long line with some other people. Germans, I think, I couldn't understand what they was talking about. The lights flickered on and off, like something wasn't working, and when they went off for a few seconds, I grabbed Joanie's hand and ran, and ran. We ended up in a place . . . almost like a farm, except some of the food was grown in troughs. We hid out there for a while, until George found us."

George says, "Yeah. I had been brought up with a bunch of guys from New Mexico, a lot of 'em were burnt and bleeding. I spread some blood on me and pretended to be dead. A couple of others had died when that son of a bitch beam brought us up and damn near crushed us. The Creepers forced the live ones to move out . . . the wounded . . . well, the wounded . . ."

He swallows. I say, "You don't have to explain."

"Okay, then. So there was a bunch of bodies there, and I figured some bug was gonna come up and clean 'em up, but I ran, Christ, did I run. I hid the best I could until I found this big-ass crack along one of the tunnel floors. I slipped in and . . . well, you wouldn't believe it. Lots of tunnels and cracks in this big rock, and once I could survive well enough, I started exploring. So here we are."

I looked around their quarters. There was bedding, some shelves made from wood or plastic, a few books, plastic and cardboard containers. The light from the oil lamps flicker, making shadows jump and move. "This . . . stuff. Where did it come from?"

Gwen says, "The bugs bring it up from Earth. They look stuff over, but if they can't use it or understand it, they dump it at various places. We're good scavengers."

I say, "Ma'am, I'm sorry, what did you mean earlier, about traveling?"

Joanie lifts her head from her mom's shoulder. "You liar! I don't know why we believed you! You liar!"

George turns to her and says, "It stands to reason, it does, that we'd be moving. I mean, they got all those parts and warehouses and spare armor parts. I thought they were going out into space."

Joanie looks to me, eyes swollen red. "Can you believe that fool? He thought we were moving in space. Going to another planet. He had these big plans, that we'd stay hidden, until we get to a planet like Earth, 'cause the bugs seemed to like a place like Earth. And then we'd figure out a way to get off the rock and get down to the new planet, and we'd be colonists, and start a new life. A new life! You damn fool, Randy here says we're still orbiting around Earth!"

Gwen says, "Don't call your father a fool."

She nearly screams. "He ain't my dad. And he ain't legally my stepdad! There was no minister, no justice of the peace, nothing!"

George says with calm, but firmly, "Joanie . . . you can't scream like that, make noises like that. The bugs could hear us."

"See if I care!" she shouts back. "You said we were making progress, that we were going someplace different, someplace safe. And all the while . . . we haven't gone anywhere."

George says, "Gwen, you tell your girl to shut the hell up, or I'm gonna have to gag her. I know she don't like that, but I'm gonna gag her for my safety and yours."

The mother hugs her daughter tight and Joanie seems to calm down, and George says to me, almost apologetically, "I know that's not right. Gagging her. Not right at all. Hell, I had a cousin, back in Los Cruces, he spanked his boy and he had to go to the police and they did a report and all that . . . but it's different up here. We gotta survive. And the bugs . . . maybe they know we're here, maybe they don't. But why make it easy for them?"

I feel odd and embarrassed, having been put in the middle of this family fight, and Gwen says, "George, we should be good hosts. Let's give . . . Randy, right? Let's give Randy something to eat."

"That's right, hon, I should have thought of that. Joanie? Daddy's sorry. Will you help your mom get some food for our guest?"

Joanie pulls her head away from her mother and I half-expect another shout of, "You're not my dad!" but she meekly nods and joins her mother.

The meal is not bad, considering we're in a cave in a large asteroid circling the Earth, filled with Creepers, and that odd thought almost gives me a fit of frantic giggles, but I keep quiet and dine on a couple of hardtack rolls that I soften by dipping in a mug of water, raw carrots, and a cold stew. George says to me, "You like the stew?"

"It's not bad," I say. "What's in it?"

"Potatoes, carrots, celery, some meat," he says. "You don't wanna know any more than that."

I give him that and finish up, and I help clean the dishes, and Gwen says I don't have to, but I say a good guest should do that. There's a small opening in a chunk of rock toward the rear of the chamber, where it looks like a Creeper conduit or cable has run through, and heat radiates from the dull blue-gray surface. We use that to heat up the water for washing, and Gwen says, "George . . . he has his moments, but he's one smart son of a gun, I'll tell you that. Me and Joanie wouldn't have survived without him. He knows parts of this rock like downtown Des Moines, he does."

We wipe the hot and clean dishes dry, and when we put them back on the shelves. George refills the lamps some more and says, "How old are you, Randy?"

"Sixteen," I say.

"What's your rank in the Army?"

"Lieutenant," I say, the word still sounding strange.

He nods and sits down and says, "Lieutenant . . ."

I interrupt him. "No need to be formal. Just keep it Randy."

"Okay . . . Randy, what did you do in the Army? Do you mind me askin'? Infantry?"

"Sort of," I say. "Recon Ranger."

Gwen is sitting next to George, and Joanie is stretched out, her head in her mother's lap. "What does a Recon Ranger do?"

George says, "Yeah. Never heard of it."

I ponder that and think, of course they wouldn't have heard of it. Recon Ranger was a relatively new MOS, created a few years after the war began, when it became deadly clear that the best way to fight the Creepers was to be small, mobile, and lethal.

"For some reason," I say, "The Creepers—unless they're gearing up for a big fight—they travel in groups of three or less. And if they want to, they can move really fast."

Gwen asks, "So, you go out and look around, and warn people that they're in the area?"

"No," I say. "I find them so we can kill them."

The three look at me like I'm a god, or a devil, I can't tell which.

George clears his throat. "You kill many of them?"

"Not nearly enough."

"And you hunt alone?"

The solid thud of emotions surprises me so much I have to turn my head, so my new friends don't see the tears well up. Damn. Oh, damn. I pretend to cough and wipe my sleeve across my eyes and say, "No . . . I have a partner. My K-9 unit. Thor."

Joanie whispers, "A dog?"

"That's right," I say. "Smartest and bravest dog you'll ever see . . . saved my life plenty of times."

Joanie says, "I always thought I'd get a dog . . . one of these days. What happened to him?"

Through my swollen eyes and throat I say, "It got too dangerous where I was, before I got captured. A lot of Creepers attacking me. So I sent him home."

"Good boy," Gwen says.

Thor and his puppy ways, turning instantly into a hunter of Creepers, and when necessary, a hunter of humans. Smelly when he got wet, always trying to steal food or steal the bed. I just nod some more and hate myself, for I can't remember the last time I had thought of him, or had wished him well on the long solo trek back to Ft. St. Paul.

My Thor.

"Some days yes, some days no," I say.

A few minutes later George wants to show me a place where he's been digging—"It sounds like a huge hollow space is nearby, and I'd love to break through and see what's there"—but when we travel through a small tunnel into a small room that's barely big enough for the two of us, he says, "Sorry, Randy, that was a bit of a lie. I wanted to talk to you without the girls nearby."

Girls. I know some young women back home in my unit that could take him down and break his neck without breathing too hard, but I let that go. "Sure, George, what's up."

He says, "It's like this . . ."

George stops.

Coughs.

Starts weeping. "Randy . . .we're so very tired. God, we're tired . . . me most of all."

I just keep my mouth shut. I'm still not used to having men cry in front of me.

He manages to take control and says, "Sorry . . . it's just, it's been so long since we've met anyone, anyone, at least, who could speak English. A while ago, shit, it must have been three or four years, we had a Chinese guy with us, an old buck, and he did what he could, but then he died, and that was that."

He stops again, and coughs once more. "Surviving . . . it's important, isn't it?"

"Very important."

"And we're barely scrapin' by. If the Creepers decided to get fancy and smart, and plug up just a few of the holes and cracks, we could be dead within the week."

I know where this is going.

"George, you need my help?"

He nods.

"You've got it."

CHAPTER FIFTEEN

A day later, I'm with George, Gwen, and Joanie, lying flat on our stomachs, peering through a wide crack in the stone that we can barely slip through if we have to, and boy, do we have to. It's been a long, grueling crawl of a slog in the dark, with George counting off seconds and turns, and the back of my head and hands are scraped and probably bleeding, but we're at our destination, a farming area built in a hollowed-out chamber of the rock.

As far as I can see there are troughs and trays of greenery, stretching out into the distance, and overhead lighting and watering and fertilizing tubes. George whispers, "Not sure if they grow this for the prisoners they're keeping somewhere else, or because they're still studying us, and I don't rightly give a shit."

"Okay," I say, and I realize I'm breathing a bit quicker and my heart is racing a bit faster, and I remember my first honest-to-God raid as a new Recon Ranger, and this is exactly the same thing. Racing out from safety to dangerous territory without knowing where the enemy might be hiding.

Strike that, I think. I know exactly where the enemy is, and they aren't hiding. They're all around us.

"We make it quick," George says. "Keep track of the time. We stay out two minutes, one hundred twenty seconds, and not a moment longer. The Creepers . . . they're smart. Not sure if they have cameras or microphones out there, but . . . two minutes is long enough."

Joanie says, "That's what happened to Tommy."

"Who's Tommy?" I whisper.

"Later," George says. "Remember, just grab one piece from one trough or tray. Don't be greedy. We go . . . now . . ."

We all crawl and scramble out, and George does something funny—tossing a bright orange rag on the stone—and then I realize he's marking our escape route. Thanks, I think, and I start running.

I have a worn and faded plastic bag from a store called Hy-Vee, and race along until I get to a trough, yank out a carrot. Next up. Radishes. Then potato. Another potato. A head of lettuce.

I check my watch.

Thirty seconds left.

Another carrot.

Fifteen seconds.

Radishes.

Drop out of my hand, fall on the stone, under the trough.

Damn it!

I reach down, pat my hand around, and can't find it.

The hell with it.

I get up and start running back. George, Gwen, and Joanie are racing ahead of me. Joanie goes in first, then her mother, and George is standing, holding the orange rag, waving at me.

"Go, go, go!" he whispers loudly.

I flatten myself out, squirm through the wide crack.

I turn and get hammered in my face by George's boots.

I yelp and squirm my way back.

George whispers, "Sorry. You'll get better as we keep it up."

"If you say so," I say, and then we humans slither into the darkness.

In our little living quarters, George checks on our haul. A bunch of vegetables that will last us a number of days, and Gwen carefully folds and puts away the worn plastic shopping bags. Something in Joanie's arms is making noises, and a little chicken head emerges. Gwen hugs and kisses her daughter. "Good job, hon, good job," she says, and Joanie nods in approval and makes a quick twisting motion with her hands, and there's a mix of snap/squawk as our big meal of the day starts getting prepared.

The three seem happy and satisfied with the day's activities, and I can't blame them. They've been up here in a Creeper prison for a number of years, they're still alive, and now they have enough to eat for at least a week.

They're surviving.

But I'm still bothered.

I can't quite figure it out.

I help with the meal and the cleanup and for a while I answer a lot of questions about what's been going on Earth since they were brought up here, and then Gwen and Joanie slip away for a nap, and I share a bit of what George calls "shine" and which tastes horrible, but something comes to me and I say, "Who's Tommy?"

"Ah, Tommy," he says, turning the chipped glass around in his rough hands. "He was with us last year. A good boy, not too bright . . . just a few years older than Joanie. A good boy . . . sometimes he just moved too slow. That's what happened. We were exploring a new farming section . . . corn. Boy, haven't had corn in a while. And I warned him, and I warned him . . . but he didn't listen. He just kept on grabbing, and grabbing . . . and a Creeper lifted itself up from the corn stalks and put a laser bolt right through his forehead. Poor boy."

"Yeah. Where was he from?"

"Maine," George says. "Thing is, he was a city boy but he learned pretty quick how to make things work." He leans over to a bottle and says, "Wanna refresh?"

"Nope, still working on it."

George smiles. "Yeah, it does take getting used to . . ." He takes another sip and says, "When Tommy died, it really broke Joanie up. They were a couple, you know? And I had hoped that at some point, the two of them could get married. Poor Tommy. Poor Joanie."

Poor us, is what I want to say, and I take another burning sip, and ask, "George, so what happens now?"

He smiles, takes a healthy sip of the shine. "Sorry, Randy, I don't get the question."

I pause, realize I need to carefully choose my words. "I mean . . . is there a plan, a strategy? Or just going week to week, stealing food from the Creepers?"

"Surviving is the plan."

I struggle again with the words. George's eyes have narrowed. "But . . . is that it? That's the long-term plan?"

"We're not in the Army, Randy. We're civilians, doing the best we can."

"Yes, of course, but . . ."

George's expression changes, like the muscles and tendon under that very light skin are rearranging and reordering themselves. "I do have a plan," he starts off, slowly. "It was in place when Tommy was here. Then it was put aside, because it didn't make sense. But now you're here. And you're part of it."

I feel like dumping the shine on the stone floor. Even the smell and the sharp taste in my mouth is too much.

"Go on, George," I say. "I'd love to hear more."

It looks like George really likes his shine. He takes a big swallow and says, "I believe in signs. Portents. The future. Things just don't happen 'cause they happen. They happen for a reason. You see what I mean?"

I see he's getting drunk, but I say, "Yes. It stands to reason."

A happy nod. "I was captured outside of Roswell. Do you think that was a coincidence?"

I have no idea what he's talking about. "It does sound doubtful."

"Absolutely," he says. "Then I'm up here alone for a while, until I come across Gwen and her daughter. Another coincidence? I don't think so. It was a plan, I tell you. A plan."

I pretend to take a sip to encourage him to keep talking, and thankfully, he does.

"It's all part of a plan," George says. "I don't know if it's God's plan, or the Creeper's plan, or anybody else's plan. But there's some sort of secret hand at work."

"And . . . what's that work, George?"

He stares at me and something has definitely changed in his eyes. "We're the new generation. We're in an ark, and one of these days, this ark is going to leave Earth and go somewhere else. Me and Gwen and Joanie, we're gonna travel with the Creepers, and we're going to land on this new planet, and start over."

I hope I choose my words well. "That sounds like . . . quite the plan, George. But have you ever thought—and I'm just asking this because I'm curious, that's all—that it might make more sense for the three of you to figure out a way to get back to Earth from here? You know, go back to someplace that's designed to be a habitat for people?"

He shakes his head. "No, damn it, that's not the plan. Not at all!"

George whips his head around, realizing his voice has just gotten louder. He leans over and says, "The plan is . . . we're part of a new species, a new line of humans. It's our destiny to travel with the Creepers and settle on a new world. A world of peace, equality, and freedom. Not to go back to old Earth, with the wars, hate, pollution."

He laughs for a moment. "Besides . . . what's left down there, hunh? Really. What's down there?"

"Probably more than you think," I say.

His eyes are hard and angry. "You telling me I'm wrong? I'm a nut?"

I'm about to truthfully answer him and I stop. Then I take in exactly where I am and where I'm living. I'm in a cave in a rock controlled by the Creepers, and only this man in front of me knows how to get in and out.

Now I know why I had that odd feeling earlier.

I'm trapped, and this loon before me is my warden, my only safe way to travel in and out of this little cramped refuge. I could try to get past him and through the cracks, fissures and openings, but where would I end up? Safely out there in the farming areas, or the tunnels? Or deeper inside this damn rock, no light, no food, no water.

"No, George, you're not wrong. Not a nut . . . it's just that, well, obviously, you've been thinking through this a lot. Over the years. And me, well, you know. I've been in the Army, and I'm just sixteen. I don't have the . . . experience. Or perspective."

His eyes don't change. Still hard and full of determination, emotion, and . . . madness? "Good point, Randy."

I pretend to take another sip of the shine. "My part of the plan . . . I guess it's to help you get the food and other supplies, am I right?"

"Partly," George says. "There's another part of the plan you're involved with."

"What's that?"

George says, "You're to marry Joanie, so we can . . . you know, prop . . . prop . . . reproduce and keep the species alive on a new world."

It's night time, I suppose, though who the hell knows. Only one flickering oil lamp is still burning, and I'm wrapped up in blanket, on a stone shelf, just waiting, trying not to think too hard. Married. To Joanie. To repopulate the species and hang up around here with my new wife, to have babies in this world to live like rats, parasites, creatures rummaging through the walls of this home.

One hell of a life that's been chosen for me.

"Hey," a voice whispers. "Can I come up?"

It's Joanie and I try to make room and she lies down next to me, breathing a bit hard, giggling, and she says, "Oh, Randy."

"Um, hi, Joanie."

"Here, I'm cold," she says. "Pull your blanket over me, will you?"

I don't say anything but I try to be polite. I shove up against the rock wall and try to make room, and Joanie comes right in and stretches out next to me. I wrap the blanket over the two of us and she whispers, "George told me the great news."

"Ah . . . yeah, great news, isn't it."

"God, yes," she says, cuddling up against me. Her breath smells sour.

"Randy?"

"Yes?"

"Will you . . . will you hold my hand?"

"Sure."

I fumble around in the dark and find her wrist, then her hand. I slip mine into hers and grasp it, and she sighs with pleasure. Her hand is warm and smooth.

"I never thought I'd get married," she whispers.

"Um . . . me either."

"But it's going to take some time," she says. "We need to get to know each other. That's what I told George."

A little lifeline came my way and I say, "Er, Joanie. You said something earlier. About the marriage between your mom and him not being legal. If that's the case . . . well . . ."

"Oh, don't worry about that," she says. "George explained it all to me. This is a ship, right? It's gonna go to the stars? And George is the head of us . . . so he's the head of the ship. That means he's the captain, and a captain can marry people on the ship. Oh, he figured it all out."

I wait for a moment, the lifeline having been dragged away. "I guess he did."

She squirms a bit and I feel trapped and confined, in all meanings of the word, and she whispers, "I sure hope wherever we land, they have those special trees. The cocoa trees."

"Why?"

"Chocolate," she says. "Oh, God, I can't remember the last time I've had chocolate. I miss it so much."

I keep quiet and hope she's falling asleep, and she says, "Randy?"

"Yes?"

"All right if I stay here for the night?"

"I guess."

"But Randy . . . don't try to kiss me. Not yet."

Her breathing slows and I try to remove my hand, but the grip is too tight.

The next day we go on another, quicker raid, and come back with a similar collection of dirty vegetables, and when we get to a free moment, I say, "George, do you think we could go somewhere else on the next run?"

"Why?"

I say, "Do you think we could go back to the tunnel where you . . . found me?"

"What's the point?"

I look to Joanie and Gwen, who are scrubbing the carrots and potatoes in a bin. I say, "There's some clothing and two rucksacks up there, with some food and other stuff."

George shakes his head. "Nah, I don't think so. Too risky. That tunnel . . . it was only by accident that we were there that day. I don't feel like going back again."

"Please?"

"Nope."

"But there's some stuff there I could use."

"Forget it."

"Some food from Nepal, some other nice stuff."

George says, "Why don't you go help the girls?"

I shrug. "All right. Too bad if those chocolate bars go to waste."

Joanie stands up from the bin, eyes wide, smiling.

And that's all it takes.

It takes a while of crawling, scraping, and with George counting, but we get to the crack in the rock that opens up to the tunnel where this little adventure had begun. Gwen and Joanie are back in the living quarters, because, as George said, "We need to travel fast . . . and you better be certain those knapsacks are still there."

George is next to me, both of us on our bellies, peering out, and then there's the blaring of the horn sound, getting louder and louder. George whispers, "The Creepers' dome must be working. The flying system."

"Flying?"

"Sure," he whispers. "How the hell we all go up here. By flying under that damn big rock."

The sound of the horns grows louder and louder, and then stops. I remember what I had seen the other "day"—however long a day is up here—when those six dazed Gurkhas emerged from under the stone cover.

And four of the survivors were led away.

We wait a bit longer and George starts to make his move and I say, "Hold on."

"Why?"

"I smell something. Cinnamon."

"Damn."

Sure enough the cinnamon smell gets stronger, and is followed by the familiar *click-click-click* of an approaching Creeper, and from my vantage point, I can't see much, just the passing armored arthropod legs.

It seems like George is going to say something and I put my hand on his shoulder, and he keeps quiet. What I can see is clear for the moment, but just for the moment.

One of the Creepers has circled back, and is paused in front of the open crack.

Click-click-click.

Then it starts talking to one of the other Creepers, in its chittering, rasping, clicking speech.

I freeze.

Hold my breath.

Try not to think of the Creeper leaning over, and letting loose with its weaponized arm that has a flamethrower at the end. But if it smells us, or senses us, why not?

Then there's a squealing, scratching noise above us that makes me want to hold my ears, and then the Creeper skitters off.

I wait.

George waits as well.

A grinding, thumping noise at the other end of the tunnel, and the grinding noise grows louder, and a *thump!* and my ears pop. Change in pressure?

The skittering noise fades away, and the grinding noise returns, and another *thump.*

George lets loose a breath.

"That was close," he whispers.

"Sure was," I say. "Did they pass through that hatch at the end of the tunnel?"

"Yeah. A . . . whaddya call it. An airlock. This area and others we've explored, it's kept at regular Earth air and pressure. Through that airlock is a passageway to the regular bug living quarters."

He taps me on the shoulder. "Let's go get that goddamn chocolate, all right? At least it'll keep Joanie quiet for a while."

We slide our way out and stand up, and George points to the wall. "There you go. This place just got marked."

I see where he's pointing to and there's two deep gouges in the stone. He says, "That bug saw the crack in the stone, our crack. Then it told its buddies that there's an opening here that needs to be closed up. That's why it got marked that way."

"How long do we have?"

"Seconds, minutes, hours. Depends if the goddamn bugs are busy or not. Let's get going."

We slide along the wall and we get to the area of the cables and conduits that marked my earlier home.

"Well?" George asks. "Is this it?"

"I think so," I say.

George now has a knife in his hand. "You better hope so."

"George . . ."

He shakes his head. "All I'm saying is, there better be two knapsacks up there, and one of 'em better have that chocolate you said is there."

"It's there," I say.

"All right," he says. "Joanie . . . she's my stepdaughter, and I've never seen her so happy to know she's getting chocolate. And I'm not about to go back empty-handed. So if this was a lie to get out or something,

I'll cut you right here and tell Joanie and Gwen the bugs got you. Savvy?"

"Oh, yeah, I savvy."

I eye again where I'm pretty sure my earlier resting spot was located, and I jump up and—

Don't make it.

Hunh?

I fall back down and George says, "What's the matter?"

I say, "Must be all the good food you're feeding me, it's weighing me down. Let me try again."

This time, I get a bit higher, my fingers brush the lowest conduit, but I fail again.

George looks both ways and says, "Kid, you're wasting my time, and I don't like being out here in the goddamn open."

"Once more."

"Last more," he says. "And I'm not fooling."

This time I step back and give it a good run, and maybe I was tired or maybe I was scared before—giving me a good burst of adrenaline— but this time I grab onto the conduit and hoist myself up. I'm about a meter further down than I should be, but there's the two knapsacks and the little bundle of clothing. I put the clothing in one knapsack and grab the other knapsack, and then peer over the edge, looking down at George.

"Hurry up!" he whispers sharply up at me. "And drop the knapsack first!"

"On my way," I say, and I keep the knapsack in hand as I let myself go. I hit the ground and have a good bounce, and George grabs my arm and says, "Why didn't you drop the knapsack?"

"I like holding it, that's why."

We get back to the open crack in the floor and George says, "Hold on, I want to see it."

"See what?"

"The chocolate."

I kneel down and open up the knapsack, poke my hand in there, and come up with a tightly wrapped foil package with a brown wrapper. George licks his lips.

"Damn . . . I wish I could have a taste right now."

"Well, I'm sure Joanie will share."

"Get in," he says. "Get in first."

I put the chocolate back in the knapsack, secure the cover, and with the knapsack in hand, I go in feet first, dragging the knapsack holding the strap. George whispers, "I hear something. Come on, make room!"

I feel trapped again.

If I go deeper, I'm not sure I can maneuver. I press myself to the left and George says, "Move, damn it, move!"

The scent of cinnamon wafts in.

Damn it!

George swears at me and squeezes in, and says, "What the hell is wrong with you? Why didn't you move?"

"I'm . . . I'm stuck."

"What?"

And I hate what I have to do next, but I see no way out. There's a tumble and a struggle, and George swears at me again, and now I've pushed the knapsack behind me, into the darkness of the split rock, and I say, "All yours, George."

Click-click-click.

I hit his head with a closed fist—not enough to hurt him, but enough to shock him—and then I crawl over him and out into the tunnel.

CHAPTER SIXTEEN

He yells out after me, "You idiot, get back in here!"

"Sorry, George," I manage to say. "I'm too young to get married."

"You're old enough to get scorched!"

Which is true, but I don't think I have time for a debate. There's shadows moving at the far end of the tunnel, the part that opens up into the huge chamber with the transport device, so I start running in the opposite direction, keeping as close as I can to the side wall.

There we go, I think, as I get to my former hidey-hole, and there's no hesitation or failure this time, and one good jump gets me up and to the conduit from before, and I haul myself up and over, as the clicking sound gets louder.

I hunch down, try to make myself small, try to imagine myself very small indeed.

Click-click-click.

One Creeper comes by, and there's a grinding and thumping noise, and the hatch must be opening up, because there's a chuff/whiff of air passing through, and the sudden decompression (or compression?) hurts my ears so much I cry out.

Then I bite my tongue. Idiot. Why not roll over and wave at the damn bug?

More clicking, and I can hear the damn articulated legs scraping over the rock as it passes through the open hatch and into the airlock or whatever the damn chamber is called, and then more grinding, a thumping noise, and then it's quiet again.

What now?

I wait for a minute or two, and decide I should get going, in case George decides to come back for me, and I'm trying to think of whether to go now or later, and then the decision is suddenly taken out of my hands.

A human voice, below me, and not a voice I've heard before up here.

"Hey, Sergeant," the woman calls up. "Get down here before I change my mind, all right?"

I can't believe what's just happened.

I stay frozen.

The voice is more urgent. "Hurry up. I don't like being out in the open when they're moving around . . . so get your ass down here!"

I roll over and up, and peer down below me.

A human is sliding over, just below me.

A woman, maybe in her fifties or so, gray hair pulled back in a tight bun, wearing khaki shorts and a gray sweatshirt that says in faded black letters, A R M Y. The sleeves have been cut off and her biceps are big and pronounced, like she's spent a lot of time in a gym.

She has no legs. Stumps that end a bit above where her knees should have been.

The woman also has black gloves on her hand, and yeah, she's moving and scooting on her bottom, propelling herself along with a sliding motion.

"Hurry up!"

I drop myself down and land next to her, suddenly dizzy and overwhelmed.

She waves at me. "Hurry up and get a move on," she says. "You don't want to be there when the transfer dome lowers down. Sometimes they sterilize and scrub the place clean and that would really ruin your day."

She starts scooting down the tunnel, working hard with her arms and gloved hands. She turns and says, "Hurry up! Jesus, I've got no legs and I'm already moving faster than you."

The tunnel ends out into the huge cavern with the domed rock, and she scoots along and I keep up with her, and she says, "We're reasonably safe but why tempt them, right? I'll take you to my quarters, Cox, and get you something to eat. You must be hungry."

I find my voice and say, "Yeah, I guess I am."

"Well, I can fix that. Follow me."

She flips herself forward, goes a few meters, and then turns back. I'm still lagging behind her and she says, "Hey, get a move on. That's an order!"

I force myself to look at her, and nothing else. "Excuse me, ma'am, just who the hell are you?"

Her face looks firm. "Major Felicia Gallagher, United States Army. So move it, Sergeant."

And I keep moving.

We go down another tunnel cut out of the rock, one I've not explored before, which curves to the right, and there are more cables, conduits, and what looks to be pressure hatches set into the smooth stone. The curved top of the tunnel seems about five or so meters up. Recessed lighting illuminates the way, and then the tunnel widens, and on the left, there is a dark green canvas-type curtain that Major Gallagher opens with one quick draw.

"There are quarters that have been set up for you a couple of meters down," she says. "But first, let's get some food into you and a bit of a debrief, and then we'll move you in."

"Ah, Major Gallagher, hold on, all right?"

She turns, hand on the curtain. "What is it?"

"Begging the major's pardon, who are you? Where are you from? How did you end up here?"

She looks at me and her face tells me she's trying to control her anger. A crisp nod. "Very well. I'm Felicia Gallagher. Originally from Ojai, in California. I'm a major assigned to the Defense Language Institute . . . if it's still there. And I got here just like you did. That enough?"

Not even close, I think, but I feel I've pushed her far enough. I follow her in and the curtain slides shut behind me.

She bustles around at a stone counter and I slowly give the place a glance, checking out her quarters, which look like they've been hewn out of the solid rock. This isn't a cave or hole scoured out by my former friend George and his family. This is organized, designed. There's a table with stone benches in the center, a number of shelves, and on the shelves are cans of food and boxes of military rations, still in their dark green plastic bags. Seeing all of those rations carefully stored and lined up makes my stomach cramp and grumble at the same time. If poor George knew what was within his grasp, just a few tunnels over . . . though Major Gallagher's upper arms look like she could take on a squad of my Recon Rangers, legs or no legs.

Other shelves have books, notebooks, and plates and pots. On the walls are old photos clipped from magazines, at least ten years old, since that's when all magazines stopped publishing. The photos are all of Earth landscapes. There's a curtain on the far rock wall, and two other, larger curtains off to the right. Sleeping quarters? Latrine? Lighting tubes curl around the curves of the rock, and there's a slow-moving fan on the rock ceiling that moves the air around.

The major is working at a stone counter, gloves now off, and there's a round stone with wires coming out that seems to be heating up. Next to it is a square sink cut out of stone.

She turns. "Any preference?"

"I'm sorry, I don't know what you mean, ma'am."

"I don't know how your body clock is set up," she explains. "Breakfast? Lunch? Dinner?"

It seems to have been a long, long time since I ate with George Cooper, Gwen, and Joanie. "If it's food, I'll eat it," I say.

"Breakfast then, it is," she says, and moving with ease in the lower gravity, it only takes several minutes for her to get two meals ready, and I try not to stare too hard at her leg stumps and the scars on her hands and face. It looks like she's missing at least four fingers.

"Ma'am," I ask.

"Yes?"

"You called me by name back there," I say. "How did you know that?"

"Ah," she says, working over a flat stone that is heated somehow. "Our hosts told me."

"They did?"

"Of course they did," she says. "Why are you surprised? Do you think anybody gets transported up here without being known?"

"But . . . my name's not Cox. It's Knox." I decide at the moment not to correct her on my real rank.

She shrugs. "Well, languages are hard, even on Earth. Between species . . ."

The smell of the cooking food fills my mouth with saliva. I swallow.

"So you can talk to them."

"Yep."

"And . . . you knew I was here?"

"Yep again. By the time I got out to the *Grantztch*, you were gone. You moved pretty quick, Sergeant. Go anyplace special?"

"Just trying to survive . . ."

She works a bit more and I ask, "And you're a prisoner?"

"I am," she says. "No offense, Sergeant, but you have a stunning grasp of the obvious."

"Ma'am . . . I'm just overwhelmed. That's all."

She taps a wooden spoon against the edge of a frying pan. "Understood. And it's been a while since I've talked to a human . . . so I tend to blather."

I take a breath, look around at how well lived in the place is. "But why was I brought up here?"

Gallagher says, "You were brought up here as a prisoner, from one of the Base Domes. They must have a reason, and I'm sure they'll let you know at some point. Were you happy there, at the Base Dome?"

After coming within moments of being executed, and seeing the other horrors where I came from, I say, "Not happy at all. But it'd be even better if I had been set free."

She turns to me for a moment, face set like the stone around her.

"Don't wish for things that can never occur."

A couple of minutes later she comes over to the stone table.

"Now that I've answered your questions, Sergeant, how about showing me the same courtesy?" The major puts down a plate with some sort of scrambled egg dish with cheese and diced up ham cubes sprinkled in, and there's orange juice and coffee. Everything was once dehydrated or dry, but I don't care. It's delicious and filling.

I say, "I was . . ." and then pause for the briefest of seconds. "I was assigned to a quartermaster column, heading into Massachusetts. The convoy was ambushed by three Creepers and—"

"No," she says crisply.

"No, what?" I ask. "I was there. I saw it happen."

Gallagher spoons up some of her eggs. "I'm sure you did. But you need to know that on this post, mister, we don't use the term Creepers."

Something flip-flops in my gut as I hear those words. What the hell can possibly be going on? I say, "Well, what kind of phrase do you prefer . . . Major?"

"Travelers," she says. "That's who they are. That's what they call themselves. The Travelers. They . . . I have lots to tell you, but this is a good start, Sergeant. One of the first rules of communications between two competing forces is to reach an agreement on terms to be used. That's the way to open up a productive line of communication."

"So what do they call us," I ask. "Targets? Game? Food?"

The major shakes her head, continues eating. "No, not that. They do understand our reference as humans . . . we'll talk more. Do go on, then. How did you end up here?"

The food is so good and filling I don't want to start talking and stop eating, but that's what I do. "I managed to break free with a couple of other soldiers, made my way away from the attack site. Eventually I was by myself . . . and then I was ambushed again. The . . . there were a couple of fighters there that took me prisoner. Led me to a Base Dome and escorted me inside."

"Where?"

"Northern Connecticut, or southern Massachusetts. Not sure."

"How long were you in the Dome?"

"Only two days . . . I think."

She nods, seems to think things through, and is about to talk, and then keeps quiet for a moment. "You were there for two days, and then you were transported here?"

"That's right."

"Were you interrogated at all in the Dome?"

"No."

"What was it like in the Dome?"

"I . . . I'd rather not say."

"Give me an idea."

"I really don't want to say anything about it."

She says quietly, "That wasn't a request, Sergeant."

I get what she's saying. "I saw one group of humans, some Army, some civilian. They were forced into combat with another group of humans that seemed to be Russian military."

"Really? That sounds . . . odd."

"That's what I saw. Two groups of humans, Russian and American, forced to fight. Or they starve."

She slowly nods. "All right then. Anything else?"

"Yes," I say. "And there was another, smaller group of humans I encountered while a Creeper, sorry, a Traveler, was taking me to another part of the Base Dome. That group . . . they were starving. They . . . I'm sorry, Major, that's it."

"I understand."

We eat and finish our plates, and I can't believe it, she offers me seconds.

Seconds!

I eat some more and feel pretty full, and I'm not sure who the major is and what she is planning for me, but as I clean up my plate the best I can without licking it, I come up with a couple of plans of my own.

I help her with the dishes, and there's even nice smelling soap to help us clean. The water comes out in a little spot and with a lever she can control the temperature.

"It took a while, but the Travelers here finally were able to get me water that adjusted for cold and hot. The first time they did it, it almost came out as steam. Nearly boiled my hands . . ."

There are cloths used for wiping, and I wipe the dishes dry and she puts them up on the shelves, and she says, "Dessert?"

"Are you kidding?"

"I'll let you know if I ever joke," she says, "and this isn't one of those times."

Chocolate bars are brought out, thick, and the labels written in German. She sits down on one stone shelf—padded with thin rectangular pillows—and I sit on another shelf, set at an angle to the first one. I unwrap the candy bar, give it a good whiff, and then take a gentle bite.

I can't believe I've eaten anything so good.

"Damn . . . I mean, Major, this is so delicious . . . where did it come from. Germany? Those look like German words on the wrapper."

She shakes her head. "No. Switzerland. They make the best chocolate in the world."

I take another bite, bigger. "You mean, they still do?"

A shrug. "There are many places on Earth where the Travelers didn't touch, never visited. Switzerland being one of them. They're one very busy country there, in the center of a blasted and burnt Europe. They do a lot of manufacturing and banking, just as they've always done, managing to keep neutral even in this little scrap of ours."

"And you were able to get their chocolate?" I suppose I should have been angered or horrified at her words about how one country was surviving, but the Swiss chocolate tasted so fine.

"I make lists, I make requests. The Travelers here fulfill them, if they can. Even after ten years, they still don't know that much about us. And vice versa, of course."

I keep on eating the chocolate, and I'm ashamed that when I finished, I'm hoping she would offer me another bar.

But she doesn't.

Gallagher carefully takes the paper wrapping out of my hand and puts it with hers, and then slides it into a canvas bag that I imagine is used for trash. She points to the curtained-off area to the right.

"If you need to wash up or you use the latrine, go right through there. Afterward, if you like, we can talk some more, or I can take you to your living quarters."

"Thanks, ma'am," I say, and I mean it, even though my belly is full and my mind is troubled. I get up—and still feel light on my feet and slightly dizzy, and I walk over and into the latrine.

I open the curtain, step in, close the curtain behind me.

Not a bad latrine. Better than some I've used in my time in the N.H. National Guard.

There's a low trough that is used for number one and number two, with water rushing through it, and squares of paper that are pretty soft. There's also a sink with towels folded up next to it, and a large, empty tub. There's also a bunch of shampoos, soaps, moisturizing creams, and other beauty doodads on a crowded stone shelf, along with brushes and combs.

The same kind of recessed lighting is used to light up the place, and there are two little black vases with flowers in them. I touch the flowers. Plastic. But the round mirror is for real, and I look at the mirror and stare, and I think my eyes are about as tired as I've ever seen them.

"Time to get to work, Recon Ranger," I whisper.

CHAPTER SEVENTEEN

I go back to her living quarters and hear music. Music! There's a box with little speakers attached to it, and I stand there and just listen to the music fill the stony room. It sounds old, classical, and I just like standing there and hearing it. Oh, I've heard music before, but usually it's from old cassette tapes or round black records, being played back on old equipment that the Creepers have left alone in their never-ending quest of destroying our electronics and computers.

Two things come to me then, one being that no matter what Major Gallagher says, they will always be Creepers to me, and the second being that the bugs don't seem to mind humans having electronics up here in their orbital base.

"Nice music," I say. "Old stuff, right? What they call classical?"

She's curled up on a rock bench that has the padded pillows beneath her. "That's right. Mozart. You ever hear Mozart before?"

"I don't think so."

She pats the area next to her. "Come on over here, sit down. In a few minutes I'll give you the grand tour."

I have an idea of what the grand tour will entail and even with everything going on in the back of my mind, I don't like the thought of going out again, like a scurrying mouse. Things seem very safe and warm in the major's quarters.

But still I sit down near her.

She says, "How long have you been in the Army?"

"Four years," I say. "I enlisted when I was twelve."

"Where's your home base?"

"New Hampshire," I say.

"And you were captured in a convoy? In Connecticut?"

"Or Massachusetts," I say. "I'm not too sure."

"How in the world did you end up there, if your home base was in New Hampshire?"

"I was detached for a courier mission that turned sideways, and which ended up with me going to New York State. After a while, things got straightened out and my orders were cut for me to go back to New Hampshire on a convoy, and that's when the convoy was attacked."

"That's too bad," she says. "This damn war . . ."

I think about what she said earlier, correcting me and my language, and I say, "May I ask you some questions, ma'am?"

"Go right ahead."

"How long have you been here?"

Her face is still smiling but a shadow slips across, like there's a cloud somewhere in this hollowed-out room. "Long enough."

"And when did you join the Army?"

"About . . . God, nearly twenty years ago."

"And your station . . . some language institute? Am I right?"

The smile looks unsteady. "That's right. The one in Monterey. In California. That's where I was stationed."

"That's funny," I say. "You from California, me from New Hampshire, ending up here."

"Not sure if it's funny, but it is something," she says.

The major plays some with the edges of her shorts and says, "How about we go for a little stroll?"

"Sure," I say, standing up from the padded bench. "Ma'am, mind if I wash my hands again? It's been a long time since I've been able to use hot water."

Gallagher says, "Go knock yourself out. I have to give the Travelers credit, once they figured out my plumbing and washing needs, they worked it until they got it right."

I'm sure, I think.

I get up, go around the stone table and go to the kitchen sink, and I play with the levers and wash my hands, and my face, once again. I dry off my face with a towel and pick up a smaller towel, and I go over to the shelves, until I find what I'm looking for.

I take it down, wrap it in the towel, put it in my pocket, and go back to Major Gallagher.

She gets up off the stone bench and says, "Let's head out, then."

Nodding and quiet, I follow her out.

She moves quickly and efficiently, and with each thrust of her strong arms, her torso and cut-off legs lift up from the stone, and she glides along. Gallagher takes me back to the large center chamber, and she pauses before the enormous stone dome. She looks up and up.

"Just look at the engineering that had to go into this," she says. "They take this enormous hunk of rock, hollow it out, seal it, pressurize it, and make it livable, for two species. It's an incredible piece of work, you have to admit."

I just grunt, not wanting to admit a damn thing. She goes on, lifts an arm.

"And there's the transport system for the Travelers," she points out. "The *Grantztch*. How does it work? I only have the vaguest idea. Somehow they're able to temporarily freeze and compress anything, from living beings to objects, and transport them down to Earth, or to another Traveler installation."

"Like the first orbital battle station?"

"That's right . . . this one, it was placed in reserve. It was fully functional. I'm sure there were humans on the first station . . . before it was destroyed. The Travelers are smart. In fact . . . their interstellar transport system, how they got here, it's a variation of the *Grantztch*. I know less about that than I know about this"—she points to the stone cap before us—"and how it works. Somehow, they're able to transport, from point to point . . . crossing interstellar space. Quite impressive."

Sure, I think, crossing interstellar space to kill and destroy. Very impressive.

"The corridors," I ask. "Where do they go? There are six of them."

"Oh," she says, "they lead to various parts of the installation. Their power plant. Their waste disposal. The living and research quarters for the Travelers. This piece we're in . . . it's only a very small piece."

"Do you get to go to the place where the Travelers are?"

"Occasionally," she says carefully. "It's been ten years and they're still terribly curious about us. And vice versa. I've picked up a good chunk of the language . . . but not nearly enough. Come along, we can go down a couple of the tunnels before I beg off."

As chance would have it, the major brings me down the tunnel where I had hidden, and where I had last seen George. She chatters on about the lighting, the different ways the Travelers control the living situation for us and them, and then we come up to the huge circular door that marks the end of the tunnel.

"There you go," she says, staring up at it again, almost in awe. "A nice piece of work. This is part of an airlock system, where the Travelers can come through to this part of their station."

"Have you been through here?"

"A number of times," she says.

"How . . . I mean, how do they get access?"

She points to an oval device secured in a corner which has a number of illuminated panels glowing softly. "Almost like a combination lock, or keypad. Those panels get touched in a particular way, and the hatch slides open."

I nod, go over, and start punching at the device.

Oh boy, does that piss her off. "Sergeant Knox, what the hell are you doing? Back off."

I do, and the panel remains the same, and the large circular hatch remains closed. "I was conducting an experiment, to see if I could work it."

"It's a code!"

"Well . . . I thought maybe something would happen."

Gallagher shakes her head. "Nothing will happen. This one is keyed into a Traveler limb, not a human hand. You were just wasting time, and irritating me, Sergeant. Don't do it again."

I nod, which for me is just an acknowledgment of her request, and not my agreeing to it. A little point for sure, but at least it made me feel better about the situation.

She flips around and we start back down the tunnel, and I take my time and see deep scratches along the rock. I stop. "Major Gallagher?"

"Yes?" She stops and comes back, as I trace the scratches. "What is it?"

I bend down, looking for the large crack.

It's gone.

Maybe it's been sealed, or maybe something closed up here, or maybe I'm just losing my mind, but the crack is no longer here.

I stand up. "Ma'am . . . are there other humans here on this station?"

She waits for a moment, and says, "Why do you ask?"

"Because . . . before you contacted me, I spent a couple of days with three people. Husband, wife, and daughter."

"Are you sure?"

"Very sure," I say. "I mean, they didn't show me any identification or anything like that, but their story seemed to check out."

"I see," she says. "And where were they residing?"

"Somewhere deep in the rock," I say. "Cracks, fissures . . . they found a few natural caves deep inside. That's how they live."

"And how do they eat? And drink?"

Gallagher seems to be interrogating me and I don't like it. I shrug. "Not sure," I say. "They got it figured out, though. I mean, I got fed a couple of times, so they had some sort of food supply."

She nods and says, "I'm sure there are a number of humans out there . . . other prisoners of war, maybe some government officials, hell, maybe a diplomat or two. But they are kept in . . . official quarters, similar to mine."

"These folks weren't official."

"Well, good for you you're not with them anymore," she says. "The Travelers . . . They like to keep their chambers and tunnels tidy. If you were spotted, you'd be instantly killed. And as to their living quarters . . . I don't doubt the Travelers sometimes try to force them out, or gas them out. To them . . . those humans must seem like vermin."

She stops talking as we emerge into the open dome again.

"But they're humans," I say. "Not vermin."

Gallagher flips around, and starts toward the home tunnel, or whatever the hell it's being called. "I'm tired now," she says. "We're going back to my quarters."

Back inside her quarters she turns on the music again, and offers me a cup of water, which I gratefully accept. As I sip from the cold water I think about Joanie, down there in the rock somewhere, and I hope she's taken my sudden leaving in good humor, and is enjoying that small piece of chocolate.

I also hope they can avoid being gassed.

Vermin indeed.

Major Gallagher is using the latrine and then she comes out, yawning. "One of the things the Travelers have never gotten used to is our sleep cycles. Sometimes they leave me alone for days, other times, they want to talk for hours and hours . . ."

She takes a seat among the cushions and I say, "Have you been alone, all these years."

That seems to catch her off guard, and she says, "Alone enough."

"Do you know why I'm here?"

She says, "I'm confident the Travelers' leadership will make it all clear."

I wait and look her over, seeing the scars, the missing two fingers, her big upper-body strength. "Major . . . with all due respect, I think you may know more."

"I'm much older than you," she says. "It's safe to assume that I know a lot more about a lot of things."

"Ma'am, please, I was referring to my status here. I think you know a lot more about why I was transported up here. I was captured, placed in a Base Dome, and then I was removed just as . . . well, just as I was about to be killed. The fact the Creepers . . . sorry, I mean the Travelers, the fact they allowed me to live and not be killed in the Base Dome, that means something. It has to."

She remains quiet.

I go on. "Hell, they took the trouble to capture me, and carefully herd me along to the Base Dome. I could have easily been burnt or lased down. But I was spared. In fact, just before I was transported up here, the . . . alien that brought me to the transport place, he bowed to me. Like he was honoring me. Why?"

Another pause from the major.

I wait as well.

She says, "Sergeant Knox?"

"Yes?"

"Why don't we take a little trip to your quarters."

I think, so that's how it's going to be, then.

I get up. "Mind if I use the latrine beforehand?"

She nods in the direction of the closed curtain. "Not at all."

I get up and go into the latrine, wash my hands and my face, avoid

looking into the mirror—I don't want to psych myself out—and then
I carefully dry each hand and emerge back into the room.

"Feel like checking out your new home?"

I shake my head. "Sorry, ma'am," I say, "I have another idea."

I step over to her, moving quickly, and from a rear pocket I take a
small towel out of my pocket, drop it, revealing a sharp knife that I
had earlier taken from her kitchen and I'm on her in a second, pushing
her back, grabbing her hair with one hand and putting the edge of the
sharp blade against her throat.

"Just who the hell are you, anyway?" I ask.

Her eyes lock on mine with her fury. "Because I volunteered, you idiot. I volunteered to be captured and sent here so I could learn their language, so we could end this damn war without humanity going extinct."

"So says you."

This time, she does spit in my eye. I try not to blink. "Up on the shelf, sealed in plastic, are my orders . . . as if I need to explain myself to a damn teenage boy. This . . . rock. This floating base, this has been my duty station for ten years. A goddamn decade! I'm well fed, mostly well taken care of, but I'm no damn collaborator. Now, let me up, or we'll stay here, and at some point, you'll have to get up to take a piss or get a drink, and unless you plan on keeping tying me up for the foreseeable future, at some point, you'll need to sleep. And when that happens, I swear to God, I'll kill you."

Hard to argue with that. I take the knife away, back off, and she stays still, watching me. I slowly get up and move around her, and go to the sink. I wash the sharp knife and put it back where I had found it. Gallagher is back up on the bench, breathing hard, and I say, "You still believe in God?"

"One of my many weaknesses," she says.

I dry my hands off and feel terribly awkward and stupid, and I say, "Major . . my apologies, ma'am."

She says, "Third shelf up there, on top of the hardcover books to the left. You'll find my orders there."

"I don't need to see them, ma'am."

"That wasn't a suggestion," she says. "Retrieve it. Now."

I go up and feel around the books, and grab a sheet of stiff plastic. I bring it down and give it a look. Inside the clear plastic sleeve is a single sheet of paper. There's a colorful logo in one corner that's faded with age, and some code groups and operations numbers, and I even note a few spelling mistakes. I check the date. About a week after the war started.

There's a numeral 1 followed by a bold SITUATION, and then a lengthy paragraph, part of it reading,

Starting on 10 October, local time 4 a.m., hostilities commenced against American military forces here and abroad, and with the military forces of other nations. Communications have been severely disrupted. NUDETs have been detected at elevations over certain areas of CONUS. Latest intelligence reports are that invading forces are now on ground and are engaging American ground units as well as local police forces. Communications with the National Command Authority have been erratic.

There's a few more depressing lines updating what was going on during that first terrible week, and then there's a numeral 2 followed by a bold MISSION, with this simple line:

MAJ Felicia Gallagher, 229th Military Intelligence Battalion, is hereby detached from this station and assigned to nearest combat area to establish communications with invading forces.

I look up at her. "Hell of an open-ended order you've got there, Major."

"It was an open-ended conflict back then," she says. "Still is, from what I'm able to gather."

At the end is a numeral 3, followed by EXECUTION, and a plaintive sentence:

Upon establishing communications with enemy forces, MAJ Gallagher will contact any surviving unit of the National Command Authority to immediately present her findings.

Sure. Pretty straightforward. There's a couple of signatures scrawled at the bottom—no time even to type in the issuing officers' names— and the paper is worn, creased, having been folded a number of times, and it has stains on one edge.

I carefully replace it back up on the books.

"Any questions?" she asks.

"A couple of hundred," I reply. "But this . . . this station. It was never known that the . . . Travelers, as you call them, had a second orbital battle station."

She sighs, folds her arms. "Have you ever heard of any force in history that didn't have a ready reserve?"

I say, "The French Army. Western front. World War II."

Gallagher slowly nods and says, "What they hell are they teaching you down there?"

"War. History of war, the current war. How to fight it, how to survive, how to win it."

"I see. Well, the Travelers did better than the poor French in 1940 and had this station in reserve. Just in case."

"Where was it located? Behind the moon?"

"That's right," she says, slowly nodding. "That's pretty good thinking. Glad to see they taught you how to think down there. But are they teaching you conflict resolution? How to arrange for an armistice? Open peace negotiations?"

"Way, way above my pay grade, ma'am."

She rubs at her face and I have a feeling she wants to say more, but she doesn't. I feel tired, worn, beat, from time I've spent here to the little fracas we've just had, and to the meal that's still filling my young belly.

Almost reflectively, she says, "All wars end, at some point. Usually in the utter defeat of the other party. Other times, the wars end when both sides have fought enough and bled enough to call an end to hostilities. One thing that surprised the Travelers, when they realized our history and background, is how often we fought over artificial ideas, boundaries."

"Not sure what you mean there, Major."

"We're all human down there. All with the same DNA, the same body type, the same everything. What's the point of fighting?"

I was going to say that history always showed there's a lot of point to fighting—some necessary, most unnecessary—but I keep my mouth shut. She's older than me, has been a prisoner for ten years, and due to her stumps and facial injuries and her hands, she's been through hell during that decade.

Plus she outranks me. One thing I've learned in my service is never to piss off your superior officer, unless you're doing it on purpose and have a necessary outcome in mind.

"Here," she says. "I want to show you something."

She scampers off her bench and I follow her to the far curved stonewall, where there's a small curtain, and she draws the curtain aside, hooks it up.

I yelp and grab onto something.

I feel like I'm going to fall.

Fall out of this room.

There's a round window of some sort, looking . . . out? Down? Near?

Below me is . . .

Damn.

Below me is Earth.

Good ol' battered and bruised Earth.

My stomach does one huge flip-flop and manages to settle down, even though my mouth is suddenly flooded with saliva. I take a couple of swallows and say, "Is that for real?"

"Of course it's real," she says. "What do you think, that the Travelers mocked up something like this for my behalf? Or yours?"

I stare down. The Earth is moving below us . . . check that, I think, remembering the few science classes I've taken. The Earth, sure, it's moving, but we're moving faster. Orbit, yes, we're in orbit.

There are lots of clouds down there. A blue expanse of something . . . a brown strip, and more clouds.

"What am I seeing?" I ask, my voice quiet with the awe.

She maneuvers so she's looking out. "Hard to tell. Might be West Africa. Since the Travelers came, there's still a lot of water vapor in the atmosphere, which means lots of clouds."

I say, "The bugs didn't just come, Major. They invaded. They dropped nuclear devices and pushed us back into the nineteenth century, and caused tidal waves with asteroids, and—"

"Enough, Lieutenant, that's enough," she says, her voice softer than I would have expected. "You don't need to revisit history. I lived through it, you lived with it. It's done."

I keep on looking down and I hold up my hand, block most of the view, and tears come to my eyes, damn it. My simple dirty, tired, and worn hand has just blocked out everything dear to me, down there on old Earth. My dad, Thor, Serena, Abby Monroe at Ft. St. Paul, and all of my fellow troopers there and other places, and Captain Kara Wallace, and even Buddy, I can block them out of existence with this brief gesture.

I pull my hand back.

Gallagher says, "Decades ago, when we Americans still had a space program, and the space shuttle, I remember buying this book at a discount, at Barnes & Noble. It was a big picture book, showing photos from orbit, taken by the astronauts."

I was going to ask her what a Barnes & Noble was, but I didn't want to interrupt. She went on.

"One of the astronauts—I don't think it was an American, he was from some other country—that astronaut said something to the effect that on the first day in orbit, they would point out the cities down below. The next day, their home nations. The day after that . . . the continents. From up here, from this vantage point, there are no borders, Randy. None at all. Just land and water and people. That's what the Travelers are hoping we understand."

"How?"

She ignores me and says, "In a few minutes we'll go into night. Then you'll see the stars out there in space, including the one that belongs to the Travelers. One speck of light, marking the home of an intelligent race, just like our sun. That's the lesson, that in distances, differences don't matter. They really, really don't."

"I think the French back in 1940 would disagree," I say.

She smiles, draws the curtain closed. "That was a long, long time ago."

I move away, my feelings all mixed up. I'm glad the curtain is closed, because my stomach was still rebelling at the feeling of looking down, afraid the window would break and I'd be sucked out.

But seeing the Earth from orbit . . .

"Ten years," I say. "Major, that's a long, long time."

She goes back to her bench. "Lieutenant, a few minutes ago you were ready to slit my throat. Now you want to be my new best friend. Forget it. You're here, and we have a job to do, a very important job."

"And what's that job, Major? Or do I have to wait until I'm older to learn your secrets?"

She starts to say something, but I don't hear what, because the curtain leading out is torn open, and a damn Creeper pokes its head and upper arms in.

CHAPTER NINETEEN

I burst out with one giant yell and propel myself to the far side of the room, near the kitchen area, and I grab the closest weapon I can get, which is a long butcher knife. I spin around and the damn Creeper is hissing and crackling, and I see that the damn bug isn't in its usual armored exoskeleton, but something I saw earlier.

There's that flexible clear plastic helmet around its head and eyestalks, and something similar covering its main arthropod. Its segment legs are open, and so are its two main claws, which have five mobile appendages. Each claw is holding something glittery, metal-like and sharp, and both claws are pointing right at me.

Gallagher yells, "Stand down, Knox, stand down!"

"The hell I will!"

"That's a damn order," she yells, sliding over, putting herself between me and the Creeper, which has managed to slide about one-third of the way in before its legs and main arthropod gets jammed up against the entrance. It's the smallest Creeper I've ever encountered, but it's still ugly and dangerous.

Gallagher then starts talking to the bug, using its hissing, crackling and snapping sound, and the Creeper replies, and without turning back to me, Gallagher yells again.

"Drop the knife! Lower your hands!"

I stay still.

Gallagher says, "You young moron, I'm trying to save your life! Do it!"

The Creeper moves its eyestalks in my direction, and then to Major Gallagher.

Damn it.

I lower my hands, drop the knife. In the lower gravity, it takes longer to strike the stone floor.

More give and take between Gallagher and the Creeper, she raising her voice louder, and then the bug slowly backs its way out of the major's quarters. The hanging curtain slowly flops back into place. She whips back to me and says, "Understand this, Lieutenant, I'm your commanding officer. You will follow my orders without hesitation, without reluctance. Do I make myself clear?"

For a moment I grit my teeth. "Yes, ma'am, I understand."

"Outstanding," she says. "Now, do me the favor of retrieving that knife and replacing it."

I do that and she slides back to her usual perch, and she says, her voice more quiet, "What the hell were you going to do? Attack that Traveler?"

"It was a thought."

"Then what," she goes on. "Try to find a door or airlock and depart?"

I say, "I guess I didn't think that far, ma'am. To be honest . . . I've been trained for more than four years to either hide from a Creeper, or to kill it. I wasn't in a position to hide. So I did the next best thing, ma'am."

Gallagher scratches her right stump. "All right, I guess that makes sense. But you better re-thread your head and change your attitude. At some point you're going to meet more of the Travelers, and you'll have to be able to do so without panicking."

"Why will I be meeting the . . . Travelers?"

"You'll know, soon enough," she says.

My legs have stopped quivering. "Ma'am . . . the apparatus around its head and main abdomen . . ."

"A breathing system, so it can move freely through the parts of its orbital base that's been designed for us humans."

"Why was it here?" I ask. "Was it protecting you?"

She scratches at the other stump. "Yes."

"They keep tabs on you . . . and me."

"Sometimes," she says. "Other times . . . well, I know they do keep watch on me. But I don't think it's every second all the time."

"And they thought I was threatening you . . ."

"Lieutenant," she interrupts.

"Yes, ma'am?"

"Later," she says. "I . . . I feel pretty worn. Let's head over to your quarters."

"Very good, ma'am," I reply, thinking I feel pretty worn as well.

And I'm glad to be moving, because her quarters stink of cinnamon.

Gallagher moves with her usual speed, skimming along the rock surface, passing through the hanging curtain. She slides left and we move a few meters until we come to another curtain hanging to the floor.

"Here you go," she says, opening the curtain for me. "All yours."

"When was it prepared?"

She says, "I think you'll find it comfortable."

"Major . . ."

"Later," she says. I slide in and she lets the curtain close behind me, and I guess I'm in my new home.

It's nearly the mirror image of her own quarters, with a bedding area, the center area with the stone-cut table and benches. There's indirect lighting as well, and in poking around, I find a small square near the opening. I touch it, tap it, and then when I slide my hand up and down, it controls the lighting. Good.

The place smells of cinnamon and something burnt. Rock, perhaps? Maybe this place was tunneled out just a while ago.

For me, or anybody else in particular?

The bathroom is the same, even to the mirror, and I use the facilities and I'm impressed with the softness of the sheets to be used for toilet paper. There's another hidey-hole next to the latrine, and it's a single-person barracks, with a smelly foam mattress, pillow, and a couple of blankets.

I go out from my sleeping quarters and one stone shelf is stuffed full with food, from boxed rations to canned goods that even have labels on them, even though some of the labels are written in French, Chinese, and what looks to be Russian. There are also some books that I plan to examine later on, and in one very weird decoration, old photos and magazine illustrations of New Hampshire. I mean, old . . . like a hundred years old. Funny looking cars on smooth highways. Smiling men and women skiing, or mountain climbing. Lots of photos and drawings of covered bridges, churches with white steeples, and maple and birch trees with their fall leaves. Even two of the Old Man of the Mountain, back before it collapsed.

Somebody—either Major Gallagher or the Creepers—is trying to make me feel at home.

It ain't working.

I bounce over to the curtain on the far wall, and pull it aside, and I'm looking out in darkness. The orbital battle station is on the night side of the Earth, and in the clouds and haze, I think I spot a couple of lights. A good sign, I hope, marking towns or even cities down there, still alive.

But for how long?

With this orbital battle station in orbit, the bugs will regain total control of their killer stealth satellites, the armed orbiters that can smear a town, village, or even someone operating a laptop computer. In the ten years since the war began, some of humanity has recovered, but only in a nineteenth-century style, with railroads, steamships, horses, and telegraphs.

And gas lamps as well.

I wonder how long those lights will remain.

Then there's sunrise, and below are more clouds, water, and brown and green. I try to puzzle out what I'm looking at, and fail. Geography is a funny subject, and after the tidal waves from ten years back, a lot of the coastlines have changed, and there hasn't been a new textbook published since then.

I keep on staring, just seeing the Earth roll by. Me, a sixteen-year-old kid, up in space, in orbit, trapped with one wounded Army major and who knows how many Creepers. Not to mention a number of human prisoners and those who scratch out a living in the cracks and fissures of this orbital station.

It feels like I can almost reach out and touch the Earth, and I think of my family and friends down there, and my buddy Thor, oh dear Thor, I surely hope you've made it back safe and sound to Ft. St. Paul. My poor Thor.

To the Earth below, I whisper, "Sweet God, please help those down there." And I pause, "And me, too, if you can spare the time."

I close the curtain and yawning, I go back to the square panel, lower the light until it's pretty dim. I slide over to the sleeping tunnel, crawl in, and take off my boots. The mattress is still smelly but I've handled worse. The blankets, though, smell fairly newly washed. I pull the blankets up and look up at the smooth cut rock, and reach out and touch it.

I feel a vibration coming through the rock. Machinery, pumps, conduits . . . who knows.

Maybe it's the movement of George Cooper and his family in the crevasses and cracks.

Or other humans. Or vermin, as the major calls them.

I draw my hand back and in the semidarkness, I think I hear things. Murmuring voices. Thumps. Whines. And whispers.

Click-click.

Click-click.

Click-click.

Remembering the Creeper that came to rescue Major Gallagher, I call out, "Sweet dreams, you buggy bastards you."

I roll over and surprise myself by going right to sleep.

I wake up later and my watch tells me I've been down for about five hours.

Now what?

I get up, put my boots on, visit the latrine, and then bring up the light. I eat over the sink, drinking my fill of the water—which is flat and tasteless—and I find a square can with French on it, open it up, and there's a rich smelling cheese and crackers. The crackers are crisp. I eat this meal—breakfast, lunch, dinner, take your pick—and then wash my hands and face, and look around once more.

The library.

I take down the books and give them a quick view, shaking my head as I do so. Textbooks, engineering manuals, paperbacks with covers torn off, and about a half-dozen different languages. There are six that are in English, and I shelve them to one side for later reading, if I ever have the time and interest to do so.

I slide out of my quarters, letting the curtain slowly flop back into place.

I'm standing in the curved corridor. Up ahead are Major Gallagher's quarters, and I walk up to the curtain covering her place.

I stand there for a minute.

Should I announce myself? Rap on the side of the rock? Or poke my head in?

Yeah, I don't think so.

One of the earliest things I learned in basic was never to bother your superior officer at any point, unless it was a life-and-death issue, and in the meantime, you could probably never go wrong by staying out of the way of superior officers.

A good lesson, either as a teen enlistee in the woods of New Hampshire, or a POW in low Earth orbit.

I move away from Major Gallagher's quarters and head up the corridor, retracing my shaky steps from earlier today. I go past sealed hatches, conduits, cables, and emerge once more into the transfer dome area. The dome is closed against the rock. Again, I tilt my head up and I can't see the top of the cut-out rock.

I move around, still trying to get used to the light motion of my feet against the surface, and I go to the nearest opening, and start down it, and then stop. There's no lighting going down this tunnel. I go until I can't see well anymore, and then reverse course, and in about a half hour, I've explored the other tunnels as well, even the one I'm familiar with. But for some reason, they're all dark.

Do the bugs turn down the illumination to reflect their own home world? Or my battered home planet? Or are they conserving their power sources?

Only one has illumination, that one being where the Major and I are residing.

Looks like the Creepers have set up that tunnel, just for us.

How damn courteous of them.

I start my way down the tunnel holding our quarters, and a loud horn blares out, causing me to jump, and I go up almost high enough to crack my skull on the overhead rock. I drop down and there's another blast, and another blast of the horn, followed by a loud hissing noise.

I flatten myself, look back out to the large room, knowing what's about to happen. Steam or some sort of vapor is escaping from the base of the rock, where the curved stone dome is fastened. The same weird vibration happens that makes the stone dome seem almost transparent.

One more horn sounds, and then the dome starts rising up, and if there's anything tugging it from on top, I still can't see it. The dome rises up further and there's a bright flash of light that makes me close my eyes, and then the dome goes up higher, and higher.

There are four Creepers on the flat stone, all Battle version, all wearing armored exoskeletons. Three of them skitter off and I flatten myself even more, not wanting to be seen, but it looks like they have other things in mind. One Creeper slips into the tunnel opening closest to it, but two of the Battle Creepers rotate and go back to the fourth one, which is barely moving. It looks like half of its armored legs are broken or damaged. The two mobile Battle Creepers grab this one, back up, and they drag and propel it down the hallway.

Horns sound again.

The stone dome lowers itself back into place, and I'm expecting a thud or a grinding noise as it mates up with the flat rock, but there's no sound. There's *click-click-click* as the Battle Creepers leave the scene, and I try to ease the shaking in my hands.

Then I get up, and move down the tunnel, as fast as I can.

I go past Major Gallagher's quarters, come up to mine, and then I keep on moving. Teen curiosity, I suppose. The further down the tunnel I go, there's more conduits, hatches, and then I come to the end, where there's a square door of some sorts, with hinges to one side, large enough to easily accommodate three Creepers moving side by side.

"Beyond here there be monsters," I whisper, as I put my hands up on the metal. I feel vibrations and I pull back, look around. There's another square panel, similar to the one back at my quarters that controls the lights, similar to the one I had played with earlier with Major Gallagher screaming at me. A little voice inside of me whispers, go ahead, try it again, see if you can open the door this time, but the bigger and smarter voice tells the little voice to shut up.

I turn and walk back, and that's when I find it.

"It" is another hanging curtain, but this one seems fastened so it doesn't easily move. But one corner at the bottom is loose, and I'm able to tug up a piece, large enough so I can crawl through.

I do so and I find myself in a third room in stone, cut out for us humans, but this one seems empty.

"Hello?" I call out, and there's no answer. I try to go in further but even the recessed lighting from the outside corridor isn't enough. I slide back through and go to my quarters, and look around to see if my buggy landlords have left me with a flashlight or some other means of lighting, but of course, they haven't.

But I keep on poking around, and then I remove one of the older books, a Russian chemistry textbook it looks like, and I tear off some pages, work them and tear them up again, and using the end of a long stirring spoon, I make some sort of a torch.

Sort being the operative word. How do I light the damn thing?

It takes me a long while, including removing some threads from my smelly socks, but I take the edge of one of the knives and strike it, strike it, and strike it a whole bunch of times until I can figure out the best way to make some sparks.

Then I get the threads and small bits of paper smoldering, and then I get the torch lit, and then I slowly but firmly haul ass, because even with some spare bits of paper with me, I'm not sure how long I can keep it lit.

Back out in the corridor, I return to the other quarters' entrance, and back my way in so I don't snuff out my flickering torch. When I'm completely in, I stand up and make an inspection.

There's not much to see. As with my quarters and those of Major Gallagher's, it has the hewn-out table and shelves, but everything is empty and clean. There's even an empty latrine, sleeping quarters, and another curtain covering a window looking out down to Earth. That curtain is also firmly in place and I don't bother tearing it loose. If I want to see the Earth, I just need to go back to my own place.

Empty.

Nothing.

I start back outside, and the torch is flickering, and then I feed it a couple of strips of paper, and the interior lights up, and I see something on the stone wall behind the near bench. I step closer and there are scratches and markings on the wall.

First of all are a number of hash marks, four straight lines with a single line going across. I hope whoever was in here was marking days, because if he or she was marking weeks, or months, well, there's a lot of hash marks stretched across the stone.

The light is dying and I lower the light further, and make out a flag, or some sort of emblem, and when I bring the torch closer, it reveals itself to be a British flag.

Below the flag are some carved letters in the stone. I wonder about the strength and determination to cut into this stone.

There are two lines, the first saying

2ND LT K. WHITNEY

Below that is

ROYAL WESSEX YEOMANRY

Under that, in smaller letters, like maybe his tool was getting dull, is

B SQUADRON SALISBURY

There are more scratchings.

I see

God Help Me

God Help Me

God

God

And then my torch flickers out and I'm in darkness.

CHAPTER TWENTY

Later I'm going through my rations, trying to figure out what exactly I have, when my curtain is slightly pulled outside and Major Gallagher calls in, "Lieutenant? May I enter?"

I turn and say, "Absolutely ma'am," and my new CO comes in, and there's something different about her, and I realize she's bathed and washed her hair, and has changed into a regular uniform blouse from the T-shirt she had on earlier.

"How are your quarters?"

"Reasonable," I say. "Considering where we are, well, not badly done. Although I'm not sure about the books the . . . Travelers have supplied me."

She smiles. "Ten years later, they still have difficulty figuring out our differences, figuring out what makes us tick." Then she lifts her face, makes a sniffing noise with her nose, and says, "I smell smoke. Do you know anything about it?"

"Not a thing," I lie. "Perhaps it's the bugs?"

Gallagher doesn't look convinced but she goes on. "If your schedule permits, Lieutenant, would you care to dine in my quarters . . . say, in an hour?"

"That would be fine, ma'am."

"Good," she says. "That'll give you time to take a bath."

"I don't think I need one."

She says, "Not a request or observation, Lieutenant. That was an order."

Then she scoots out and the curtain closes behind her.

I go into the latrine and examine the cut-out stone tub. There's a drain with a round rubber-type stopper, and I move a lever around until water starts coming out, moving and dropping funny in the lesser gravity. On a stone shelf are cloth towels, and little wrapped bars of soap, each one saying HILTON. I wonder who Hilton was and why he had so much soap named after him.

I slowly get undressed, wait, and then go to the kitchen area and return with a knife.

Paranoid, perhaps, but if there's any place to be paranoid, it would be up here in the Creepers' battle station.

I put the knife on the side of the stone tub, check the water, and then slide the lever shut and slide myself in. The hot and clean water feels great, and I just lie down and let the water soothe my muscles as I stretch out. The bugs have made this a large tub, and also did something funny at one end, so it's at an angle, making it more comfortable, and I run my fingers along the surface and find its spongy. Soft rock? Who knew.

I unwrap one and then two bars of soap, and then spend the rest of the time washing and rewashing myself, and watching the water ripple and sway in odd ways So the bugs have artificial gravity. Plus a transport system that can drop you down and bring you up to Earth. And a similar system that has given them interstellar travel.

I use one and then a second towel. Plus they're advanced enough to keep human prisoners in some sort of comfort.

But for what reason? Pets? Entertainment? Food?

I remembered some days ago—days, it seems like months!—when I was back at the naval station in New York State. The night this second battle station appeared in orbit, Serena's young brother—who hardly ever mutters a word—looked up at the glowing disk and had said, "Sister . . . Please don't let them bring me back up there again. Please."

Her younger brother Buddy had learned the Creeper language, just like Gallagher. But he had been sent back to Earth.

Why?

Why him, and why not Gallagher? Was she a spare, like the station itself?

I lean back, dunk my head in the perfectly warm water, wash and re-wash my hair, and decide it's better to be on time with my new CO than to spend more minutes trying to figure things out.

I dry off and look at myself in the mirror, see and feel the growing bristles on my face.

But no razor or shaving device.

Yet there is a comb, also from Mister Hilton, and I run that through my wet hair and get dressed, and I feel squeamish putting these damp and smelly clothes back on, with the smelly socks. I take one of my damp towels, do the best to clean off my boots, and then its time.

I slip out of my quarters and go up to hers, and I'm not sure of the protocol. Barge right in? Stick my head past the curtain and announce myself?

I reach in and rap the side of the rock with my fist, as loud as I can.

"Major Gallagher, it's me," I call out, which I instantly reflect is pretty stupid. Who else would it be?

She calls back, "Enter!" and in I go.

The place has changed some since I was last here. The lighting is low but there are candles lit here and there, even giving this rough-hewn rock a more lived-in feel. The major is in the kitchen area and swivels around, and says, "Right on time, Randy. Have a seat."

She's moved some cushions to the stone benches on either side of the carved table, and I say, "Can I help you, Major?" and with her back turned, "No, not now. Cleanup, yes, but we're all set. Just sit still."

Gallagher has on some sort of short black dress that's belted around her waist, and that billows around her severed legs. Her hair is washed and there's even silver earrings dangling from her ears. For some reason the candlelight, the smell of cooked food, and seeing her in civvy clothes causes me to be tongue-tied for a moment.

But only a moment. As she puts down plates and cutlery, she sniffs and says, "Your clothes . . ."

"Didn't have time to wash them, ma'am. Sorry."

She says, "Not a worry. I'll put in a . . . request. We'll get you some clean clothes. Enjoy the bath?"

I rub my chin. "I could have used a razor, ma'am."

Gallagher nods. "I'll put that on the list. Anything else?"

"Well . . ."

"Be practical, all right?"

I try to look like a sheepish teenager, confessing something to teacher. "I . . . hate to admit this, ma'am, but I took a long nap earlier, and when I woke up, I had a nightmare. I was scared. It seemed really, really dark. Any chance you might have a spare flashlight, or something like that, to help?"

"Hold on," she says, and she slides her way over to the shelves, comes back with a skinny black flashlight. "Fresh batteries in there. But don't break it, lose it, or do anything stupid with it."

I take the flashlight from her warm hand, slip it into a pants pocket. "I understand, ma'am."

"Good," she says. "Let's eat."

I'm not too sure how she did it—a decade of practice, I'm sure—but the meal is fine indeed. A hot beef soup, followed by a thick pasta dish with sausage and vegetables inside, and even bread. The bread's a bit stale but there's real butter that I smear on. Our drink is a cold fruit juice and she says, "Wine. I haven't had wine in . . . well, a very long time. The Travelers don't like to see us get intoxicated. Still, how's the food?"

"Best I've had in a very long time, Major."

She laughs. "Randy . . . let's relax, all right? We're a couple of hundred miles away from the Earth, we're the only two humans in the vicinity, and I think we can relax the military formality for the foreseeable future. So stop with the major."

"Yes, ma'am."

Gallagher gives my wrist a playful slap. "And cut it out with the ma'am! You make me feel like an old crone . . . which reminds me, how old are you?"

"Sixteen, ma'am . . . sorry. Sixteen."

She nods, spoons up some of the pasta. Fetta-something it's called. I can't remember. "Sixteen . . . and you're a lieutenant?"

"I am."

Gallagher eats in silence for a few more minutes, and I try to restrain myself from eating everything in sight within seconds. She looks up and takes a sip from her juice. "What's it like, back home?"

That surprises me in the middle of buttering another piece of bread. "Excuse me? I thought you'd know via the . . . Travelers. I mean, how things are."

A purse of the lips, a shake of the head. "No. I get bits and pieces. The occasional old newspaper, and if I'm lucky, it's in a language I know. I've asked for a radio receiver over the years but I've never gotten one."

"You wouldn't miss much," I say. "There might be some local low-watt stations here and there, but the only ones with national reach in the States are the Voice of America and the Armed Forces Radio Network. Sometimes we can get the BBC, or Radio Paris."

That makes her smile. "After ten years . . . that'd be so wonderful to hear." Then she looks at me and her face gets more serious. "Again, what's it like, down there. Tell me."

This is a very odd position I'm in, being the one telling an older person and a superior officer information she doesn't know, but then I convince myself I'm just providing a debriefing of sort, and being polite.

I say, "Best I know, the food situation is improving across the United States, as well as the medical system. There's not as many food shortages as there were, even from a few years ago. It's been at least four or so years since there was a major food riot in a city . . . at least in the States. And it used to be, some years back, that the flu would kill off tens of thousands." I take a bite from the bread, loving the thick butter spread on top. "The siege of Denver was lifted a few weeks back, that was pretty big news. And the capitol got attacked a while later from the killer stealth satellites."

"Really? Where's the capital now? Harrisburg?"

I shake my head. "No. Albany. But word I got was that the President and most of the Congress escaped before the sat strike."

She says, "But the people . . . tell me about the mood of the people."

"I'm sorry, ma'am . . ."

"Felicia," she insists.

"Felicia," I repeat. "I'm not sure what you mean about the mood."

"Oh, how they're feeling. How they're surviving. What they're hoping for. Stuff like that."

I chew slowly and try to come up with a good answer for the curious major, and I'm not sure if it's good or bad, so I just let it fly.

"Most people are surviving, that's what they're thinking about," I say. "Living day to day, having enough to eat, living in a town where there's a doctor nearby. Maybe the telephone's working again. Maybe some electricity. For a while it was just living, just scrambling around to get enough to eat. Now, some jobs are coming back. Railroad engines. Roadwork. Bridgework. People seem like they're looking ahead . . . well, from what I can see. Which is pretty limited, being mostly the Northeast."

"And what about the Travelers?"

"Most have given up caring one way or another. It's like . . . some teacher told me, it's like the peasants in Italy, living at the base of that volcano, Mt. Vesuvius. You sit there, you get on with your life the best you can, knowing that any moment, the mountain might blow . . . or an alien might come through, burning and lasing everything in its path. No sense to it, no rhyme, no reason. It's like the . . . the Travelers themselves don't even know why they're here. It's not like they're trying to occupy the planet."

"Is that what you think?" she asks.

"No," I say, now getting the feeling this isn't a relaxing, have a nice talk with your CO kind of dinner.

"Then tell me what you think, Randy," she says, trying to keep her voice casual, but I sense something else in what she's asking me.

The truth, I think. Let's give that a try again.

"They can be hurt," I say. "They can be killed. We should keep on hurting them and killing them until they leave. Or until we figure out a way of killing them all."

"Surrender? How about if they surrender?"

I shake my head. "Bugs . . . they don't surrender."

"Travelers."

"Ma'am, you can—"

"Felicia, you can call them Travelers, searchers, explorers, whatever you'd like. It doesn't change anything at all. They're invaders . . . and they started it. And we're damn well going to finish it."

That brings out a slight smile. "They've taught you well."

I shoot back. "A lot I learned on my own, when I was six years old."

"I'm sure," she says. "Who . . . who have you lost over the years?"

"Didn't take years," I say. "Started off the first week. The . . . Travelers killed my mom and my sister. Plenty of uncles, aunts, and cousins. I don't even remember their names anymore. My dad tried over the years to teach me their names but it never stuck."

She starts picking up the empty plates and piles them up. "I was lucky, I suppose. My husband and my two sons, we had a weekend place in the Sierra Madres. After everything started, we stayed put for a couple of weeks, until I left to join up with my unit. I think they're safe. I hope they're safe. We had supplies there, it was in an out-of-the-way small town . . ."

Her voice gets soft, reflective. "My parents were in San Francisco. I hope . . . it was quick for them. But my boys . . . sometimes at night, just before I go to sleep, I look out the port here, hoping the weather is clear over California. Sometimes it is, sometimes it isn't."

Gallagher's eyes moisten. "You know what's worse? It's seeing that part of California, when it's clear. There are no clouds. No cover. No illusions. Just seeing what's really down there . . . that's the worst."

We have cups of instant coffee and stay quiet, and I clear my throat and say, "Felicia . . ."

She waves a hand at me. "I know, I know. Lots of questions. You have lots of questions. I understand."

I say, "No . . . I was going to say, ma'am, you made this wonderful meal. Will you let me do the dishes?"

I think I get the biggest smile ever on her face since arriving here. "The time I say no to a male, asking to do dishes, is the day I've certainly given up on life. Go right ahead. Soap and such is over there by the sink."

I get up. "Ma'am . . . Felicia, I owe you. Really. This is one of the best meals I've had in a long, long time."

She says, "Now you're teasing me."

"No, I'm not," I say. "And I realize that . . . getting resupplied must be a challenge from the . . . Travelers. Getting the right kind of rations and foodstuffs. And then you shared your rations . . . for us troopers on the ground, having somebody share their food and water is about the highest form of trust and thanks you can give to another soldier. So I thank you."

Gallagher wipes at her eyes with a clean white cloth. "I thank you, Randy. Honest. That was nice to hear."

I get up and take the piles of dishes, and go over to the sink and get to work. I rinse and wash and rinse some more, and there's movement and I glance back, and she's stretched out on the stone shelf with the cushions, head resting against a pillow. At this angle it's hard to see that her lower legs are missing. As I finish up the dishes I decide to snuff out the candles, and on the shelf with the kitchen supplies, I find wooden matches in a cardboard box marked in Indian, it looks like.

I turn back to Major Gallagher.

She seems asleep.

I take some of the matches, slip them into my pants pocket.

I poke around some more.

There are scores of tubes of liquid soap, piled in a basket. I take two of the largest, slip one in each pocket.

Then when everything seems safe and secure, I leave.

Having violated the trust that she's placed in me.

I'll have to decide later if that was a good or bad thing.

CHAPTER TWENTY-ONE

I go back into my quarters, hide the matches and the liquid soap. I take the flashlight out and slip into the corridor.

No noise from Major Gallagher's quarters.

I decide against searching Lieutenant Whitney's quarters again, thinking I can always return back there later if I'm still curious about what else might still be in that chamber. Instead, it's time for me to relearn the first skills from my original unit's job—Recon Ranger—and find out what I can up here.

Even though there must be some sort of surveillance system emplaced around here—explaining the small Creeper that burst in to "rescue" the Major—I'm not going to just sit on my nice well-fed butt and not do anything.

I owe the American taxpayers that, at least.

I move flat along the side of the tunnel until I come out again into the huge expanse that has the concrete dome, part of the *Grantztch* system, and using the flashlight, I find something I missed before: a cutout in the rock that contains panels and instrumentation.

I flash the light around, trying to take in what I'm seeing. There's a low black expanse of some sort of metal and plastic, and built in are panels in different shapes: circle, square, three types of triangles, rectangle, and another circle.

That's it.

I reach out and touch the circular panel, and even the slightest touch causes it to light up.

"Damn it," I whisper, backing up.

Did I just trigger something?

I look around.

I'm still alone. There's no noise. The light coming up from the circle has illuminated it from within, and it looks pink.

The light fades away.

All right, trooper, I think. Looks like we dodged that laser blast.

Then I recall what Felicia had told me, that it takes a Creeper touch to actually do something to the access control panels.

Again, so much for the intrepid trooper learning the secret code from the bugs, and transporting his young butt back to Earth.

I back out, go around, and head to the first opening that's not ours, and that I've not been in before. I go in deeper and switch on the flashlight, cup the beam in my hands so it's not too bright, and hug the wall again.

There's something different in this tunnel. I can't quite explain it. There's an odd shape, or geometry, or something going on. The tunnel with my quarters and Gallagher's are smooth and linear. This one . . . it goes down, it goes up, widens, tilts, and there's just an oddness to it.

It's a tunnel for Creepers.

Not for humans.

It widens and constricts and then comes to an end, with another, similar hatch as from the tunnel I call "ours." I flash around my light and see another panel, like the one back at the dome. Another series of geometric shapes. There are scratch marks all around the panel area. I see in my mind what might happen. The Creepers come here and using their articulated armored legs, they manipulate these shapes and open the hatch.

Crude but also simple.

Probably the same way they use their transportation dome.

I trot back up the tunnel, and decide to go down one more before returning to my own place. This tunnel starts off even wider, and becomes an avenue, scores of meters wide. I lift up the flashlight and barely make out the overhead rock. Impressive. I move along and it gets even wider, such that I become even uneasier, and I hug the wall even more, like a mouse in a barracks trying to be inconspicuous.

Then I take a step forward and fall.

Damn it!

But with the lower gravity here, I don't hit hard when I land, and in fact, I bounce before I settle down.

My flashlight falls and falls, going down a terraced set of steps. I get up and move down, skipping from step to step, reaching the flashlight as it rotates like a little beacon.

When I get to the flashlight, I pick it up glance around.

The damn place looks like a stadium. There are wide terraced seats rising up all about me, and before me is an open area. I step out onto the wide flat area and illuminate where I can. Wide, very wide indeed.

There's another, smaller opening set against the stone. I aim the flashlight at the opening, revealing a small cavern. There are piles of something in the corner. I step closer, lower the light.

Torn clothing.

Leather lumps of what was probably belts and boots.

Bones.

Human bones.

Looks like three or four humans, dead and decayed, stuffed in a forgotten corner of the universe.

I back out and go up the terraces. Even with the lower gravity, my legs are screaming at me when I get to the top of the arena.

Time to go back to my home.

When I make my way down the tunnel designed for us humans, I hear music coming from Gallagher's quarters, and I envy her. I wonder how long it'll be before I can get a musical device for myself, which causes me to wonder how long I'll be up here, and that leads to other dark thoughts and I just let it be.

Inside my quarters it feels right damn snug and comfortable after exploring that second tunnel, and I keep the lights low. I strip off my clothes and then take them to the stone tub, and do my best to wash, rinse, and then wash again. I squeeze the water out and slap the clothes against the near stone wall, and I move around, and find that if I put my hand up against the light tubes, they emit a little bit of heat.

I hope it's enough. I manage to arrange my clothes so that they are warmed by the lights, and then I go to bed. Naked, I stretch out on the itchy wool blankets.

No problem.

I've slept on worse.

Breakfast is in Major Gallagher's quarters and is dehydrated eggs and ham, and an orange-flavored drink called Tang. It tastes delicious. She raises the ceramic cup and makes an odd toast, saying, "Here's to the drink of space travelers everywhere."

"Hunh?"

"Oh, you're too young," she says. "Actually, so am I. My father told me about it. In the 1960s, this drink was used by astronauts when they started going up into space. Even though Tang wasn't made for NASA, that was always the misconception. For decades it flew up with the astronauts, even though Buzz Aldrin said it tasted awful."

I reach back into my schooling and say, "Second man on the moon, right?"

That rewards me with a smile. "Very good. Nice to know they've taught you more than just killing and fighting."

I pick up the dishes and start washing them, and she says, calmly and with no forewarning. "School starts today. Are you ready?"

"Yes, ma'am."

"Felicia," she says.

"Yes, Felicia," I say.

When the dishes are dried and put away, she leads the way and says, "Your clothes look and smell better, Randy."

"I washed them last night."

"They dry out?"

"Good enough for government work," I reply, which makes her laugh again.

We go out in the hallway and bear right, and then head again to the stone dome. She looks up to it almost in awe and says, "I've been here for ten years and I still don't know how this works. It's a transport system, of course, but how it can transport Travelers and supplies in a tight beam . . . I just don't know. I've worked very, very hard to get the explanation but the language . . . it doesn't make sense to me."

"Can it transport to any place on Earth?"

"I'm sorry, I don't understand what you're asking."

I say, "The *Grantztch* . . . does it reach down and deposit what's being transported, or—"

"Oh, I see," she says. "No, it's . . . connected, somehow, to the Domes. There's a mirror *Grantztch* system in every Dome. It's like there's a . . . connection between the Domes and here."

I step closer and ignore the opening I had spotted some hours earlier. "Like a subway system, perhaps, with one terminus?"

"Like what?" she asks.

I was thinking it through and said, "Let's say you have a train station. And there are a dozen stations it runs to, on single tracks. You can take a train from the terminus—like this station—to a particular Dome on Earth. Like that?"

"Very good, Randy," she says, and maybe she's not doing it on purpose, but she does sound a bit dismissive. "That's a good analogy."

"Did the *Grantztch* work from this station to the first one?"

"It did," she says carefully. "That's how I ended up there. I was transported from California to the original station, and from there, to this one, in orbit behind the moon."

I push it. "Are there any other stations out there?"

A quick hesitation. "Not that I know. Come along, now."

We circumnavigate the transport dome and she points out the different tunnels as we go around. "One is used for those Travelers heading out to the dome. Another is used for Travelers coming in."

"Why two?"

"There's . . . a ceremony that happens when they leave. And a different ceremony when they come back. That's why there's two separate tunnels."

"Can we go down there?"

"Not now," she says. "Later."

"How much later?" I ask as we keep on moving, staying next to her as she slides along, propelling herself with her strong arms.

"Eager young lad, aren't you."

"Ma'am . . . Felicia, I want to know why I'm here. And why you're here."

"Me? I'm here to communicate with humanity. I've spent the last ten years of my life learning to do that."

"And me? Lieutenant Randy Knox? What's my role?"

She glances up at me, and with all seriousness says, "You're here to help me save the world."

❋ ❋ ❋

One tunnel is abandoned—and that's the one I went down, the one with the terraced steps and human bones—and she won't tell me why it's abandoned. One other tunnel is used to ship supplies in and out of the dome, and I say, "So . . . those two tunnels, they're used for the Travelers only. And the third over there is used for supply."

"That's right."

I say, "It sounds like there's some ceremonial or religious reason why the Travelers use those two specific tunnels. Like it would be . . . forbidden, or taboo, for anyone or anything else to use those openings. Am I right?"

She stops and stares at me. Stares at me for what is probably just a few seconds, but seems much longer.

"You . . . you're smart one, you are."

"Not that smart," I reply.

"Why's that?"

"Because I ended up in the Army, and a POW."

A smiling nod, and she says, "Anything else?"

I point to the last tunnel, which is taller and wider than the others. "This one. Where does it go? What's its purpose?"

"That's the main tunnel," she says. "It goes deeper into the station. There's lifts, ramps, storage units . . . living quarters for the Travelers. Power, communications, life support."

"How many of them are here?"

"Enough."

"And . . . humans?"

"There are other prisoners, I'm sure."

I'm more than sure, I think, and I say, "What about the other ones, the escapees, the ones that live in the cracks and crevasses?"

"Don't worry about them."

"They're humans. They're up here with us. Why shouldn't I worry about them? Or is it just because they're . . . vermin?"

"We two are your focus," she says. "That's all you should care about."

"That's not a good answer, Felicia."

Her eyes narrow. "Only answer you're getting today, Lieutenant."

"Oh," I say, my voice sharp, echoing in the stone. "Now we're back to the usual command structure."

"We are," she says. "Any more questions?"

"Lots, Major," I say. "But you keep on pushing me back, saying later, saying not right now. What's the point?"

"Try me," she says.

"All right," I say. "Why the Travelers? Why do you call them that?"

"That's what they call themselves."

"Why?"

"That's what they do. They travel from star system to star system."

Doing what, I want to ask, but I say, "But not this chunk of rock."

"Go on."

"It's . . . a chunk of rock. I find it hard to believe that the bugs . . . the Travelers . . . would travel light-years in a piece of rock."

"They didn't," she says. "They used . . . well, *craft* is too broad a term, but no, you're right, they didn't come with this structure. Like I said earlier, their interstellar travel . . . it's based on the *Grantztch*."

"Where did they get this rock?" I ask, slapping at the near surface. "The asteroid belt?"

She shakes her head. "No. The Kuiper belt. They . . . were on the move. They came to the Kuiper belt. They secured two structures that would serve their purpose . . . and with other . . . pieces, they arrived in the solar system."

"Why wasn't there any warning?"

"They didn't teach you that in school?"

I say, "All I remember is that—"

A low-sounding growl interrupts me, and I turn to the tunnels, thinking something awful and alien is coming out, but there's nothing, and the growl increases in sound and pitch, until it's a siren, and then it gets louder and deeper and I look to Major Gallagher, and she looks scared out of her wits.

"What's wrong?" I ask. "What's going on?"

"Something bad."

"How bad?"

Gallagher says, "Under-attack bad. C'mon, we've got to haul ass. Now!"

She leads the way to the tunnel that holds our living quarters, and there's a hissing sound and a loud *thump!* and she says, "Shit, shit, shit, we're not gonna make it."

I see what's wrong.

Hatches or doors are sliding down for each of the six tunnels, and the way we're moving, we're not going to make it.

"Randy!" she yells. "Don't wait for me! Haul ass!"

I think about that for about a second and instantly dismiss it, and I say, "By your leave, ma'am," and I scoop her up, and after a few seconds of fumbling, she's riding my back, her stumps grasping my hips, her hands on my shoulders.

I really start running now, and she yells in my ear, "We're still not going to make it!"

"So what?" I yell back. "What happens if we're stuck out here?"

She says, "Once the doors shut, this place is eventually opened to vacuum . . . better to gradually drain it of atmosphere than expose everything in here to explosive decompression."

I bend down and really kick it up, and while the lower gravity helps me in building up a nice head of steam, having Gallagher's body on my back is throwing off my balance and center of gravity.

But I won't leave her behind.

It's not how was I trained.

It's not in my nature.

Closer.

We're getting closer.

Gallagher suddenly shifts, like she's trying to push herself off, and I don't let it happen. I grab her wrists and twist them hard, and she yelps, and it feels like she's no longer struggling.

We're closer but that damn door is sliding down, and a little voice inside of me whispers, give it up, give it up . . . a few seconds of misery when the air is vented out and then it'll be over, you won't be a prisoner anymore among the Creepers, and you'll see Mom and Melissa again, and no more worries, no more pain, and you'll be finished with it, finished with the fear and fighting and—

I yell out from frustration and exertion, and I flip Gallagher over and fling her in front of me. With her lower body mass and with the lower gravity, she sails in front of me, hitting the stone floor, and sliding and tumbling into the tunnel.

I slide in on my belly, scraping my hands and face, and something kisses the tip of my right foot before the door whispers shut behind me.

CHAPTER TWENTY-TWO

I get myself up off the stone floor and Gallagher rearranges herself as well, and the lights in the tunnel are bright, and even though the thick sliding door is shut, I can still hear the siren as it climbs higher in pitch.

I check out my scraped hands. "What now?"

"My quarters," she says. "You, too."

"Is there a hatch there, to seal us off?" I ask, puzzled. I don't remember having seen one, but what the hell, they are aliens. Maybe the major has a sliding door that appears if you add water or something. Right now I'm still giddy and overwhelmed at what's going on.

She shakes her head. "No. No hatch. But if we're going to get hit, I don't want to die alone. Move it."

That little phrase digs into me, and I follow her as she moves along, going through the curtain, and then to the far end of the room, where the round window looking down at Earth is located. The major moves up and pulls the curtain aside, and I stand next to her.

The same old battered Earth, in daylight, in clouds and smoke and more clouds, and then as we watch, it slides into darkness.

"What are you looking for?" I ask.

"If I see it I'll let you know."

Below us the cloud cover seems pretty thick, but I see one dot of light, and then another. It warms me, seeing a city alive down there, but the two dots of light . . .

They're moving.

I can hear Gallagher sigh.

"Here it comes. Looks like two . . . no, wait, there's three."

I blink my eyes and see the grouping of three lights, moving slow, and now sliding faster up toward the battle station, and maybe it's my imagination, but I actually think I can see little flares of flame from underneath the moving dots.

"Missiles."

"Yeah," she says. "Ten years later, you think the folks down there would have run out of them. Or know how useless they are."

"Then why all the excitement? The doors closing down? The main chamber back there being evacuated of air?"

"Because we up here have to be lucky all the time," she says. "Down there . . . they just have to be lucky once. Like last month, when the original station was destroyed."

The lights come closer.

"Nukes?"

"Perhaps. We'll find out soon enough, won't we."

Closer, rising closer.

My chest is tight and I suppose I should feel fear, or terror, or sadness that it might all be over in a few more seconds, but I'm feeling none of that.

I'm full of pride.

We humans, we're still fighting back.

There's something warm in my left hand and it's Gallagher, holding hands with me.

"Not much longer now," she says, and I don't know if she means before the missiles are intercepted, or before we and everything else on this orbital battle station are destroyed, and then the round window goes black.

Remains black.

Then it's clear again, and the little dots of light are balls of expanding light and colors and soon fade away.

Gallagher lets out a breath of air. "Made it."

"The Creepers destroyed them? How?"

She quickly removes her hand from mine, like she's suddenly ashamed to have been put in such a vulnerable position. "Various weapons they have. They've traveled for millennia . . . they know how to defend themselves, Randy."

"The window . . . what happened?"

"A reaction from the light," she says. "When the missiles and their warheads were destroyed, there would be a very bright flash of light that might have blinded us, or hurt our eyes. The Travelers designed this window, and others, so that it instantly becomes opaque."

Below us the fading balls of light are sliding out of view as this endless orbit continues. "Who do you think launched them?"

She seems to peer closer through the window. "Not sure. Based on where we look to be, I'd say what's left of Russia. Or China. Maybe Japan. Poor folks. Whoever launched those missiles, they're going to get hammered pretty soon."

I say, "You sound happy about that."

"I'm happy that I'm alive and that they failed. Aren't you?"

"No," I say, without hesitation, which surprises me. "No, I wish they had made it. I'd stop being a POW, the Creepers would be dead, and maybe this time humanity would have won . . . for real this time."

"But what kind of victory?" she asks.

"What do you mean, what kind of victory?" I move away from her.

"You heard me. Let's say the Travelers are destroyed. Doubtful, because they are quick learners, and they learned a lot from the attack that destroyed the first orbital station."

"Don't be so sure," I say.

"I'm sure because I know facts, and I know them," she says, voice rising. "All right, Lieutenant Knox. In your dream world, your dream universe, let's say this orbital station is destroyed. Humanity is again alone in the universe. What then?"

"Then we recover," I say. "Rebuild. Bring back the power, the electronics, the computers, the Internet, the—"

"The greed, the infighting, the wars between brothers and sisters. So we can go back to a time when we were hell bent on destroying each other and this planet."

My voice is louder and sharper. "For real? Major, the goddamn Creepers seem to be doing a pretty good job destroying us and the planet."

Gallagher pushes her way back to the stone couch. "They've interfered, yes, but for a reason."

"What reason?"

"You stupid kid, haven't you figured it out by now? The Travelers . . . they're not here to destroy us."

⊕ ⊕ ⊕

I think maybe a minute or so passes before I find the ways to speak again. "Major . . . explain yourself."

"I don't have to explain anything to a dumb kid like you," she says, face bright, tone furious.

I step over, and soften my approach. "Begging the major's pardon, and indulgence . . . please. I don't understand. I want to . . . be a good officer."

All right, I nearly choke on those last words, but a Recon Ranger needs information most of all.

"Really," I continue. "I need to know the situation. Major Gallagher, if I may, isn't that a reasonable request? From a subordinate officer?"

She stares back at me and says, "I'm not sure you're ready."

"I believe I am."

"But . . ."

"Please."

She looks away and says, "Sit down. Now, Lieutenant."

I sit down at one of the benches. She slowly turns back to me and says, "You've seen their capability. We've all seen their capability, back on October tenth, when they made their presence known. In less than a week, a good portion of humanity was dead, the cities depopulated, what was left of civilization tossed back into the nineteenth century."

To say this is old history is an understatement, which is what I want to tell the major. I lived through the first attack, I know what it meant, and how we survived.

"Lieutenant . . . Randy," she says. "If the Travelers really wanted to kill humanity, would they have taken such a heavy-handed, sledgehammer approach?"

"No," I reply. "They would have studied us further, investigated our ecology and environment, and devised a virus that would have killed us all. Or they could have just kept dropping nukes from orbit until the whole planet had a radiation level high enough to eliminate humanity."

"But they didn't do that. Why?"

"That's above my pay grade, ma'am. Lots of reasons out there."

"Yet the fight continues, correct? Each time a new power plant is built, or someone tries to set up a television station, or a computer network, it's terminated very quickly thereafter. No matter how small the . . . infraction."

I don't say anything. The major says, "You know I'm right, don't you."

"Yes," I say. "Years back, when I was in the Boy Scouts, we were doing search and recovery of some homes in Massachusetts. Recovering canned food, bottled water, other salvageable stuff. We had strict orders not to pick up anything electronic or computer based. One kid ignored the orders. There was some sort of handheld computer game that he started up, sitting in a road, the game in his lap . . ."

"And what happened?"

Obliteration is what happened, I think. "He was killed. Matter of minutes. Looked like a particle beam blast or a laser burst from orbit."

"That's right. The Travelers, they took away our technology, and our technological way of life. And why?"

"To punish us . . . or to convert us to their belief system. I guess."

She shakes her head. "No."

There's a long moment or two. "Randy, they are our saviors."

I try to see if she's joking or not, because the Major doesn't have a particularly jovial personality, and I try to think of something to say that won't piss her off, and the best I come up with is, "They sure have a funny way of showing it."

"But it's true. They're here to rescue us."

"From what?"

She rearranges her stumps. "The Travelers . . . they frighten us, they've killed millions of us, drowned and destroyed our cities. So many of us know them as all-seeing, all-powerful monsters. But can you imagine something more monstrous that would even frighten the Travelers?"

I don't want to imagine anything like that, but the major continues. "Years and years ago, the Travelers only existed on two home worlds in a star system . . . I'm still not sure which star system it is. My language skills with them . . . enough to ask for food and clothing, not good enough for astrophysics and astronomy. But what I do know is that they were in this star system, which included asteroid settlements and deep space probes, living peacefully, expanding, learning. Then . . . one day, the Other came."

"What do you mean, the Other."

She says, "The name of the ones who came to their home system . . . they still can't mention it in public. It's taboo. Unmentionable. You know the old fantasy books, the Harry Potter ones? There was an enemy in those books that was called 'You-Know-Who' or 'He-Who-Must-Not-Be-Named.' He was so terrifying that even his real name scared people. Do you remember?"

"Not really."

"I thought all kids read those books," she says.

"I read the first one," I say. "I was bored out of my skull."

"You . . ." In exasperation, she continues, "Those who came were so horrible, so destructive, that they wiped out both home worlds . . . used burrowing nukes that cracked both planets, causing volcanic eruptions and earthquakes, laid down genetically engineered plagues that had no cure . . . on and on. They then went after the asteroid settlements, and other locations, until about ninety-nine percent of the Traveler race was wiped out."

Gallagher takes a long look around the rock, and she seems overwhelmed at what she's telling me. She touches the stone. "So many of them dead in less than a week."

Me, being the coarse and callow youth that I am, want to say that I wish the Creepers' enemy had done a better job, but I keep my mouth shut.

I say, "Then they left?"

"After some time had passed," she says quietly. "The survivors . . . they had to find each other. To see how many had escaped their holocaust. And then the survivors, after more time, they decided they had to leave their star system. Like the Roma, or Gypsies, on Earth, they left their homeland, to travel forever, and never to return."

"But . . . they came here to save us? By killing us? By beating us down?"

"Randy . . ." She shakes her head. "You're still not getting it. Those surviving Travelers . . . they decided they survived for a reason, for a cause. To warn others of the . . . Other. To make sure that other civilizations, other lives, wouldn't catch the attention of the Other. That became their mission in their surviving civilization . . . to never return home, and to live to warn others."

Now it comes to me, like waking up from a bad dream to realize you're waking up to a worse reality. "The Travelers never wanted to kill us all. They wanted to destroy our modern civilization. If we relied on steamships, locomotives, and telegraphs . . . then the Other, or whatever the hell they are, would ignore us."

"That's right."

"But . . . they killed so many of us! Destroyed so much!"

"Yes, to save us."

"They had no right!"

"Says who? Yes, this current generation would say that . . . but in another century, if the world is finally at peace in a self-sustaining, agricultural civilization, then humanity will survive. And the Other will ignore us, and move on."

I say, "I . . . why . . . damn it, they should have just come here and warned us. That's all! They didn't have to kill so many and destroy so much!"

"And humanity would have listened?"

"They should have given us that chance!"

"Randy . . . really? A species that still fights among itself over religion and skin color, you expect them to come together as one and listen to the Travelers, about what to do to prevent being exterminated by the Other? Really? And who would speak for humanity? The President of the United States? Or France? Or Russia? Or the United Nations? Please."

"The Travelers . . . they should have tried something else."

"Like what?"

I don't have a good answer. I don't know if I could ever come up with a good answer.

Softly, Felicia says, "They were like professional, cold-blooded surgeons. They needed to cut out a part of humanity to save the rest."

"So why didn't they move on after . . . the drowning, the killings, the burning?"

"Because they needed humanity to agree with them, to . . . conclude a pact that we will follow their insight."

"Their religion, you mean."

"No, not quite," she says. "Their way of life. And when they are satisfied that we have chosen the right path, that we won't be a target for the Other, then they will depart."

"And go find another civilization to destroy?"

"Not destroy, Randy. Change. For the better. To put them on a way of life that means they won't be a target for the Other."

To say everything seems surreal and unbelievable is an understatement, listening to a superior officer utter such statements. Yet she looks calm, relaxed, like she was telling me the history of the Battle of Hastings in 1066.

"Major . . . earlier you said you and I, we're going to save the world. How? By convincing the folks down there to surrender, to give up the fight, to agree to a nineteenth-century life?"

She nods. "That's exactly what we're going to do. You and I, we're going to be emissaries, humanity's ambassadors, and we're going to save the Earth and what's left of humanity, and ensure we survive."

I don't know how to respond to that, but it's okay, because the major takes care of it for me.

"It starts tomorrow," she says. "You're going with me to meet with the senior Travelers to agree to do just that."

CHAPTER TWENTY-THREE

I can't sleep that night, and I don't think anything I do will make sleep happen. I toss and turn, toss and turn, thinking of what Major Gallagher has told me, and what she tells me I'm going to do tomorrow.

I'm going to meet the bug leadership, and I'm going to agree to join the major to save humanity.

Right.

I think of my life, my half-remembered years up to when I was six, of fun times, warmth, lights, hot water, plenty to eat . . . and Mom and my older sister Melissa.

What about them?

What about the millions—hell, let's be real—billions of the dead out there? What was my duty, my responsibility to them? To work with the major, to . . . work with these damn invaders, these killers, who've come such a long way and wrecked so much, burned, destroyed, severed, blasted, and left shattered families and countless orphans? Was that my destiny, my job?

I had been picked Major Gallagher had said, for this mission, to put an end to the war and save humanity.

But save humanity for what?

To live the next centuries and millennia as peasants? Laborers? To live simple lives and die, knowing that in some distant time, their ancestors had a glorious life and future that was snatched away by aliens, who thought they were doing right by us, by battering us down to save us from the Other?

Toss and turn.

Toss and turn.

The rumbling goes on, deep there in the rock. Out there are the Creepers, working and planning to keep on killing us. There are also humans here as well—the escaped ones living in the cracks and crevasses, and the other prisoners—all living here, rotating around the broken Earth below us, every ninety minutes.

Toss and turn.

Then I stop.

Stare up to the bare rock overhead.

Enough.

I get up and fumble around, and find the switch to bring the lights up.

They illuminate my quarters.

My cell.

My prison.

I go through and take a sheet off the mattress, and dump everything I own into it, tie the four corners, grab the flashlight, and slide my way out, past the curtain. Pause in the corridor.

Wait.

I walk past Major Gallagher's quarters.

Something tugs at me, to pause, to ask permission to talk to her, to explain what I'm doing.

No.

Won't work.

I keep on moving, and now I'm out in the main chamber. The huge dome of the *Grantztch* is locked into position. I slide around the edge of the chamber, holding the sheet with my stuff close to my side. I go down the corridor where I had been discovered by both the major and the Cooper family—George, Joanie, and Gwen—and at what I feel is the right point, I drop my sheet and then try to propel myself up.

Surprise, surprise, I make it on the first attempt.

I scramble up and bump my head, and then find the spare knapsack I had left behind.

Good.

Having the knapsack gives me a glimmer of hope and happiness.

One more thing.

I run my hands over the rock and find the crack from before, and gingerly slide my hand in, feeling the harsh bite of the curved knife I had earlier taken from the dead Gurkhas. A dim memory comes to me. It's called a kukri. I run my fingers along the metal and grasp the handle, and pull it out. I find a way of hanging it from my belt, and then I drop the knapsack onto the stone corridor. I lower myself down and then pick up the knapsack, and start moving again.

It's good to be moving.

I go out to the main chamber and it's quiet, but I still move to the side and stay away from the tunnels.

Before me is the lowered dome of the *Grantztch*. Something heavy inside of my gut makes itself known when I realize that if I could only figure out how to use the damn thing, I might be able to return to Earth. But I remember what the major had told me, that somehow, the *Grantztch* here had to be coordinated with a *Grantztch* Dome back on Earth, and that it took a Creeper arm to manipulate it.

So I'm not going anywhere.

I'm stuck.

I trot around the *Grantztch* and see what I'm sure is the control panel, and above that panel are fissures and cracks of rock. I make sure my knapsack and my salvaged kukri are fastened tight enough, and I start climbing. Even with the seven-tenths gravity I take my time, because I have nothing to secure me if I were to fall. I go up a number of meters where I find a wide rock shelf that has a series of cables and conduits running through it, and it's a good enough place for now.

I flip over and take a break, undo my knapsack, spread out a few things.

I take a drink from one of the bottled waters.

Rest.

Look over from my vantage point, which gives me a great sky-eye view of the chamber, the *Grantztch*, and the six tunnels.

"Recon Ranger Knox, on duty," I whisper.

For the first couple of days, the Recon part is all that I worry about. I check out my new lodgings and find more cracks, fissures, and places to check out. Twice at night, just before going to sleep, I hear Major Gallagher below, calling for me, and I look down and I shouldn't feel smug, but not once does she look up.

"Knox! If you can hear me, get your ass down here! That's a direct order!"

And I cock my head, so that my left ear, the one with the twenty percent hearing loss, has a hard time making out her words.

On the third day I really luck out after a brutal climb into the upper reaches of the carved-out stone, and I find a conduit that must be transporting something cold indeed, for frost has collected around the entire surface. I gently scrape off the frost into a plastic bottle and I now have a fairly reliable source of water.

Food is okay for a few weeks, and I know that this will probably be enough.

Being alive at the end of a few weeks is an impossible goal.

So why not be busy and have some fun in the meantime?

Five days later I'm on the lower part of the chamber, waiting. I've waited for two days, and I'll keep on waiting. I'm chewing on a bar made of nuts, raisins, and apparent sawdust when the sounding horns make me jump. I carefully put the rest of the food bar away and put my hand on a small cloth bag.

And wait.

Nothing's approaching from any of the tunnels but the dome starts to lower, which means visitors are coming up here from Earth.

Perfect.

I jump down, get to a lower part of the chamber, and then propel myself to the stone floor. The *Grantztch* is now flush with the circular stone base, and I know I don't have much time. I go to the part of the stone that has lots of scratches and gouges, marking the departure point for the Creepers, and I undo the small cloth bag, and take out the three bottles of liquid shampoo I had earlier stolen from Major Gallagher's quarters. I pop the tops open and squirt and squirt them until all three are empty.

I toss the bottles aside, and I get back up to the side of the stone, hunker down, and wait.

The blinding flash of light returns as before, and the stone dome of the *Grantztch* lifts up—still without any means of support—revealing three Creepers, of the Battle form.

Click-click.

Click-click.

Click-click.

The standard cinnamon smell lifts up to me and the three Creepers move as one off the stone platform, and their arthropod legs slip, slide, and tangle into each other.

Click-click.

There's chattering, clicking, and for a few minutes they're tangled up and can't move. I watch with pure pleasure, the best feeling I've had in a while. It's not much, but I've managed to piss off three Creeper fighters, and that's a pretty good day.

The next few days I look for sabotage opportunities, and I take them where I find them. Up over the wide tunnel that is supposedly used for exiting the chamber, I climb up and up—finding my climbing skills are improving—and I find some loose cables that I manage to tug free. Nearby is a terrace of stone that leads to an instrument panel, and using the base end of the kukri, I smash as much as I can and then make my escape.

There's also a screened ventilation system I find, and I carefully collect my personal waste and dump it past the screens, hoping it fouls up something deep within the orbital station.

At night I'm filled with dreams, of being lased and scorched, of seeing Dad—in my dreams he still has both legs—and my boy Thor, along with Serena and her brother Buddy, and my dear friend Abby from Ft. St. Paul. In all of the dreams there is food, cold drinks, lots of laughter, hugs and kisses from both Serena and Abby, and most of all, lots of play time with Thor, tossing a ball back and forth on a wide green lawn, his tongue flopping in pure dog joy, his tail wagging, him jumping on me with his front paws, both of us happy to be out of the war for a while.

It's those moments when I wake up that I feel the most blue, because like anyone else in my situation, I wish I could stay in dreamland.

But reality always roars in.

A week after my escape from Major Gallagher, I escalate things, and I'm proud that I do it. I hear the familiar *click-click-click* sound and I peer over and there's a Creeper moving along the bottom of the chamber, but this Creeper isn't clad in its usual arthropod armor, it's wearing the bulky breathing apparatus that allows the bug to move around in this human reservation. It might be the same bug that rescued Major Gallagher from my attention a couple of weeks ago, but I'm not sure.

But it's alone, and out in the open.

I start moving, climbing down the rock surface, knowing from memory where all the cracks and openings are that allow me to use my feet and hands.

I'm on the surface now.

The Creeper with the breathing apparatus is slowly going down the tunnel, the one that has the wide terraced auditorium, where I had earlier found human bones and scraps of clothing.

I hunker down, start running after the Creeper, now flattening myself against the near tunnel wall. The bug ahead of me is moving relatively slowly—I've seen the little bastards move quickly and go over the horizon in a matter of seconds—and I'm able to close up to him in less than a minute.

The heavy curved Gurkha knife is in my right hand. I see the Creeper's two main articulated arms are carrying something metallic and shiny, and I'm not sure if it's weapons or instrumentation, but I'm going to guess it's something dangerous, and I take that into account.

And I get close enough, and then I attack. I swing the kukri at the near left leg, and slice it in half. The Creeper squeals and tries to spin around, but I slide under its abdomen—trying not to gasp at the cinnamon scent—and I take out two other legs, rolling over the stone floor as the bug collapses, spraying out a yellowish fluid that must be from its circulatory system.

Another screech comes out from the Creeper, echoing in the large stone chamber, and I slit and cut away its breathing apparatus, and the mouth moves and chatters, the eyes on the end of the stalks glare at me, and I say, "Thought you were safe, hunh? Thought wrong."

Then I take off his head.

I get back to my hidey-hole when the proverbial shit storm arrives, a half-dozen Creepers in their full battle rattle, and they cluster around their dead friend, and I slide back in and wash the kukri with some of my precious water, and I wait, chest thumping, breathing hard, trying to relax.

I take a few minutes to assess the strategic situation, just like I was taught in school, just like I learned on battlefields in Maine, New Hampshire, Connecticut, and New York.

I'm certainly behind enemy lines—or above or constrained by enemy lines, hard to figure out since I'm in Earth orbit—and I'm currently conducting insurgent warfare against the Creepers. What I have in my favor is my quickness of movement, no need for supply lines or logistics at this moment, and the growing awareness of my surroundings. If I'm careful, I can keep on doing hit-and-run raids.

Which leads up to the Big Question, why? Right now I'm an irritant to the Creepers, and at some point, they'll probably decide they have had enough, evacuate Major Gallagher and any other humans they have here, and flood the place with a human-specific gas to kill me and whatever other human vermin are in hiding.

More chattering and chittering from the stone floor.

So I'm an irritant.

So what?

I'm still fighting, and for me, that's what counts.

Two days pass, and I've reconnoitered the tunnels again, and the hatch system, and the colored shapes that control them, and I try to puzzle out the code by looking at the scratches from previous use. I take notes of which shapes have been used more, but from my cryptography classes way back when, trying to figure out the pattern would be one hell of a challenge.

That night, I munch some more on the Nepali rations, thank their cooks for the tasty spices that they've made them with, and I roll myself in a blanket and try to get some sleep. Major Gallagher has so far given up looking for me, and since I killed that last Creeper, the chamber has been empty and the *Grantztch* hasn't been used once. Maybe things are quiet in Creeper-land, or maybe they're starting to get afraid of the human spirit who lashes out when he can and kills and causes trouble. If so, I'm pretty happy about that.

With the lower gravity it's easier to fall asleep, and sure, I'm alone, but there's been plenty of times before when I've been alone, out on Recon, curled up in a trench or a barn, nestled in old hay, and then there's a lump in my throat and the tears come up, and I know how wrong I am.

I've never been totally alone in those times. I've always had Thor at my side, either sleeping or standing watch, and I try to swallow and it's hard, my throat is so thick, and I hope he's made it back to Asgard, back to Ft. St. Paul. The guilt just stabs at me, at how I ordered him away, nearly hit him with a thrown rock, and I hope that some part of his doggy mind realizes that I was doing this for his own good. I couldn't have assumed that the Creepers would have captured both of us, and I know that if he had gone into that Base Dome with me, he would have been slaughtered for food by my fellow starving humans.

"Miss you boy," I whisper, and I hope he's back safe at Ft. St. Paul, being spoiled and treated by the base vet, and I like to think he'll have it easy for the rest of his life, but I know the Army and how it works. Thor is one experienced and able K-9 unit, an Army piece of equipment, and at some point, he'll be reassigned to another Recon Ranger. And he'll relearn these commands from his new handler, and will run with him or her, hunt, and play and be treated well, and God, I sure hope that some dim part of him remembers me, remembers me and I hope has thoughts that for the most part, I had treated him well.

Hard to confess, but I sob a few times before I roll over and try to go to sleep, and then the dreams come, of voices, voices talking to me.

"Randy . . ."

"Randy . . ."

In my dream I can't quite understand who's talking to me.

"Randy . . . please help . . . please . . ."

My head then hits a bit of stone, and that's when I realize I haven't been sleeping.

I sit up in the darkness.

I distinctly remember hearing a human voice.

And one I recognize.

Was it Major Gallagher? George? Joanie? Gwen?

I lean over my hidey-hole, look down.

The lights are low and there's the *Grantztch*, the tunnel entrances, and nothing else.

But there's a faint murmur. I strain and strain to hear it.

It sounds like my name.

"Randy . . ."

I get dressed and grab my kukri, lower myself down, about two-thirds of the way from my vantage point, and stop on a fairly wide ledge.

I was going to call out but thought better of it. Major Gallagher might be down there, trying another, softer approach to get me to show up.

So I wait.

The kukri is in my hand, and I wait.

Wait a bit longer. Shiver from something. The cold? Fear? Not knowing what's going on?

"Randy . . ." comes the loud whisper.

I almost drop the Nepalese blade.

I lean over, still don't see anybody. I whisper down, "Buddy, is that you?"

"Oh, Randy . . ." and there's a sob. "I've been looking for you for a long time . . . please help me."

I start down. Buddy Coulson, twelve-year-old younger brother of Serena. He's . . . different, having long moments of not saying a word, but he's chillingly scary, and he knows the Creeper language pretty well, along with having what's called a photographic memory.

That night back at the naval installation, when we thought everything was fine, that peace was finally coming our way, the second orbital battle station had appeared, and Buddy had said, "Please don't let them send me back."

I keep a close eye on my handholds and footholds. Serena told me that some men had taken Buddy away, and had brought him up to the original Creeper installation.

Damn it, they must have gotten back to him, whoever "they" were.

"Randy, are you coming? Please hurry up!"

"Shhh," I whisper down to him. "Keep quiet!"

Just a few meters more, and I'm starting to think about how in hell I'm going to get him back up to my hideout, if I can lead him by taking off my shirt or something, have him hold onto it, maybe that'd work climbing back up.

And Buddy with his intelligence, his memory, he might be able to help me get deeper into the orbital battle station, to raid some of those farming areas to get more food, maybe have some more fun sabotaging.

Lots of problems for sure, but boy, lots of possibilities.

"Randy . . ."

"Almost there, pal, almost there . . ."

Just over a meter left and I let go, and drop easily down to the rock surface.

"Randy?"

I'm lit up by some sort of floodlight and I stand right still.

From a recess in the rock wall, two Battle Creepers come out, in their full arthropod armor, their weaponized arms lowered right in my direction.

The thought of problems and possibilities is now gone.

Major Gallagher emerges from behind the two Creepers, holding some sort of device in one hand, and a tiny speaker in the other. I don't know how she and the Creepers did it, but they've imitated Buddy's voice.

"Lieutenant, you're very late," she says, voice serious. "It's time."

CHAPTER TWENTY-FOUR

It seems like an hour has passed, and now I'm in the upper reaches of the orbital battle station, my legs tired by all the walking, even in the lower gravity. Led by the two Creepers and Major Gallagher, I enter a room with wide terraced steps leading up about twenty or so meters. The wide terraces are crowded with Creepers, and there's some sort of shimmering curtain separating the terraces from where I'm standing, along with Major Gallagher and the two bugs in their arthropods.

All of the bugs seem to be looking at me.

I don't like being in this spotlight.

A while ago I realized Major Gallagher is dressed in parts of an Army uniform, complete with a black beret and black socks over her stumps. Must be a formal occasion, and in any other location, I'd be embarrassed by what I'm wearing, dirty old fatigues with tears and rips.

About a half hour into our journey, she says, "It took me a while to make up a convincing story so they'd let you live."

"Thanks," I say, not feeling guilty about the killing I did a few days back.

"Don't thank me yet," she says, irritated. "The day's not over yet. They took a dim view of you disobeying orders."

"But . . ."

"But what?"

"Nothing," I say. So that's what pissed them off. Not me killing one of their own.

Aliens just being aliens, I guess.

Now the smell of cinnamon is as strong as I've ever experienced, and I look up and up the terrace. There must be at least sixty or so of the Creepers looking at me, and I do my best not to let the fear and terror roll over me by staring at just one of the bugs. So I let my eyes pass over them and then look down at the stone, and Major Gallagher says, "This is an important ceremony."

"All right," I say.

"Don't screw it up."

"How can I screw it up?"

She says, "By saying no, by not being cooperative."

"Suppose I don't feel like cooperating? Or I want to say no?"

Major Gallagher says, "Then you'll be dead. And I'll be pissed for all the time I wasted trying to save you."

The major slides forward a meter and in a loud voice, starts talking in Creeper language, the odd series of clicks, chattering, and whirs. The Creepers start paying attention to her, which makes me feel a little bit better.

She pauses, waits, and one Creeper in the center row of the near terrace sputters out a sentence.

Major Gallagher keeps looking up but talks to me now, in English. "Are you Knox, of the warriors from the hive called Merka?"

Boy, if we were on Earth and I wasn't so outnumbered, I could have had some fun with this inquiry, but I snap to and say, "Yes, I am."

Major Gallagher talks to the bug, and the bug talks back.

"How long have you been a warrior?"

"Four years."

Major Gallagher says, "You mean, four orbits of this planet around your star."

"That's right."

There's low chattering and then the main bug talks to the major, and she says, "Look up the screen, about midway up . . . is this you, warrior Knox?"

And by God, I don't know how the Creepers do it, or what technology and magic they possess—after all, they have traveled between the stars—but up there, looking about three meters high, is me! Sergeant Randy Knox, in the field somewhere, carrying a small knapsack and my Colt M-10, helmet on, MOLLE vest, and—

Running across a grassy field, tongue flapping in the air, one happy Thor, coming straight to me.

"Stop it," I yell. "Stop it!"

But Major Gallagher doesn't say anything, and I watch as the huge Thor before me rolls to a stop in front of the "me" up there, rolls over and presents his belly, and the "me" up there leans down and rubs him.

"Yes, that's me," I yell. "That's me."

A burst of chatter, and Major Gallagher says, "Warrior Knox, is this you?"

Another visual of me up there, marching along a road.

"That's me."

And . . . my God, it's from a long time ago, when I was fighting a Transport Creeper in a swamp, all by myself. The scene is at night, and trees are burning, and there's me, attacking the Creeper, only carrying a knife. In this scene, I'm jumping up on the main arthropod, and I'm stabbing, and the scene fades out . . .

I don't wait for Major Gallagher.

"Yes, that's me! And proud of it!"

Several of the Creepers on the terraces are chattering loudly, and the one that's been leading speaks loudly, and Major Gallagher interprets and says, "Warrior Knox, that is you, affirmative?"

"Affirmative," I say.

"Do you know who you . . . expired?"

"A Creeper," I say. "That's all I cared about."

More chattering. Major Gallagher chatters back. There are no more displays up on the shimmering screen.

Major Gallagher says, "Warrior . . . the . . . hive member you expired . . . he was a . . . royalty? Special? I'm not sure what they're telling me . . . it seems . . . you killed a prominent member of the hive that traveled here."

"Big deal," I say, trying to stay brave. "It was a bug, I killed it."

"It was an important Traveler to them, that one you killed."

I say, "If it was so important, why was it out there, traveling by itself?"

"It was . . . being brave. It was demonstrating it could be out on its own . . . and you killed it . . . without any weapons . . . save your hands and bladed weapon."

"So what?"

"Randy . . . it means, without a doubt to them, that you are a Chosen. Someone brave, a warrior, a survivor who can conquer incredible odds. Why do you think you're alive? You have earned their respect. They may hate you, despise what you've done, but in the end, they honor you. They respect you."

I remember being back on Earth, captured in that Dome, about to be transported up to the orbital battle station, and the Creeper that had escorted me . . .

It had bowed to me.

Now it makes sense.

Major Gallagher says, "To them, you're someone who can talk to other humans and who will be respected. Someone that other humans will listen to. Someone key to ending this useless war. That's why you're still here. You're a Chosen."

"I'm not a Chosen."

"They say you are, and that's settled," Major Gallagher says.

Then the lead Creeper starts chattering some more. Major Gallagher nods, and then says one more sentence in bug language, and then says to me, "You are a Chosen. You have . . . I can't explain it, but they think you're some exalted warrior of a spiritual nature. You are a Chosen, and you will return back to Earth with . . . er, with me . . . and the two of us will convince the Earth species to submit, to agree to Traveler rule, to . . . adjust our way to the new life, to the new order."

"For how long?" I ask.

"Randy . . . forever."

There's not much going on then, some muttered chattering, and Major Gallagher says, "This . . . hive agreement, this council, they're waiting for your answer."

"My answer? To agree to be a Chosen, to agree to go back to Earth and convince humanity to surrender?"

"Adjust, Randy, not surrender."

"Oh, okay."

I take a breath, look up at the flickering screen where my actions and my boy Thor have been displayed, and I say, "Here's my answer. No."

"Lieutenant Knox . . ."

"That's my answer." I step forward. "No! And you can all go to hell!"

Major Gallagher doesn't say anything, which doesn't matter.

One of the two Battle Creepers in full armor skitters over, and picks me up with its right pincer. I'm lifted up and up, and the grip is firm but not too hard. I kick and struggle, and then the Creeper grabs my right arm, stretches it out. It squeezes hard, and my hand opens up.

The second Creeper comes over, and there's a bright flick of light, and on my right hand, I lose my pinky finger.

I'm dropped to the stone surface, screaming, holding my injured hand in my other, rolling back and forth, back and forth. There's the light stench of burnt flesh, which I've been so accustomed to over these years, and but now it's my turn to get scorched again. I've been struck in my left ear, my shoulder, and other bits and parts of my body over the years, but I've never lost a finger.

The pain roars right up my hand to my wrist and arm, and seems to explode in my head. I grit my teeth and take deep breaths, one after another, and the pain merely goes from excruciating to barely tolerable. I cough, choke, and sit up. The armored Creepers have moved back. I hold my right hand with my left, looking at the cauterized wound. Not even a stump. Lasered right down to the hand.

Bastards have had a lot of practice.

Tears are rolling down my face and I hold my hand, hold my hand, and about a half meter away is a little tube of pink and black, and I turn away from it.

Major Gallagher is ignoring me, looking up at the rows of Creepers looking down at us. The shimmering curtain that rises up from floor to curved ceiling continues to shimmer.

The Creeper speaks out, and Major Gallagher says in a flat voice, "Warrior Knox, do you agree to return to Earth, with Speaker Gallagher . . . and convince the Earth species to submit, to agree to Traveler rule, to . . . adjust to the new life, to the new order."

I grit my teeth. The pain seems to be coming back again, wave after scarlet wave.

"Warrior Knox."

Damn them, damn them all to hell.

"Randy . . ."

I look over and Major Gallagher is looking at me, her eyes filling up with tears. "Randy, please, please say yes . . ."

I stumble up to my feet, stare at them now, no longer filled with fear, just refilled with the hate that's been with me for more than ten years, and I say, "Go to hell. Humans will never surrender . . . never give up . . . we'll fight you with sticks and rocks if we have to . . . we'll never give up . . ."

I'm grabbed again by the near Creeper, lifted up, and I try to struggle but I'm much more weak this time around, and with another, almost bored *flick* of light, I lose the pinky finger on my left hand.

I'm consumed with pain, with the raw blowtorch of fire on my hands, and I'm curled up on my side, moaning, and with one nasty shudder, I vomit and spew bile and foul-smelling fluids across the stone, and I'm weeping, moaning, and a hand is on my forehead, stroking me, and she says, "Randy, give it up. Say yes. What difference does it make now? Your original commanding officer is still back on Earth. I'm you're commanding officer, and I urge you to agree."

I grind my teeth and try to roll away from her, but she holds me still, which doesn't say much, because I think a pair of puppies could have done the same thing without too much effort.

"Randy . . . do you think the Army cares? Or the human race? No, they don't . . . we're up in space . . . we could be orbiting Pluto for all they care. But you and I, we have a chance to go back to Earth, as emissaries, as ambassadors, to end this war, to save millions, and millions more when the Other arrives here and sees an agrarian species that will pose no threat to them."

The Creeper up there speaks, and Gallagher replies with the same low chittering and chattering, and she continues to stroke my head. "That one simple word, Randy. Yes. Just say yes, and then there'll be a brief ceremony, and then you'll be back in my quarters. I'll take care of you . . . and you'll feel much, much better in just a while. I promise."

The Creeper sounds off again, and it sounds harsher.

"Lieutenant . . ."

I manage to speak, though my mouth is filled with spit and my throat is clogged. "It . . . hurts . . . so . . . damn . . . much . . ."

"I know, I know," she says soothingly. "But I can make it better. Like we can make it better for the world. Just say that word."

The pain in my hands is driving me now, and I don't care about the Creepers or the Earth or anything else, it's just the pain where I've been mutilated, and I struggle to my knees, and lift my head, and I hold my hands up and away from my body, shaking and trembling, and spit is dribbling down my chin.

Major Gallagher says in a loud voice, "Warrior Knox, do you agree to return to Earth, with Speaker Gallagher. To convince the Earth species to submit, to agree to Traveler rule, to adjust to the new life, to the new order."

I don't hesitate. I just gurgle out "Yes," and then roll back down onto the cold raw stone floor.

I'm on my right side, trying to keep my scorched hands still, trying to keep my hands away from my body, and there's a chuff of air, and more chittering and chattering, and I hear the sound of Creeper legs scrabbling across the stone. A shadow falls over me and I open my eyes, look up to see a Creeper segmented abdomen overhead. The abdomen isn't covered with the standard exoskeleton armor, which means this particular bug is out here with us two humans, wearing some sort of breathing device.

So what.

I don't care.

Gallagher says, "Randy, close your eyes. Close your mouth. Don't breathe."

I close my eyes and mouth, try hard not to breathe, even with the pain radiating across my poor hands.

A fine mist coats me, a strong stench of cinnamon, with other scents mixed in, and I just lie there, until there's more skittering, and then the shadow is gone.

"Okay," she says in a soft voice. "It's over now. You can breathe again. Just take it easy."

I get up, feeling sticky, woozy, and still groggy from the pain radiating up both trembling arms. She tugs at me and I lower my upper torso and with a scrap of cloth, she wipes at my eyes and face.

"What the hell was that?" I ask.

She puts the cloth away. "You've been initiated, Randy, and you've been marked by their scent. No matter where you go, either here or on Earth, the Travelers will always be able to find you."

I have a memory of raiding two Domes with Kara's Killers so very long ago, and seeing what I thought was a Creeper "sniffing" bloodied human clothing some time later. And I remember seeing a Creeper being held prisoner at an underground Air Force installation, and how it screamed and seemed frightened when I got close enough for it to smell me.

Was I being watched back then as a possible Chosen, someone who could betray his Army, his country, his fellow humans? Was I already known to the Creepers as a warrior who could kill them with such ease?

"Is that it?" I ask.

"In a way."

"What kind of way?"

Gallagher gently touches my side, as I keep both hands up and out. "Randy, you're now part of the Traveler hive. You're no longer in the Army, no longer a human. You're now a Traveler."

CHAPTER TWENTY-FIVE

The rest of what passes for a day is spent in Major Gallagher's quarters, and she helps me into her sleeping area. It seems to be about the same size as my own, and that's where the similarity ends. The bedding seems more soft, the blankets in better shape, and there are candles and incense sticks that give the place a homey smell. Hard to describe, but you could be in there and convince yourself that you were back home, in some sort of odd hotel.

There are books and pamphlets, two glass bottles, stone shelves with carefully folded clothing, and a mirror and another, smaller shelf, holding stuff that I really have a hard time identifying. But from where I am, it looks like brushes, combs, and little bottles and containers of makeup and lotions.

She sits on the bed next to me and opens up a small black satchel.

"Hold out your left hand first," she says, and gritting my teeth once more, I do that, holding it out. She takes it in her soft hand and goes, *tsk-tsk*, and tilts my hand back and forth, and says, "They sure know how to slice and cauterize, don't they. Don't move."

For once I follow her orders. I don't move.

Gallagher takes a small tubelike device out of her satchel, flips the top open, and sprays the burnt area on my hand that once held a finger.

I take a deep breath, and whisper, "What?"

There's a tingling in my hand and then pain is gone.

Just like that.

Which makes my right hand hurt even more.

"Other, please," she says, and I move my right hand into position. Another cool spray and again, the pain just slips away.

She replaces the cap, puts the tube back in. "The Travelers have studied us for a long time. They still struggle with our thoughts, emotions, desires, our psychology, but they have an excellent handle on our physiology. Hold on again."

This time Gallagher comes out with what looks to be a round stone container, and she removes a stone lid, revealing some sort of cream or soft gel inside. She scoops up some of the gel and I wince in anticipation, but I don't feel a thing as she rubs the gel into one scorched area, and then the other. She wipes her fingers, deftly replaces the lid, and then rummages around some more, and puts on little squares of some gauzelike material that sticks to the skin and molds itself, and then she nods in satisfaction.

"There," she says. "In about twenty-four hours or so, the healing will be completed, and then the bandages and a slight . . . crust, I guess you can call it, will come off. Then you'll be fine."

I say, "Major . . ."

She gently pushes me on the chest and I flop down.

"Sleep is what's best for you, all right?" Gallagher slides off the bed and comes back with a thin, clean, light-blue cotton blanket. With some difficulty the major drapes it over me and then I'm feeling fuzzy and lightheaded.

"There's . . . something in the . . . cream."

"Yes, there is," she says. "To make you sleep. So sleep."

And I quickly drift off, just as I think I feel her kiss my forehead.

I think.

I wake up refreshed, hungry, thirsty, and wondering where the hell I am, until all those memories from before come roaring back in at me, like a thunderstorm suddenly breaking. I sit up and look at both of my hands, and the tight Creeper-supplied bandages are still there.

I wiggle my other fingers. They feel fine.

I stare at the little bandages, and a little hysterical voice inside of me says, Congrats, bud, you've just earned your third Purple Heart. Maybe you can request that desk assignment, as a persistent rumor I've always heard is that those who get three Purple Hearts can request a transfer to a softer billet, but since there's no such thing as a front line or a safe area in this war, it really doesn't make much of a difference.

Still . . . I wiggle my eight fingers again.

Adjustment time.

I think I'll still be able to get dressed, tie my shoes . . . but what about handling a weapon?

I lie back down. I think my weapon handling days are now finished. I'm a Chosen, a special person, a diplomat.

A traitor to the human race.

I wipe at the sleep crust in my eyes and look around, see a few things I had missed earlier. There are drawings hung up on the far wall, done by pencil or charcoal, not sure, and they are drawings of a man and two boys. The boys look like twins.

The major's family.

How did she get them?

The curtain slowly slides open and Gallagher pokes her head in. She's in old shorts and the A R M Y sweatshirt with hacked-off arms that she had worn one of the first days I had met her.

"You up?"

"Yes, ma'am."

"You've been asleep for nearly a day," she says. "Need to use the latrine?"

"Um, no, I think I'm okay for now."

"Good," she says. "Stay put. I'll get you something to eat."

The curtain falls back into place and I stare at the drawings of the man, who has bright eyes, a thick beard, but a smile that makes it through the beard. Both boys seem to be about eleven or so, fishing off a dock, wearing T-shirts and shorts. The drawings are very well done.

The curtain comes open, and Gallagher scoots along using her butt, bringing a tray with her. There's a bowl of what looks to be broth, some bread and butter, and a mug of that Tang stuff she had told me about earlier.

I sit up and balance the tray on my lap, and Gallagher hoists herself up to a shelf, pushing aside books and magazines. "How did you sleep?"

"Ah . . . I find it hard to believe, but I slept like a rock," I say. "Best I've slept in a long, long while."

She takes a folded piece of soft paper out, places it under my chin. "The Travelers . . . so much more advanced than us, in so many ways."

"But . . ."

"Yes?"

I take a spoon of the broth—beef—which tastes thick and oh so warming. "When I was being . . . interviewed"—I had almost said interrogated, but I didn't want to go there—"the . . . Travelers said something about my encounter with that Transport . . . unit. They said it was by itself because it wanted to show its bravery. That it was a special Traveler, one that might be royalty. Then why? Why expose itself like that?"

"Eat up," she says. I do that, taking in a few more spoonfuls of the broth. I can feel strength returning to me, as odd as it sounds.

Gallagher says, "Earlier we've talked about if the Travelers wanted to kill us all, they could have done that in just a few weeks. Correct?"

"Yes," I say.

"Then why didn't they do it?"

I can't believe how moist the bread is. "Because of their mission . . . what they want. They want us to regress, to . . . save us from the Other, whenever they show up."

"Then why go down to the Earth's surface? Why fight against us?"

"To keep on punishing us? To make us surrender, finally and totally?"

"True . . . but Randy. What's the only weapon the humans down there have against the Travelers?"

"The binary gas weapon that's used to kill the Creepers, I mean, the Travelers."

"What's it made of?"

I shake my head. "I don't know. It's a binary gas weapon, that's all I know. Two substances that mix together when the round is fired off, and when it explodes, the gas cloud penetrates the arthropod breathing membrane."

"Randy . . ."

I finish off the broth, wipe the bowl clean with the bread. "Yes, ma'am?"

"The humans down there have used the gas weapon for a few years now, right?"

"Yes."

"Then why haven't the Travelers redesigned their breathing system? Adjusted the membrane? Done anything to prevent the gas from killing them?"

I finish chewing the bread, take a solid drink of the cold Tang. "Ma'am . . . I. Well, I don't know. Above my pay grade, I suppose."

She checks the tray, gently removes it from my lap. "Randy, you've seen what they've been able to do. They were able to hollow out this planetoid and transport it to Earth orbit. They have a system of nearly instantly transporting living creatures and objects from the Earth's surface to here. They've developed a medical system that will heal your hands in less than a day. Don't you think they could come up with a way to prevent their Travelers on Earth from dying from gas attacks? Really? Gas attacks?"

I take another swallow of the Tang. It tastes slightly off.

"Randy . . ." and she reaches out, gently touches my knee. "The Travelers that are on the Earth's surface . . . they're like monks. Holy warriors. They go out knowing they will be attacked, fought, and most likely will die. That's why they haven't made a defense against the gas. They go into battle willingly."

"But . . . why?"

She says, "They want us to grow. They want us to be tough. They do want us to fight . . . but only fight long enough to realize the futility of it, and then realize the only true way forward is to submit and follow the Travelers' way."

I think of the battles I've been in, the close calls, the number of Creepers I've killed over the years.

I've been so proud of those victories.

But now?

How can I be proud if my enemies went into battle, knowing and reveling in their weaknesses?

"Ma'am?"

"Yes?"

"I think I need to use the latrine."

She slides off the bed, balancing the tray in one hand. "Go right ahead . . . draw a bath if you'd like."

"I can do that in my own quarters."

Gallagher slides out. "Not until I get you off today's sick list, mister."

⊕ ⊕ ⊕

I'm in her latrine and I draw a bath and sink in, holding up my wounded hands, and I just rest in the water, quietly weeping, thinking of all the deaths, the destruction, and my own part in it, thinking I'm fighting to save humanity, while in actuality, I was helping the buggy bastards fulfill their mission, their passions.

I slide into the bath until my mouth and nose are barely above the water surface, and I wish I could just stay like this forever, and then a bit of memory clicks in.

I can't believe it.

Randy, you stay in there any longer you'll come out looking like a raisin.

My Mom's voice, suddenly cutting through my thoughts.

My poor dead Mom, and my older sister Melissa.

Mom! Randy won't get out of the tub!

Melissa's voice, now.

Am I hallucinating? Dreaming? Or had some random memory in my brain finally came up to the surface?

I slowly rise up, the water dripping off me, looking strange in the seven-tenths gravity. My hands are still up in the air, and then, without warning, they start itching.

Itching something terribly.

I grit my teeth, try to move one hand against the other, and then the small bandages on each hand tighten very hard, loosen, and then fall off into the water.

There are little dark-brown patches where my pinkies used to be.

I dunk each hand into the water, and when I bring them up, the scabs or scales have fallen off.

My hands look pink and fine, except for the fact I have eight fingers now, not ten. I wiggle the survivors. "All right, pals," I whisper. "Let's see how we do with just eight."

I clean up the latrine and Gallagher calls out, "Sliding clothes to you, Randy," and a square pile of clothes are thrust under the closed curtain. I dry myself and pick up the clothes, which are standard dark green Army fatigues—crisp clean, complete with socks and underwear!—and I get dressed, feeling refreshed no matter what had happened to me yesterday.

I pile up the dirty clothes, drain the water in the tub, and think of how I was sprayed, or marked, or made part of the tribe yesterday. I don't smell anything but that doesn't mean squat. The bugs obviously have a very good sense of smell, like a dog's, like my Thor—

I push back the thoughts of Thor.

I don't want to go there.

Instead I go out into Gallagher's quarters.

At first I can't find her but the curtain to her bedroom is open, and she motions me in, and I sit on the edge of her bed, and say, "Ma'am, where did you sleep last night?"

"Aren't you the considerate one," she says, smiling.

"Well . . . you gave up your bed for me. I wanted just to express my thanks."

She says, "I bunked out in the main room, on one of the stone couches. It was all right. Comfortable enough."

I sit on a stone shelf to the left of the bed and she says, "Tomorrow, your training starts. And education. And language lessons. You've got a lot to learn . . . before they send us back to Earth."

Back to the surface, I think. Places to run, places to hide, places to get away from everything . . .

Except I'm marked.

I'm part of the hive, now.

No matter where I go on Earth, I'll be able to be tracked and scented by the Creepers.

"That sounds . . . interesting," I say. "Any idea how long that might take?"

She shrugs. "As long as it takes. It all depends on you, Randy."

"And why the two of us? Why not just you?"

"Strength in numbers," she says. "Male and female. Young and old. Both service members. If it goes well, we'll be able to meet with those officials who have influence, who can reach out to others."

I don't know what to say about that, so I look again at the drawings. "Ma'am, is that your husband . . . and boys?"

"God, yes," she says, shifting in her bed. "That's Brad up there. Good ol' Brad. Financial adviser."

"What's a financial adviser?"

She smiles even more. "You know, he told me lots of times, and I never quite understood what he did, with investments, bonds, and securities. But it's like this. People back then could make lots of money. And there were ways of using that money to . . . make more money. There was a saying, 'Making your money work for you.'"

I guess I look confused for her smile gets a bit wider. "I know. It does sound strange."

"The . . . drawings. How did you get them?"

She says, "The protective screen, the one with the photos that were displayed . . . at some point, the Travelers allowed me the privilege of seeing my family . . . and I sketched them, the best I could do."

"You did a very good job," I say.

"Thanks."

"And your boys . . ."

"That's them, all right. Peter and Paul. My two apostles . . . apostles of raising hell."

I don't quite know what she means by that, and I say, "The Travelers, how do they get those photos?"

"They have a constellation of hidden satellites around the Earth. That's known, isn't it?"

"Yes, ma'am. We call them killer stealth satellites. They hit us with laser beams, particle beam weapons, rods from God . . ."

"They also do surveillance. That's where the information comes from."

"Are they occupied? By Travelers?"

She says, "Yes . . . why?"

"It's always been a mystery," I say.

"The mystery has been solved, then," she says. "Tell me . . . would you like to do the same?"

"Excuse me?"

"At some point, you will earn the trust of the Travelers. That will bring you some additional benefits. They can show your friends, your father, your dog."

Hoo boy.

"I guess I'll wait."

"Good," she says. "The Travelers . . . if you cooperate once you've joined the hive, you will be rewarded. If you don't, you'll be punished."

Something in her voice strikes me. That last sentence has weight to it, a different tone.

She stares at me and I say, "Ma'am . . . how often were you punished?"

Gallagher brushes at her lower torso. "How do you think I lost my legs?"

CHAPTER TWENTY-SIX

It's night. My belly is full, my hands with the two missing fingers don't hurt, and I have fresh and clean bedding.

I should be asleep.

But I'm wide awake, staring up at the stone ceiling.

What the hell have I done?

I slide out of bed and go to my main quarters. Supposedly mine but it still doesn't feel anything like home, or even temporary quarters. I go over to the tarp covering the round window looking down at the Earth and just watch the landscape, clouds, and oceans slip by as the orbital battle station makes its ninety-minute sweep across the day and night sky. I see a big chunk of land that might be India, but I'm not sure. The tsunami strikes during the first week of the war drowned a lot of cities and rearranged a lot of the landscape. My poor Earth. I rub my hands together, feel the queasiness inside as I miss the two fingers.

"How do you think I lost my legs?"

I'm in a deep funk, mourning my wounding and how easily I surrendered, how easily I betrayed everyone and everything down there on the not-so-green hills of earth. But I think of Major Felicia Gallagher, up here for a decade, learning the bug language, sometimes cooperating, other times not, and the bugs chop off her feet, her lower legs, and then above the knees.

Yet she keeps on, trying to keep me in line, trying to convince me that the only road forward for us and the survivors down there is to change our ways, to become part of the Creeper's race, adjust and cooperate.

And she still bears witness to her husband and her boys.

I sniff my hands and wrists. All I smell is the soap I used a while ago to wash and rewash myself, scrubbing until my skin is pink and nearly raw. That's it. But deep down, maybe on the molecular level, maybe all the way down to the bones, I've been marked for life.

To the Creepers here, I'm no longer human.

I'm part of them, their tribe, their hive.

I look down to the Earth again. The clouds have parted, allowing me to see a bulge that looks to be the upper west coast of Africa, and then an expanse of ocean, then more clouds.

I put my hand up against the thick glass, whatever it's made of. All I wanted to do in my life was to grow old enough to fight the Creepers, fight them until final victory, and then . . . choose a life. Maybe stay in the Army. Maybe go back to school. Maybe take pen to paper, or typewriter, or—who knows—a computer keyboard, and write my memories of the Creeper war.

Those were my plans.

Now?

All gone.

Down there is everyone I've ever known, dead or alive, save for the major, George, and his family. Long days have passed. I wonder if my father or my old unit has been notified of the firefight that took place in Connecticut, when the golden carpet convoy was on its way to taking me back to Ft. St. Paul. Something heavy just goes *a-chunk* in my chest when I realize they all will think I'm dead. How could it be otherwise? After a firefight like the one I was in, if I haven't turned up wounded or wandering along some road, then I'm dead. I know they won't think I'm a deserter—even with what I'm doing up here that's not who I am—but I also know that without any other evidence, they'll think I'm just a charred corpse somewhere in a field or woods, whose bones and ID might be found later by a Graves Registration Unit or some lucky civilian.

The clouds have cleared again. I see a huge expanse of water that seems to be the reconstituted Great Lakes, and below, a flat part of the Midwest. Little—

Fireflies?

Flicks of light?

Yeah.

Little flickers of light, almost too quick for me to notice.

There.

Again.

God, now I know.

From hundreds of kilometers up in Earth orbit, I'm watching a battle below me, as the aliens—Creepers, Travelers, bugs, whatever the hell you want to call them—are killing and scorching targets below me. American soldiers, civilians, human beings.

I put my hand on the glass again.

"Sorry," I whisper. "I can't help you anymore. I've surrendered."

When the dark clouds return, I go back to bed.

After a quiet breakfast I'm with Major Gallagher at the hollowed tube near what I think is the control panel for the *Grantztch*, and which is a score or so meters away from my last hidey-hole, up there in the cracks and fissures of rock. I'm dressed in clean fatigues and new boots—well, new for me—and the major has on a plain black T-shirt and cut-off dungaree shorts. She's also carrying a small red knapsack over one shoulder. We approach a circular hatch or door, with a smaller control panel nearby, and she says, "This is your first day. Make it a good one."

She runs her fingers over the lit geometrical shapes and the hatch shudders, squeaks, and starts to roll to the left. Gallagher sees my expression and says, "Looks complicated, doesn't it, but it really isn't. These lit panels . . . they're symbolic in some way to the Travelers, like a prayer chant or a Bible verse. It means the way is now opened."

I say, "Is that how the *Grantztch* works? Same concept?"

"That's right," she says.

"But . . . I thought you said the *Grantztch* only works by the touch of a Traveler."

"That's right. This one is keyed to humans . . . you'll see why. Now, don't be scared. Follow me."

I take four steps in behind her and freeze.

I'm very scared indeed.

There are rows upon rows of Creepers in their armored arthropods—all three types, Research, Battle, and Transport—and they seem to be all looking at me.

I can't move.

I've never seen so many of the damn bugs before in my life.

Gallagher stops scooting along and looks back at me. "Randy . . . come along. There's nobody in them. They're empty."

I take a deep breath, clench and unclench my hands. Overhead is a rectangular roof with lighting and ductwork, and stretching out in the distance is more of the Creeper armor. I take a step, and then another step forward.

She's right.

They're not moving.

The air is still drenched with the smell of cinnamon, but it's an old, stale smell. The closer I get, I also see that some of the armored arthropods are covered with scorch marks, soot, and other dirt and debris. There are some with dents, dings, and broken armored legs. I feel a little tug of pride, knowing that my fellow humans down there have done this. They may not have permanently destroyed them, but they have left their mark.

Then the little bit of pride fades away.

According to the bugs running this station, I'm no longer human. I'm one of them.

Gallagher says, "As a pilgrim, as someone who's a novice, you have to start where all supplicants begin, Randy."

"Like at boot camp."

"Very good."

Up ahead there's a low, wide platform made of stone and I give it a close look, and there's brushes, some type of rolled-up cloth, round stone stubs containing a paste or gel.

"Cleaning up?" I ask.

"That's right." She maneuvers around the low table and says, "These armored units, before they're used again and sent back down to Earth, they need to be cleaned . . . blessed. They're considered . . . well, taboo in a way, that they've been dirtied in the service of converting humanity. We can't do the blessing, but we can do the cleaning."

Gallagher then spends a while explaining the cleaning process, how the brushes scrub away the easy stuff, how the cloth—which feels squiggly in my hands, like it's almost alive—and the gel is used for the deep cleaning and polishing. I look at all the armored units and say, "There are so many."

"Once you get into a pattern, once you learn how to do it, it moves faster." She pauses, picking up a brush, and then putting it back down. "Trust me, I know."

She removes the small knapsack, hands it over to me. "There's water and a lunch in there. I'll leave you be."

Gallagher starts scooting away and I call out, "Hold on, ma'am, you're leaving me here? Alone?"

"Not alone," she says. "George will be here to supervise."

"Who's George?"

There's a skittering noise, of segmented legs moving over stone. "That's George."

She heads back to the open entrance and a Creeper comes into view, and this time, I'm scared for real.

It moves slowly in my direction, and it has the same kind of breathing apparatus around its head and abdomen that allows it to be here, in Earth pressure and atmosphere.

"That's George," Gallagher calls out. "Don't get him angry."

She passes through the large hatch opening, flicks her hand over the control panel, and the hatch rolls in and seals shut.

George skitters up to me and he has something extra hanging off of him, some black object that looks like a keyboard with lots of colored shapes and symbols, and a ball hanging down from a cable that swings back and forth. He leans over, the two eyestalks wide open and focused through the clear membrane of the hood.

My legs are shaking. I can't help it.

One arm comes up and I see the end of it, with a number of long and short mandibles, and he brings the mandibles to the keyboard and moves them in a frenzy.

A human voice comes out of the round ball.

"Interrogative. Warrior. Knox."

I step back. "What?"

The mandibles move again. "Interrogative. Warrior. Knox."

Human words, spoken in a human voice, but three different voices. The first sounds like American South. The second is . . . British? Irish? The third sounds like a young girl.

Again.

"Interrogative. Warrior. Knox."

"Yes, I'm—"

The other arm whips out and catches me straight in the middle of my chest.

In the lower gravity I'm really propelled some distance, hit the floor with my back and upper shoulders, and I skid across, and I roll up and hit the wall with one bone-quaking thump.

I untangle myself and I can't get up. The bug called George is right over me, looking down. Hearing the human voices mixed in with the sight of the Creeper over me causes me to shiver. A mandible moves and the voices come back, louder.

"Interrogative. Warrior. Knox."

My chest aches from where I was hit. The bug leans into me, and the cinnamon stench makes me gag.

I cough. I say, "Knox. Just Knox."

The Creeper backs away. "Work. Now. Work."

I get up and go to the curved counter, my chest still hurting.

"Work," I say.

I go to the closest Creeper arthropod, examine the front legs, note dirt and scorch stains. The other four legs are also marked up. The bug called George watches me. I go back to the counter, remove a brush, and get to work.

Long hours slide by. I scrape away at the scorch marks and dirt, until the legs look pretty clean. I keep the horror away of what I'm doing by just focusing on the job right before me. I try not to look at the lines of Creeper arthropods stretching out to my left, and I also try to ignore the bug named George, who's busy doing whatever bug tasks he's up to.

After I get one leg completed and go to the next, I hear a clicking-whirring sound, and I step back to see what's going on. Down at the very end of the line of Creeper exoskeletons, George has positioned himself in front of one, with cables running from his two pincers to the center of the empty arthropod. George gently moves his pincers in slow movements, and the piece of armor moves with him, like some sort of toy that I've only seen in the old movies and newsreels shown back home at Ft. St. Paul.

This exoskeleton must have been cleaned and repaired to George's alien satisfaction, and the two of them nearly move as one, until they come to a low rectangle that slides up, showing a tunnel. The two enter the tunnel, the rectangle door comes back down, and I go back to work.

Scour, rub, repeat.

Scour, rub, repeat.

I manage to get into a good pattern and rhythm of work, even though I'm still getting used to only having eight fingers, and a little voice reminds me, *Be thankful you still have two legs.*

There's more skittering and clicking, and George returns from the square-shaped tunnel, and comes over closer, and working the instrumentation below his chest, says, "Move. One meter."

He doesn't tell me where to move one meter, so I just step back. He takes the left pincer arm and lowers it down to where I've been working, and there's more movement of the mandibles.

An inspection.

Great.

He stays in position and then moves back, looking down at me.

The mandibles go back to work on the communication device.

"Acceptable."

George stares at me with his twin eyestalks and open mouth, all visible through the clear hood. Even with the horror and distaste of being so close to a Creeper, I almost laugh. An interstellar traveling species is communicating to another intelligent tool-making species about a cleaning job.

Not really the tales of science fiction I'd read and seen over the years.

I think he's waiting for me to say something, so I say, "Thank you."

He pauses. The smell of cinnamon comes at me in waves. The eyes blink. The open mouth closes and open.

I pick up the brush. "Back to work."

The mandibles move again. The sweetest, warmest female voice I've ever heard repeats what I've just said.

"Back to work."

I do more brushwork, cleaning off all of the legs, and I grab the squirmy cloth and take it one step further, cleaning every speck and piece of dirt I can. When George inspected my work, I had a flashback to when I was twelve years old, in basic training. One of my drill sergeants—Chesak, I think?—took joy in flipping over our bunks even though they had been made correctly and without a single flaw.

At one point he had said, "Kiddoes, stop crying. You want to know why I flip your bunks like that, even though you did the job right? Because I could. Because life's not fair. So suck it up and get back to work."

At the time I thought Chesak was overdoing it—being survivors of a ten-year-old war and semioccupation by the Creepers certainly had proven to all of us that life wasn't fair—but I was glad George didn't feel the need to demonstrate that to me.

Small favors.

The gel has a bitter smell to it, and stings my hands, but I find if I put some of it on the cloth that moves in my hands, it removes the final dirt and grime. My stomach eventually starts grumbling at me and I check the time, and see that four hours have passed.

There's three stone bowls of water on the low stone table and I wash and rinse the best I can, and then take out the small knapsack left for me by Major Gallagher. I zip it open and find an apple, some lengths of carrot, and a little package wrapped in plastic. I unwrap it and reveal a sandwich made of a light brown bread, a meat spread, and a cheese spread, plus what looks to be mustard.

Something else falls out, a square piece of paper. I unfold it and read in neat handwriting:

Randy . . . have a good day on your first step as a Chosen . . . Felicia.

I read it a couple of more times, rub the paper in my fingers, and remember something.

Then I eat lunch and get back to work.

The afternoon goes by as slowly as the morning, and I find a metal stool in between two of the Creeper exoskeletons, and I make good progress on the main section of my first project. The legs are the hardest part, since they are so close to the ground being chewed up and tossed around, but the abdomen and the interlinking sections start out cleaner than the legs.

I'm straddling the back, rubbing and moving the cloth around, when the hatch slides open and Major Gallagher scoots in. She ignores me at first and goes over to George, who looks to be transporting another empty exoskeleton to deeper parts of the orbital battle station.

I finish up the best I can while a representative of humanity and a representative of the Creepers/Travelers talk back and forth, and then Gallagher comes over and says, "George says you did an okay job."

"Thanks," I say, letting myself down to the rock surface. "Okay is what I was looking for. I didn't want to wear myself out on the first day by doing some exceptional work."

She cocks her head and says, "Was that a joke?"

"An observation, that's all."

I go to the bowls of water, rinse my aching hands and eight fingers, and she comes closer. "You doing okay?"

"I guess," I say. "I'm aching and sore . . . but on the good side, I've been sharing these quarters with a Creeper, er, Traveler these past hours, and we haven't tried to kill each other."

Gallagher seems to ponder that, and I interrupt her chain of thought by saying, "Thanks for the lunch."

"You're welcome."

"No, really. It was simple and filling, and it fit the bill. Thank you. And thank you for the note."

She's giving me an odd look and I think she thinks I'm teasing her, and I try to reassure her. "Honest, Major, I—"

"Felicia."

"Thanks," I say. "Force of habit. No, I'm serious. It was . . . reassuring. Comforting. Like it tells me that I've chosen the right path."

Gallagher smiles, nods. "Ready to come back to quarters? I've made a stew for dinner."

I wipe my hands dry with a rough piece of cloth that at least didn't squirm in my hands. "Felicia . . . that'd be great. But could I ask for a favor?"

She shrugs. "Ask away. You can at least do that."

I say, "This is going to sound strange . . . but could I have some blank paper? And a pencil? Or a pen?"

She sounds suspicious. "Why?"

I say, "For years, ever since basic, I kept a diary. Or journal. I know it was against regulations, but I did it anyway. I always thought that at some point I might write a book . . . if the war ever was finished, and I had lived through it."

"Go on," she says.

"A couple of the volumes are hidden back at Ft. St. Paul, and one was in a knapsack that got left behind when I was lost in battle. It's . . . a habit, and I want to start it up again. I think keeping a journal up here will help me—I mean, us, when we get back to Earth."

She slowly nods. "You know, I don't see why not. I'm sure I can rummage something up. Come along, let's go."

And I fall in step with her, and at the other end of the cavern, George sees me, and I wave bye-bye at him.

He doesn't respond.

That's okay.

I don't take it personally.

An Excerpt From the Journal of Randall Knox

I've done a lot and seen a lot since the war began, but I think this bit will set a record: I've restarted this journal while being about three or four hundred kilometers up in space from the Earth's surface.

Yeah, hard to believe.

I'm aboard the Creepers' second orbital battle station, which they had left behind the Moon during the first ten years of the war. A month or so ago, the original battle station was destroyed, and they brought the second one into Earth orbit to continue their . . . well, their religious and cultural crusades. The Creepers are here to beat us down, to bring us down to a pre-computer and electricity civilization, so we will be protected when and if a more destructive species ever comes across us. From what I've learned from Major Gallagher—even though she insists I call her Felicia—this other species (called the Other by the Creepers), would see humans as a nonthreat because of our lack of industrialization and capability of going into space. Otherwise, if we're seen as a threat, the Other wouldn't hesitate to exterminate every last human.

In this way, I guess, the Creepers are our saviors.

Though I have to admit I have a hard time believing this, comprehending and understanding this. All my life, since I was six, I was taught and retaught that the Creepers were our mortal enemies, and that it was my eventual duty in life to join the military and destroy them.

Felicia says that's to be understood, for how else would we comprehend what had happened to us? And she says there's much more to learn, because to learn that the Creepers are here to save us would mean humanity adjusting itself to realizing that it can never, ever be more than just a simple, agrarian-based civilization, in order to save lives.

As Felicia has told me, "The Creepers came here and did a type of surgery upon us. We suffered mightily, we bled and we wept, but in the long run, it will be a much, much better place for all of us."

High-sounding words, but what I've done these past several days hasn't been particularly high sounding. I've been tasked to clean and help rehabilitate armored arthropods that the Creepers (I should call them the Travelers, their preferred name, but I still find that old habit hard to break) used while fighting on Earth. It's truly grunt work, a dirty job that reminds me of some of my old KP duties back at home, but in the end, it's somewhat satisfying. I can point to something and say, this job is done. These dirty and soot-covered objects are now clean, thanks to me.

Plus . . . and I still have a hard time considering this, but the Creepers here, at least their leaders, consider me something special. A "Chosen." Someone with special talents and skills—and mind—to return to Earth as a sort of ambassador, to talk to and reason with the surviving Earth governments, explain that we should stop fighting, stop killing and dying, and accept our new station in life.

My working for the Creepers in doing this cleaning work, it's some sort of trial, or test, to see if I can subdue my normal urges and do what the Creepers require. Maybe so, but right now, the work is okay, and I'm getting fed pretty well, and sleep okay at night, and I don't have to carry a weapon anymore, or worry about being killed.

But sometimes there are things that worry me, like the other night when I had dinner with Felicia, and I asked her, "Felicia . . . aren't you worried, when we get back to Earth, that the Army might not like what we've done up here? I mean . . . some might think we were traitors, or collaborators."

And she said, "Don't worry about that, Randy. We're doing our jobs, ending this war. Not with a bloody or scorched victory, but something just as important . . . a peaceful understanding."

And I said in return, "That sounds good up here . . . I'm just worried what a general might say once we get back to Earth."

"Simple," she said. "We'll just tell him we got promoted."

"How's that?"

"Promoted," she said. "From war maker to peace maker."

CHAPTER TWENTY-SEVEN

About a month after I restarted my journal, it's another day, another stroll off to the Clean, Repair, and Re-Anoint chamber—my name, not anybody else's—and by now, I can walk there and back by myself. I carry my knapsack with my lunch and journal—sometimes I keep it with me, and other times I leave it behind—and I stroll to this chamber like I own the joint. At the keypad I touch the colored shapes—broken square, triangle, skinny triangle, circle—and the hatch slides open, and there's George at the other end, working on one of the arthropods I had cleaned a while back.

He's got some sort of tools that he's working with his two arms, and he just spares me a quick glance with his two eyestalks as I go to my workbench and call out, "Hey George, you ugly bastard. Working hard or hardly working?"

He goes back to his work. Or her work. Or its work. I still don't know, but he rarely ever communicates to me, and he pretty much leaves me alone. I drop off my knapsack and then start right in, and this time, the legs of this new arthropod are really encrusted with dirt and some other sticky stuff. I start off with the brush and work it, and work it, getting the worst of it off, and then I move on to water, gel, and the squiggly "alive" cleaning cloth that seems to scrub itself.

Dull, boring, and most days, pretty satisfactory. Sounds stupid, but there's a real sense of accomplishment when I'm done, and it makes me feel good.

But this isn't one of those days.

⊕ ⊕ ⊕

I'm working on the port rear leg when I spot it, sticking out from one of the leg joints. It's cloth-covered, dangling, and I look closer and see—

Dried, decayed flesh.

The jagged edge of a bone.

And I realize the cloth is part of a sleeve.

Good God.

George is whirring and clanking at the other end of the large work cavern, so he can't see what I've found, or what I'm doing, which makes me happy. I give the object a closer look and try to tug it free.

It won't move.

I try again.

Nothing.

I go back to the workbench, find a skinny brush with a long stone handle, and I go back and I jam the end of it up into the joint, and use it as a lever, and the object pops out and falls to the stone floor.

I kneel down. It's an upper arm and a hand. The hand is small, with a torn black glove on the palm and some of the fingers. I gently pick it up, turn it over, and see the fingernails are covered with red nail polish.

A young woman, or teen girl.

Fighting the Creepers.

I gently lower the severed arm back to the stone, return to the joint, work it again with the brush handle, and pieces of metal and wire dribble out from where the hand had been. I look back at the hand, work it through my mind. Young woman soldier in the midst of a battle, has some type of hand grenade or explosive device that she shoves into the joint, hoping it might disable the Creeper. But the device doesn't work, it's crushed, and the arm is either torn off or lasered off.

God.

I go to the workbench and get a scrap of cloth, and I wrap up the severed limb. George skitters back in front of me, and gives me a stare, and I go back to work.

Scrape, scrape.

Scrub, scrub.

Wash and polish, get through the day, looking down, again and again, at the wrapped-up object on the stone floor.

A female warrior, trying to hurt an enemy, and suffers oh so much for it.

And what am I doing?

Cleaning the arthropod so it can eventually be repaired, and sent back to the surface, to kill more young boys and girls.

As my day ends and I leave, I carry the severed hand and wrist with me, not wanting to leave it back there with George. At the end of my workday, there's always a pile of soiled cleaning cloths, broken scrub brushes, and piles of soot and crusty dirt, and I imagine George or someone else cleans it up, for it's gone by the time I go back to work the next morning.

What now?

Beats the hell out of me.

I just don't want it to be tossed out with the trash.

I leave the tunnel and go to the main chamber, and I hear the same old familiar noise.

Click-click.

Click-click.

Click-click.

Five Battle Creepers emerge from a near tunnel, marching in line, heading to the *Grantztch*. The horns sound out and the large dome moves up as four of the five Creepers march up onto the round surface, with the last one going to the recessed control panel.

I see as it types in the familiar pattern with the end of its right arm: squished circle, triangle, broken square, squiggly line, squiggly line.

Then it comes to me.

I run over to the *Grantztch* and toss the severed arm onto the surface.

The Creepers ignore me. The one who manipulated the control panel scrambles up and joins its comrades.

A thought comes, of joining them, but I don't know where I would end up, and how I would be when I got there.

And if I did end up in a Creeper Battle Dome, somewhere on Earth, what next?

A quick laser blast to the head or a burst of flame to my body, and that would be that. And Major Gallagher would eat by herself tonight.

I back away.

The horns keep on sounding.

The dome lowers itself down and there's a sharp flicker of light through the crack, and there's a shimmering, and then that's that.

The Creepers and that bit of a human being have gone down to Earth.

At least that bit of bone and flesh has gone home.

Dinner with Major Gallagher—all right, Felicia—and she's made us a stew with a fresh salad, and white bread again—and she says, "Randy, how was your day?"

What to say?

"Routine, Felicia, routine."

"Good," she says, stirring up her stew. "I know this is boring, dull work. But to the Travelers, they're seeing you do what has to be done, to lower yourself before them in order to come out in a new place, as a Chosen, one to help us end this conflict."

I remember something from one of my New England history classes at Ft. St. Paul, and I say, "You and the Travelers, you're like the Shakers."

"The who?"

"The Shakers. A religious group in New England, Ohio, and elsewhere. Their whole intent was to humble themselves before God, to bring themselves down to the lowest level before making themselves into something different."

She smiles, picks up a piece of bread, butters it. "I've never heard that. Whatever happened to the Shakers?"

I say, "They went extinct, maybe fifty or sixty years ago."

Another week slides by and I'm going off in the morning, when horns start sounding. I'm near the *Grantztch* and the noise makes me jump and drop my knapsack. I bend down and pick it up, and I don't see anything approaching, so this means there's an incoming transport scheduled. Knapsack in hand, I make a quick stroll to the tunnel where my work station is located.

The large dome comes down and slides shut, and there's a bright light, the same vibration and quivering, and I'm curious to see what comes out when the dome lifts itself up.

Some days it doesn't pay to be curious.

The sharp light coming from the crack dims and there are more horns, and the dome returns to its normal position. There are two Research Creepers, and they skitter out, and a number of humans stumble after them.

Humans.

Damn.

There are about a half dozen of them, in uniform, staggering out, faces twisted in pain, covered with soot, some helping others, lots of burn injuries and bloody bandages.

A Battle Creeper comes after them, sending out little bursts of flames from its left weaponized arm, herding them in the direction of a far tunnel. They gather together like a herd of frightened animals, surrounded by predators.

Then I'm spotted.

"Hey!"

"Over here!"

"Hey, mate, can you help us?"

"Help us!"

"We're from Townsville! Second Cavalry Regiment!"

"We need a doc!"

"Hey, mate, please!"

"For the love of God, help us!"

The Australian soldiers are herded down one of the corridors, and I stay frozen in place until I can't hear their pleading voices.

Then I go along to my traitorous work.

I'm on top of one of the Transport arthropods, scrubbing away, and stuck in the crevasses I find some old plastic dolls. I just sit for a bit, examining them, turning them over and over, wondering if these dolls had been held by young girls, and if so, when, and if the girls were still alive or were turned into carbonized flesh and bone. I've seen Transport Creepers move lots of stuff over the years, from human artifacts to bones and to food down there in the Creeper Dome where I was kept prisoner.

A little girl.

I think of my older sister, Melissa, who died with my mom when the war began, ten years back . . . damn, now starting to come to year eleven.

I guess I should toss the dolls over the top of the open transport bin, but to hell with it.

I stick them back in, climb back on top of the arthropod, and start cleaning and scrubbing, my eight fingers still looking unsettling.

When I take my lunch break, I sit against a bug leg, take out my new journal. It's not a book of any sorts, just a thick sheaf of papers held together by a black binder clip. Hard to believe, but I've missed writing since the Connecticut ambush. My English instructors back at Ft. St. Paul always praised me on my writing, and I'd sort of taken it under the proverbial advisement. There was a war on. What did I care about writing?

But the more I wrote in my journal, the more I realized I was creating something that might be of value, if and when the war ended. I had written a book that saw the war from the grunt's point of view, when you don't care about grand tactics or strategy, but just cared about the guy or gal next to you, or your K-9 unit, out there in the woods and hills, chasing down a Creeper.

For some reason, the writing has grown into something comforting, something useful, and I plan to keep on with this writing until the war ends, if it ends from up here or on the Earth.

I pause, remove a sheet from the rear, scribble some more.

Another bit of knowledge pops up from my schooling.

The pen is mightier than the sword.

But is the pen mightier than an interstellar species?

Damned if I know.

An Excerpt From the Journal of Randall Knox

Since I've submitted to being a Chosen, Major Gallagher's whole attitude and way of dealing with me has changed. She's no longer the tough major, lassoing a lieutenant into doing what's right by the Army. Now she's a fellow human being, imprisoned among the Travelers, convinced that she and her eight-fingered acolyte are destined to end the war against humanity.

I admire her change of attitude and the way she deals with me. It's quite the refreshing difference.

I never thought I'd say this, but I can see what she means. I've taken to looking out the small window port in my quarters during our "night," looking down at the Earth's surface. There's still lots of cloud cover and smoke, but it's nice to see the few lights of cities still making it ten years later. It makes me wonder, when the war is over and peace has been achieved, will those cities go dim when humanity agrees to give up power lines and transmissions? And will oil lamps and gas lamps be enough to work, without attracting the notice of the Other?

There are still millions of people down there, alive. Is it too much to ask that in order to survive, they live in peace like their great-great-grandparents?

There are other lights as well, little flashes of light, and glowing lines as space debris burns up into the atmosphere. So much debris from when the war started, when the Creepers came in and destroyed every satellite in orbit, and then a lot more debris from a couple of months ago, when the first orbital battle station was destroyed by the U.S. Air Force.

Lots of space junk up here, lots of debris that will be burning up and hitting the Earth for decades to come.

The other day I found out that the major has the same habit I do,
when I entered her quarters a bit early for dinner. She was up at her own
viewing port, and turned with a sad smile as I came in.

"Just watching the evening show," she said, patting the cushions next
to her. "Come join me."

I sit down and she looks . . . content? At ease? Not happy, but the
major looked like things were finally coming together.

"I've lucked out," she said. "We've made two orbits and both times,
the sky was clear over California. I saw the two rivers in the mountains
where Taunton is located. That's the place where my husband Brad and
my two boys are living. From what the Travelers have shown me, they're
still alive. Still waiting for Mom to come home."

I said, "The Travelers have told you about your family. Do you think
. . . they've done the same? Do you think they've told them that you're still
alive, up here?"

Then she surprised me, by taking my right hand and squeezing it
hard, but not hurting, even with the missing finger.

"I hope so," she said. "I really, really hope so."

CHAPTER TWENTY-EIGHT

A few weeks after the hand-holding, we're having breakfast together and it's the same freeze-dried eggs, and bacon, and instant coffee, and that Tang drink. When I had first come here with the major, I had loved this food, found it tasty and filling. Now . . . it's got a dull, chemical-like taste. I think of the food I've eaten back on Earth and sure, some of the old canned stuff was way beyond its expiration date, or stale, or close to being spoiled, but it was local. And then there was food we got from local farmers or stores, and that was fresh stuff, good indeed. Maybe not a lot, but it was fresh, and it was ours.

"Problem with your breakfast, Randy?" the major asks.

"No, not at all, ma'am," I say.

She smiles, looks down at her plate. "I really wish you would stop calling me ma'am. It makes me feel . . . old."

"Sorry, Felicia, it's force of habit. And you're not old. Honest."

Felicia smiles. "You making a move on me, Randy?"

My face flushes. "Ah . . ."

"My turn to be sorry," she says. "I'm just teasing you. You got any girls back home?"

"Ah . . ."

"Well?"

"Ah . . ."

She laughs. "It sounds complicated. Is it?"

I spend the next several minutes telling her about my relationship with Abby Monroe, combat courier, who's in my unit back at Ft. St. Paul, and the lovely Serena Coulson, who got my attention the very first time I met her.

"So which one do you want?" she asks.

"Not sure . . . Felicia."

"Want a tip from an old broad like me?"

"Sure," I say.

"Flip a coin. Abby is heads, Serena is tails. Toss it in the air. When the coin falls, part of you will be wishing it lands on one side or the other. Your subconscious will tell you."

I say, "Is that how you picked your husband Brad?"

Another slight laugh. "No, not hardly . . . we met at school, where he was studying business, and I was in ROTC. One thing just led to another . . . then we got married. Got lucky enough to have twin boys, and then even luckier to have our careers be located in the same area. Finance for him in San Francisco, me at the language school. I was good at the languages, and the Army wanted me to stay there for the foreseeable future."

She looks mournful for a moment. "Who knew the future would include alien visitors, coming to rescue us?"

I said nothing.

Felicia says, "Come along, let's get the dishes done. I'm coming to work with you this morning."

"How's that?"

She says, "I want to talk to George, see if you're ready for the next step."

"What step is that?"

"Grab your plate, all right?"

Side by side, me washing dishes, she drying them, I decide it's time to ask her a question that's been in the back of my mind for the past few months.

"Felicia . . . I have something to ask you."

"Go ahead, sport."

I take a deep breath. "Who was K. Whitney? A British soldier, right?"

She shudders, drops a fork on the floor. "Damn you." She scoots around, picks up the fork, gives it to me.

"Wash it again," she says, her major voice returning. "And you . . . you weren't supposed to go into his quarters."

"I didn't see a sign," I say.

"You should have asked."

"Felicia, I didn't see a sign." I rewash the fork, hand it back to her.

She dries it and says, "You're too curious for your own good, you know that?"

"Probably."

"Second Lieutenant Whitney . . . Damn, I loved that man's accent. And his humor. Nothing like a British sense of humor to lighten up your day."

"Was he a Chosen like me?"

She pauses. "Why do you ask?"

I say, "It just makes sense. Another male soldier. Quartered next to you. It would seem to be logical. I don't think the Travelers would go to the trouble of bringing up a soldier and having him live without having a purpose for him."

She slowly wipes another fork dry. "Yes . . . he was. He was a Chosen. He had done incredible things while fighting the Travelers in the UK, and he had the attributes of a Chosen."

"What happened?"

"He gave up."

"Why?"

She shrugs. "Who knows what goes inside a person's mind, Randy. Let's go, time for you to make your lunch."

There's not much in the way of a lunch choice—meat spread and cheese spread once more—and after tossing in some raw vegetables and a bottle of water in the knapsack, I say, "Let me run to my quarters for a sec and I'll be right back."

"I'll meet you in the corridor."

"Fair enough, Felicia."

I go out through the canvas-type curtain, duck into my own place and take my journal and its loosely bound pages with the metal clip off the near shelf. I stuff it in my knapsack and I go out, and Felicia is waiting in the corridor.

Outside of Lieutenant Whitney's quarters.

She's on the stone, arms closed, staring at the nearly hidden entrance.

I slowly go over to her and she keeps on looking, and then starts speaking in a low and quiet voice.

"Whit was a real hard case from the start. You think you were tough, Randy, being on the loose for a week or so? He was gone for months. The Travelers wanted to hunt him down and kill him, but I said no, they had made . . . an investment into bringing him up here." A dry laugh. "Investment. Brian would have loved that, me using his terminology. But eventually he got hungry, thirsty, tired of running . . . and when we got together, he was still a hard case. Refused to accept my authority, my oversight. Even though he was a second lieutenant and I was a major. But eventually . . . I convinced him that I had the authority over him, us being NATO forces."

"I see."

"Then . . . it even took longer for him to understand what I was saying, about ending the war, about being a Chosen. But he eventually saw the reasoning, and agreed to cooperate with me, to end the war."

"How many fingers did he lose?"

Another dry laugh. "He was smarter than you, smarter than me. No fingers, no toes. He went at it with some . . . enthusiasm. He had lost a lot of family members, lots of friends in his unit, and God, he just wanted the war over."

"How many arthropods did he clean?"

"More than you, Randy."

"Then what?"

"Language lessons, of course, and then history lessons, about the Travelers and the Other, and how the Travelers ended up here . . ."

"How long did he stay here until . . ."

She moves forward, touches the curtain. "Almost a year, Randy. Almost a year . . . and then, he tried something and it didn't work. And then the time span of everything just came crashing down on him, that's what I guess."

"What did he try to do?"

Another touch of the curtain. "Marry me."

"But . . ."

"I know, I know, I'm married, right? But . . . try not to be shocked, Randy, but we were lovers. We were about the same age, he was a widower, I was practically a widow . . . and he wanted to make it official, as best as we could, up here among the Travelers."

"You said no, then."

"Nice observation, young man," she sighed, moving away from the curtain. "I said I'd be his helper, teacher, mentor, and lover up here, but once we got back on the Earth's surface, I would have to seek out Brad and my boys. I just had to."

"That . . . sounds reasonable."

"He didn't think so."

"The time span . . . what did you mean about the time span?"

"Oh, I told him that we might be up here for another year, two years, or even five years, before we'd go back to Earth, and he couldn't handle that. I tried to tell him that the Travelers don't see time in the way we do, that they really, really took the long view . . . So he killed himself."

"I'm sorry."

"Well . . . at least he had the courtesy not to do it in front of me, or in these quarters."

"How did he do it, then?"

"Come, now."

We start out of the corridor, and before I have a chance to ask her again, she says, "He went to work like any other day. George was absent. But he knew the access codes for going deeper into the station. So he passed through the airlock, and then entered quarters for the Travelers. Died nearly instantly."

Out in the main chamber, I'm taking my time, walking slowly, as we go by the inactive *Grantztch*, and Felicia says, "You dragging your butt for any good reason, Randy?"

"I've got another question."

"Make it quick," she says. "We're already late, and I don't want George complaining to the Travelers upstairs."

We head toward the familiar route to my daily chores, and I say, "When you said the Travelers took the long view, what did you mean?"

"Meant what I said, Randy," she replies. "They don't see time in the same way we do."

Then something like a wet, heavy, and disgusting blanket falls across my shoulders, weighing me down.

"How long has it been?"

She ignores me and I stop.

"Felicia, how long has it been?"

She stops, doesn't turn around.

"Felicia?"

She turns and says, "You're not ready for this information."

"The hell I'm not," I shoot back. "According to you and the bugs, I'm—"

"The Travelers."

I swear and say, "I don't care if they call themselves undocumented immigrants, Holy Rollers, or the Pope's Own. According to them, I'm a Chosen. I've been selected to be educated for an important job, a vital task, to end the war between them and us. So I'm goddamn ready to receive this information."

Her face looks worn, tired. "Ask your question again."

"How long has it been since the . . . Travelers were attacked by the Other? When did that happen?"

"Randy . . ."

"Tell me or I'm going on strike."

"Randy . . ."

"I'll skip out and you and they will never find me," I say. "And I won't fall again for that same trick, using a computer voice to imitate Buddy Coulson."

She bites her lower lip, runs her hands across her face, and says, "A hundred. Maybe two hundred."

"Two hundred years?"

"No," she says. "Two hundred thousand years."

Now I'm struck dumb.

All the deaths, all the destruction, all of the heartache, all of the tears and burnt bodies and drowned cities, all of the aircraft that dropped out of the sky that October tenth, my own mom and sister, dead, my buds in the Army burnt or crippled, the millions that have starved, or died from the cold, or from diseases that had been eradicated centuries ago . . .

All of the efforts by them to beat us down, to save us from a threat that . . .

A threat more than two thousand centuries old.

At about the time *homo sapiens* began its long march from Africa.

"I . . . Felicia . . . I can't believe it."

"Randy . . . that's why I told you that you had to wait. You're not ready for this information. After you learn more, after you get exposed to their languages and their culture, you'll still see that they're coming here was the best thing that ever happened to us."

"They killed us all because of a threat two hundred thousand years old! How in hell was that in our best interest?"

"Randy—"

"Are you nuts? Is that it?"

Her eyes light up with anger and her retort to me is drowned out by the sound of horns blaring. I turn and the dome for the *Grantztch* begins to lower. The horns get louder. Felicia moves away a bit and I join her. The dome matches up with the elevated round surface and we wait.

The shuddering of the dome commences, along with a leakage of a very bright light around the base, and then the dome starts to lift. The horns stop their blaring. The dome lifts high enough to reveal the visitors here, three arthropods, all of the Transport class.

Felicia starts arguing with me again but I ignore her.

Something doesn't seem right.

The three Creeper exoskeletons aren't moving.

Usually when the dome is clear, the bugs quickly move off, heading to one of the tunnels.

Nothing is moving.

By now Felicia notices something isn't right.

"Randy . . . what's going on?"

"I don't know," I say, as something fierce and bright starts growing inside of my chest. "I don't know."

Then, from inside the near arthropod, I hear something I've not heard for months.

A barking dog.

"Thor!" I yell, and I start racing to the three arthropods, as they break open from underneath and a number of heavily armed American soldiers tumble out.

CHAPTER TWENTY-NINE

A few are armed with the standard infantry M-4 rifle, while others have the Colt M-10, but two are wearing some sort of exoskeleton that allows them to bear a heavier weapon than I've ever seen before. And all are carrying heavy-looking satchels on their backs.

Two soldiers with M-4s come to me and I lift my arms and I start to identify myself, as a Belgian Malinois races from the second arthropod and knocks me over.

I fall in the light gravity and hug and hug Thor, and my face is licked and licked, and I'm bawling, rubbing his fur, saying all sorts of nonsense things, until someone kicks my feet and a familiar voice says, "This is all heartwarming and crap, Lieutenant, but we're in the middle of a raid. Get off the goddamn floor."

I pull Thor off of me and his fur bristles from smelling all of the nearby Creepers, and before me is Captain—correct that, Colonel— Kara Wallace, whom I last saw months ago, as she and her unit of Kara's Killers were heading back to their base in New York. She looks thinner, a bit more haggard, and there's fresh burn scar tissue on her left cheek, but I'm still quietly bawling, seeing another familiar face from Earth.

"Great to see you, Colonel," I manage to choke out.

"Same here, Lieutenant."

"It . . . it worked."

"Oh yes, it worked quite well." She turns and yells out, "Squads, one through six, get to work! Now!"

Felicia—Major Gallagher—scoots over, her face shocked, hands shaking. "Who . . . what . . . what's going on?"

I say, "Colonel Kara Wallace, this is Major Felicia Gallagher, from the Monterey Language Institute . . . she's been with the Creepers for ten years."

"Jesus Christ," Colonel Wallace says.

Thor is still growling and I rub his head and fur, and I whisper, "Stay, okay? Stay."

He leans into me, growling but at a lower tone. I say, "Colonel . . . what's he doing here? I sent him back to Ft. St. Paul, just before I was captured."

"Good question," she says. "Your furry friend managed to find me instead . . . and then we went back to that Dome in Massachusetts, the one you and Buddy Coulson made surrender. I kept him around and just as we were about to . . . dispatch up here, the guy jumped in with me. Too late for us to start over, so here he is."

Major Gallagher regains her composure and says, "Hey, will someone tell me what the hell is going on?"

Colonel Wallace's eyes narrow and harden. "What do you think, Major? Isn't it apparent?"

At Wallace's side, something crackles. It's a black rectangular box and she picks it off her belt and holds it up to her ear, and I can hear words.

I can hear words!

"Squad one in position."

"Two in position."

"Three locked and loaded, Colonel."

And so forth until all six of her squads are in the position.

She pushes a switch on the side of her radio—a working radio!— and says, "All squads, acknowledged. Keep this circuit clear unless you get visitors. And anyone who shoots first will get a beer from me when we're done. Wallace out."

From somewhere in the battle station, I both hear and feel a deep *thump*. My hands feel funny, even though I'm used to only having eight fingers. Somebody out there has just set off an explosion. Another *thump* comes along, too.

I need to have a weapon in my hands.

Gallagher says, "Colonel, please—"

Wallace cuts her off. "Do you have any actionable intelligence I can use, right now?"

"Ah, I can speak the language, I can—"

Another brush-off. "Sorry, the time for talking is over. Knox."

"Ma'am."

"Nice work," she says. A soldier moves by, carrying both an M-10 and an M-4. She grabs him, strips her of the M-4, hands it over to me.

I can't believe how good it feels to hold it.

"How many of them got through?" I ask.

"Enough."

She turns and there are four soldiers emerging from the far open arthropod, each pair carrying an object between them, a circular metallic thing nearly as tall as I am, and wide enough so that I'm not sure I could reach around with both hands.

"Weps!" she yells out, checking her watch. "You know the drill. Ten minutes . . . and be snappy about it."

While one of my hands is still rubbing and stroking my dear Thor, the other one is suddenly grabbed by Gallagher.

"Randy . . . what did you do? For God's sake, what did you do?"

I pull away, check the M-4, flip off the safety, work the action. "My duty."

She grabs my hand again. "Tell me, what did you do?"

"I sent messages back to Earth. Telling them everything I knew about the Creepers up here, the layout of the tunnels, how the *Grantztch* works, the codes for making it work . . . pretty much anything I could think of."

She's practically crying. "You young fool, how the hell did you do that?"

"I wrote messages with the paper and the pencil you provided me, stuck them in the joints and crevasses of the arthropods. I figured if any one of them got whacked down on Earth, when the evaluation teams examined the dead Creepers, they'd find my notes, no matter what country they were in. I hoped even if they got whacked in Brazil or Japan, the information in the notes might be sent back to the States."

"Randy, they could have been found here!"

The four-man crew holding the two metal objects scurry out into the main chamber, escorted by an officer wearing eyeglasses that Wallace called Weps, and then they halt. One of them seems to be taking some sort of measurements with the help of a clipboard, pen, and a little computer. A computer! Another also has a pair of binoculars that she's using to look at the area.

"I guess they weren't, then, ma'am."

The crew stops at the command of Weps. Odd name.

Then it comes to me, from an old, dirty, and torn paperback I had gotten from the Ft. St. Paul library some time back, when I was just a corporal. It was a Cold War tale, America versus the Russians (or Chinese, I forget) and one of the main characters was an Air Force officer, nickname of Weps.

For Weapons.

Special Weapons.

Now I know what that four-man crew has in its possession, and I know Weps is trying to situate the two nuclear devices for maximum impact.

Nukes.

Hoo boy.

"Randy . . ."

I turn to Gallagher, feeling almost pity at the look on her face, realizing that her decade-long confinement and work is coming to an end that she probably couldn't even have imagined.

"Randy," she says again. "But . . . your journal."

"All lies," I say. "I figured you'd be reading it when I wasn't around."

"But you're a Chosen!"

"Begging the major's pardon, but that's a mistake," I say. "I'm a lieutenant in the N.H. National Guard, attached to the 26th Division, Army of the United States. And I'm back on duty."

Then Colonel Wallace's radio starts crackling and things get real interesting, real quick.

"Contact, contact," a voice calls out on the radio, loud enough for even me with my bum hearing. "Tunnel Bravo . . . hatch has opened up, have engaged the enemy."

I can make out the echoing *BLAM!* of someone firing off an M-10, along with the quick rounds of an M-4. Wallace swears and says, "Damn it, I could use more firepower. I was hoping the bugs wouldn't respond this fast."

And I can't help it, I'm off to the sound of the guns, like an eager recruit, and God, it feels good to be running again, even in the seven-tenths gravity, M-4 in my hands, Thor racing after me. Wallace screams at me as I race away, and I tap my left ear in the usual style, pointing out that I'm partially deaf there and can't possibly hear what she's ordering me to do.

Tunnel Bravo is where I've traipsed these past months going to work as a slave, and it's harshly lit up by a set of portable flood lamps. There's one soldier with an M-4, another with an M-10, and a third, bulky-looking woman wearing the metal harness with the odd looking weapon hanging over her right shoulder.

A sergeant looks at Thor and me as we join their huddled group. Ahead of us is the round hatch, which is stuck open about a third, and a dead Battle Creeper is lying half in and half out. A smoky haze obscures the view inside of what I had called the Clean, Repair, and Re-Anoint chamber. There's rock rubble in front of us from a crater on the side wall, and the sergeant says, "I don't like being out in the open like this, so I made a shelter with a shaped charge. You're Knox, the prisoner, right?"

The prisoner, I think. Yeah, that's what I am.

"That's right."

Thor barks, whines, and I rub his head and back again. If I were to be killed right now, I'd be the happiest I've been in months.

He says, "A minute or so ago, the smoke cleared, and it looked like there was a goddamn line of Creepers ready to come out after us. Why aren't they moving?"

"Because they're empty," I say. "It's a repair facility for damaged exoskeletons they bring back up from Earth."

"I still don't like it," he says. "Debbie!"

"Yo, Sergeant," the woman with the harness says.

"Hose the interior of that room, five rounds."

"Yes, Sergeant."

She moves forward, rests herself against a large piece of rock, manipulates some switches and handles, and—

BLAM!

BLAM!

BLAM!

BLAM!

BLAM!

Whoever Debbie is, she's got a Colt M-10 variant that's a semiautomatic weapon, unlike the single-shot weapon I've been used to the past couple of years. Her harness bucks against her but she stays upright, and the rounds go through the opening and into the room, and there are smaller explosions as the binary gas rounds do their job. Outstanding. What I wouldn't have given to have had that weapon in my past, back when you fired once at Creeper, and hoped you reloaded in time to get another shot off before you got lased or burned.

A shout from behind us. "Cease fire, cease fire, that's an order, cease fire!"

The sergeant says a series of obscenities and we turn and by God, there's Major Gallagher, scooting along, and then scrambling over the rock barrier. "I'm Major Felicia Gallagher, U.S. Army, and I'm telling you to cease fire!"

The sergeant then says, "What the . . . you, Knox, is she on the level? Is she a major?"

I answer only half of his question, and I say, "Yes, she's a major and—"

Gallagher yells again, "This ends now! I'm an Army-trained linguist and I can talk to them and make it stop! Cease fire!"

Debbie lowers herself down from the rock barrier and says, "Sarge, I think she's gonna get her chance. Look what the hell is coming out . . . shit, the damn bug should be dead for all the rounds that went in there."

What's coming out is George, wearing his breathing apparatus, and the reason he's still alive is that he's protected from the binary nerve gas that Debbie just plowed in our mutual work area. His exit is blocked by the dead Creeper so he has to scramble over, and a soldier says, "Sarge, look at that ugly bastard."

The sarge doesn't say anything and Gallagher moves forward, holds up her arms, and starts talking to George in Creeper talk, and even though it's the alien language, I can hear the urgency in the clicks, hisses, and snaps.

"Damn," Debbie says. "The Major speaks Creeper."

Sarge says, "She better make it quick."

His radio sounds off with harsh words from Wallace, and George gets free, is about three meters in front of Gallagher, and she's shouting, beseeching, and George's arms have objects at each end, and he brings up his right arm and points it straight at Gallagher.

I can't explain it.

From fighting Creepers all these years, I know what's going to happen next.

I get off a quick three-shot burst as a laser beam flashes out and knocks Gallagher back.

My three shots trigger more fire from two other soldiers armed with M-4s, and George's breathing apparatus is torn away and he collapses, legs twitching, fluid oozing out, a serious stench coming over us in one thick wave. I climb up over the broken rock and debris and grab Gallagher's left shoulder, pulling her up.

She's alive.

There's a burnt furrow of hair and skin on the side of her skull, just above her left ear. The skin has been cauterized from the laser and there's no bleeding. Gallagher whispers, "He was trying to kill me . . . I was trying to help him . . . and he tried to kill me . . ."

From behind the barrier the sergeant yells out, "Hey, Knox, the colonel says you better haul ass back to where she is! And now!"

I say to Gallagher, "Are you all right? Can you move?"

She slaps my hand away. "He . . . tried to kill me."

I call out, "Thor! Come!" and we start running back to the central chamber.

When we get there, Colonel Wallace has two soldiers near her, one with an M-10, the other with an M-4, and she checks her watch and swears again. "Running out of time . . ." She yells out, "Weps, what's the problem? We can't stay here all goddamn day!"

Weps doesn't answer, working frantically on the two nuclear devices, with the other four soldiers trying to help him. Wallace says, "What the hell happened in Tunnel Bravo?"

"Two Creepers attempted a breakout, ma'am. They were stopped."

"Any casualties?"

"Major Gallagher was scorched on her head, but she's fine."

Wallace says, "She right, about speaking to the Creepers? Knowing the language?"

"Yes, she is right," I say. "I've seen and heard her."

"Hunh," she says. "Too bad her language skills are going to be pretty useless in five minutes . . . that is, if Weps can hurry the hell up."

"Ma'am, you should know, Major Gallagher says the Creepers have the ability to decompress this whole chamber in a matter of seconds, if need be."

"Do you or her know how to prevent that?"

I hear the soldier called Weps start swearing loudly. "No, ma'am."

"Then keep your trap shut. Hey, Weps, you got three minutes!"

"Colonel Wallace."

"Yes?" I've seen her in action before, seen how her face can get hard and set, like it's been carved out of stone, but this day is certainly different, fighting a possible suicide mission in the Creepers' home.

I take a deep breath. "Ma'am, there are a number of humans being held prisoner here. POWs, civilians, some that are living on their own in caves and crevasses."

Her voice is sharp and to the point. "Do you know how to rescue them in the next two minutes?"

"No."

"Then shut up. Weps!"

The soldier known as Weps breaks away from the other four soldiers and runs back to the Colonel, legs and arms slipping and sliding awkwardly in the low gravity. He skids to a halt in front of her, his plump face bright red, his eyes filled with tears.

"Colonel Wallace, there's a problem."

"Go," she says.

"The timing devices . . . we even had two spares. But the transport up here, it screwed them up. I've tried, and tried . . ." He starts sobbing. "I'm sorry, Colonel, I really, really tried."

Wallace says, "What do you mean?"

"Ma'am, the timers don't work. We can't explode the bombs."

CHAPTER THIRTY

Before any of us can say a word, Colonel Wallace's portable radio crackles again and there's a frantic voice, "Delta Tunnel, Delta Tunnel, we're under attack! Repeat, we're under attack!"

Wallace picks up the radio, says, "Acknowledged, Delta Tunnel. Hold your position."

She says to Weps, "Figure something out."

"I can't. The timing devices don't work. The two spares don't work."

Her radio snaps to again. "Colonel Wallace, this is Echo Tunnel. Creepers are coming through an opening. We're returning fire."

"Message received," Wallace says, and she says to Weps, "I don't care what you have to do, or how you do it, but we don't have the time. Get those bombs to work."

"I can't!"

"You have to!"

Weps starts sobbing again and I say to him, "The timers don't work. But can you trigger them . . . manually?"

Wallace looks to me, and then Weps, who wipes his arm across his eyes.

"I . . . it's possible."

"Then do it," Wallace says sharply. "Now."

"But, ma'am . . ."

"What?"

Weps looks at all of us, including Major Gallagher, who's joined us and who's still gingerly touching the wound at the side of her head. The slight sounds of gunfire in the distant tunnels starts to get louder. The Creepers seem to have decided to come right at us. No decompression or poison gas then.

He coughs. "Ma'am, that'll mean somebody will have to trigger it . . . somebody will have to connect the switch."

"Do it," she says. "Quick as you can, before the bugs decide to pull the plug on their transporter."

"But who'll do it?"

"You don't worry about that," she says. "Just make it happen. Now."

"Yes, ma'am."

Weps runs off and starts yelling orders to his four-man squad, and then Wallace sighs, removes her helmet, runs a hand over her close-cropped red hair. She looks at the eagle insignia on the front of her helmet and says in a soft voice, "Damn, I didn't even have you there long enough to get used to it."

"Ma'am?" I ask.

She puts the helmet back on, tugs the chinstrap tight. "My job. Nobody else's. Knox?"

"Ma'am."

"You're the highest ranking officer I got here, except for the major, but Major, no offense, you're not a line officer. Lieutenant Knox has combat experience. Knox, when Weps is done—"

And in an astounding coincidence, he yells out, "Colonel Wallace, it's set up!"

Wallace offers a little grim smile. "As I was saying, now that he's done, I'll assume the position, and order a pull back. You make sure my guys get back to Earth. Sergeant Houlihan, he knows what to do."

I don't know what to say then. Part of me wants to be noble and volunteer to detonate the nuclear bombs, to sacrifice myself for the others, but the hell with that. I'm only sixteen, I've volunteered enough for some crappy missions over the years, and if Colonel Wallace wants to do it, I'm not going to try to argue her out of it.

A cowardly approach, I know, but I'm tired of being heroic.

"Very good, Colonel."

She nods, and says, "Major Gallagher, I—"

"No," she says.

"What? Major, we don't have time for this. Lieutenant Knox is going to be in charge when my troops enter that transport chamber. That's final."

Gallagher is still gingerly touching the fresh wound at the side of her head, looks up and says, "No. I mean, no, you're going back to Earth, Colonel."

I think we all know what she's saying, and Gallagher makes it perfectly clear.

"I'll stay behind and detonate the weapons," she says.

There's a brief and violent argument between the two women, and Colonel Wallace checks her watch, looks at me, and says, "Randy . . . straight up, no bullshit. Can she be trusted? Can she?"

Straight up. No bullshit.

Good God, my legs are trembling, and so are my arms, and I know what I want to say, what I should say, but I can't do that.

"Ma'am, she's been turned," I say. "She can't be trusted."

Wallace mouths a very vile obscenity and says, "All right, thanks, Randy. That's that."

Gallagher moves quickly over to the two nuclear bombs and the crew, and Wallace and I follow, and she yells, "Don't let her near that, Weps! Don't!"

Two of the soldiers hold onto her and Weps—holding a little instrument connected to a series of wires—looks confused, and Gallagher turns and says, "I've got to do it. I've got to."

Wallace says, "Sorry, Major, you can't be trusted."

"I can be trusted, and I can prove it."

Wallace swears again, and now sirens and horns are blaring in the chamber, echoing about the walls. The soldiers here all look around and bite their lips, and finger their weapons, and I know what's going through their minds:

Being captured or dying here, hundreds of kilometers away from home.

Gallagher says, "I speak the language. You soldiers start evacuating, I can hold them off, at least for a few seconds."

"Not good enough," Wallace says.

"I was wrong . . . I've been so for very, very long . . . I thought I was helping my family, and the world . . . but I was wrong. Please, Colonel, let me make it right."

Her radio is crackling with more messages of Creepers coming at us through the tunnels.

The major's voice softens. "Colonel, I've had my Damascus moment. Honest. And Randy . . . look up my boys later, will you? Tell them . . . well, tell them enough to make my boys proud of their mom."

A very long second or two passes by.

"Weps," Wallace says.

"Ma'am."

"How does it work."

He holds up a little box with a gray button in the center.

"Press the gray button, it's activated. Release the gray button . . . it, uh, it then works. Ma'am."

Another long second passes. More frantic radio chatter.

"Give it to the major."

She whispers, "Thank you," and takes the instrument in her hands, and then Wallace bends over, and it looks like she kisses her on the cheek, and she says, "Weps! You and your crew . . . move!"

I'm bawling again, silently, and Gallagher smiles and blows me a kiss with her free hand, and says, "You promise?"

"I promise."

"Then get the hell out of here, Lieutenant."

I salute her.

"Yes, ma'am."

Then I run along with Wallace, and my boy Thor runs along next to me, tongue hanging out, happy in his ignorance of what's going on around us, but so happy to be with me, even if it's forever, which just might be a few seconds from now.

On the round platform Weps and his guys crawl back into one of the exoskeletons, and Wallace pulls her radio free and says, "All squads, all squads. Redeploy, redeploy. Let's go home."

More gunfire erupts and then one, and then two, and then all squads come racing out from each tunnel, running toward us. There are distant explosions and I say, "Ma'am?"

"Landmines," she says. "Gorgeous little development. It should hold them off just a bit longer."

She starts counting off the soldiers that come in, and one, and then two are holding up arms that are missing a hand, grimacing and trying to keep it together. Then I have to turn away for a brief moment as one soldier is carried in, supported by two others, missing a head.

"That's Jonesy," a soldier pants out. "I sure as hell am bringing him home."

Wallace just nods and calls out, "Houlihan, we're all here! Do it!"

While other soldiers are crawling back into the exoskeletons, a sergeant with a large knapsack peels away and runs over to the control panel. He dumps the knapsack on the ground, opens it up, and brings out what looks to be the end of a Creeper joint. There are tubes and bottles at one end, and at the other end, he touches the control panel in a series of moves.

Nothing happens.

"Houlihan!" Wallace calls out.

Again, he touches, and she says, "Take your time, take your time."

Behind me someone says, "What difference does it make, we're dead anyway . . ."

Houlihan goes slower, more deliberate, and another horn joins the cacophony, and the overhead dome of the *Grantztch* starts to descend over us. Houlihan then runs over to join us.

The dome moves so goddamn slow.

"Charlie Tunnel, Charlie Tunnel," someone yells, and a Creeper emerges, dressed like George, in a breathing suit that will protect him from our nerve gas, and as the dome continues its slow descent, I kneel down and carefully empty out my M-4's magazine with three-shot bursts, tearing into its abdomen and breathing apparatus, as it slides to the floor.

That's the last thing I see as the dome closes around us.

I was hoping to see the major one more time, but it doesn't happen.

In the darkness someone lights up a flashlight, and Wallace grabs my upper arm and says, "Haul ass with me, or who the hell knows what might happen next."

With Thor near me, I'm dragged into an exoskeleton, jostling and finding a place, and I say, "What did Houlihan have back there?"

"A Creeper arm that our white-coats managed to keep living," she says. "We were hoping it would fool the control panel here into letting us off the base once we were done. We did the same thing on Earth when we hid in the damaged Creepers."

I say, "When did you test it?"

"About ninety seconds ago."

The world inside gets blindingly bright, something crushes my chest, arms, legs, and skull, and there are screams and yells, and Thor barks and whines, and again. I close my eyes tight but the blinding light still seeps in, and I'm falling, falling, and—

It stops.

We're in darkness.

There's more sighs, curses, and then I feel heavy, very heavy, and I flop out from the exoskeleton, and I'm nearly trampled as other soldiers do the same thing. Light emerges from around the base, and by God, this dome starts lifting up, and we're in a Creeper Base Dome, and looking at us are a number of soldiers and civilians. The civilians are staring, mouths agape, and they push through and start asking questions, and the soldiers are all heavily armed with Colt M-10s, and what looks to be rapid-firing cannon, and there's even two old Abrams tanks there, long barrels pointed at us.

Wallace says, "Make way, make way," and grabs my hands.

We push through and some of Wallace's soldiers make a lane, and we all start running, and then there's a wide ramp in front of us, and I feel heavy and sloggy, being back in normal Earth gravity, and we emerge into a familiar-looking field. Thor's keeping pace right next to me, barking with joy.

The place where a long, long time ago, the Creepers had first surrendered to me, back when I thought the war was truly and really over.

I'm on Earth.

I'm home.

Thor licks my hand and I rub his head, and I say, "Pal, whatever you beg, whatever you want, it's yours. Forever."

It's dusk. The sun is near the western, wooded horizon. A crowd has gathered around us, and there are two generals, more well-dressed civilians, and Wallace yells out, "Anybody know the orbital elements? Anybody?"

"Less than a minute!" an older woman yells back, and then we all quiet down.

No voices.

A grumbling of diesel engines somewhere, but this crowd of about fifty or sixty are keeping their mouths shut, as we all look up to the darkening sky.

"There it is!" comes another cry, and we all crane our necks even further, and Thor, like he's sensing something important is happening, sits down next to me and leans into my legs.

The deadly familiar and well-lit shape of the Creepers' orbital battle station comes into clearer view, as it makes its way across the sky, and I just feel the first taste of bitter disappointment when the shape is replaced by a sharp, bright light, expanding with starfish like filaments, and then contracting, and then darkening as it fades from view.

It's over.

Wallace clears her throat, takes my hand, leads me over to the two generals, one male, the other female, both of whom are silently weeping.

My colonel salutes the two.

In a quavering voice she says, "General Perkins, General Blaine, I'm pleased to announce Kara's Killers, detached, have completed Operation Trojan Horse."

The generals can't speak. Neither can anybody else.

Wallace says, "We await further orders."

CHAPTER THIRTY-ONE

A month has passed since Victory Day, and I'm back home at Ft. St. Paul in Concord, N.H., feeling itchy in a brand-new full dress uniform. I stand before the mirror in my near empty quarters, tugging at this and that, hoping I've left enough room for a third Purple Heart. When you lose two fingers from Creeper action, the award evaluation period is pretty brief.

In the corner Thor is sleeping on my bed, all four legs sprawled out and draped over the edge, like his bones have turned into soft cartilage. My good boy is snoring, and he's about the only familiar object in my quarters. Since my capture many months ago, I was first listed as MIA, and then KIA, so some other trooper has my old room here at the fort. In the near closet is a small cardboard box with just a handful of personal items, my spare clothing and footwear having been distributed among my surviving platoon mates in the usual tradition. My battle pack—bloodied, soot covered, and damp—is also there, having been recovered from the ambush site back in Connecticut and in a small miracle, it ended back up at my duty station. All my rations and spare clothing are gone as well, but I was happy to see my journal had been left behind.

At least my thieves didn't steal it for toilet paper.

The room smells new, and I really haven't found myself entirely comfortable here. On the bureau is a slim envelope. I don't need to read it. The message is clear in my mind.

Dear Randy,

I can't tell you how thrilled I am that you've made it back home, and that—again!—you're a hero. When I found out you had been killed by the Bugs . . . well, having you back is a miracle.

I'm also praying for another miracle. Buddy ran away soon after we last saw you. He's officially listed as Missing and perhaps he'll be found, but we both know how long that list is.

I'm happy to tell you that I'm engaged, to a Gus Fonda that I met at Stratton. He's a lieutenant in ARC and we're going to be living at the Detroit Arsenal after the marriage.

Oh Randy . . . if you're ever in Michigan, please look me up. I'll do the same if I ever get back to N.H.

The times we've spent together . . . I'll always cherish them.

And you'll always be a hero. Forever.

Yours,
Serena

ARC.

Asset Recovery Command, fastest growing command in the Army, as the computers get fired up, the lights come on again, and the jets and trucks begin moving.

Just as the dead Major Felicia Gallagher had warned would happen.

Well, if so, it's by our choice, not the choice of others.

I check my watch and say, "Thor, come."

He snaps to in an instant, leaps off the bed and joins my side, as I leave my empty quarters.

Outside it's a crisp spring day, with lots of leaves starting to show on the oaks and maples, and Dad is waiting for me. I was hoping to see someone else, but I still put a smile on my face.

Hard to believe how long I was gone, hard to believe I missed Christmas and New Year's, and so much else.

He's in uniform as well, wearing the rank and insignia of a major in the Intelligence Corps, and leaning on a cane, he limps to me, smiling back. He's thin and tired looking, but at least the Army has given him a new pair of black-rimmed glasses. It's been a while since I've seen him in full dress uniform, and he's got a shiny Purple Heart to mark when his leg got burned off in New York State a long time ago.

"Walk with you?" he asks.

"Sure, Dad," I say, and he comes to me, slips an arm into mine, and we slowly walk to the parade grounds, still glancing around at the soldiers trickling by, looking for one special young female soldier, and not seeing her.

"How's your new leg working out?" I ask.

"Oh, it's doing fine," he says. "There a lot of prosthetic specialists in the VA who know how to fit a limb and train the user. War gives them a steady business."

The walkway to the parade ground is nearly deserted, and we come out in an open space beyond the buildings and trees, and Dad stops, and I stop as well. There's a schedule to be kept, I know, but I also know some things just won't start without me. Around us are the brick buildings of Ft. St. Paul, and already there's talk about negotiations to close the base and transfer the property back to the few alumni and teachers left from the old prep school.

Dad sighs, leans into me and for a brief, horrible moment, I think he's about to faint or collapse. "Gorgeous day," he manages to say.

"Sure is," I reply, and Thor trots off to a bit of green and finds a tree trunk, lifts his leg, and does his morning business.

"It was a day as pretty as this, when the war started, when we lost your Mom and Melissa."

I keep my mouth shut. He's never, ever, told me what happened on that awful day.

"My fault," he says, voice cracking. "For more than a decade, that's what I've carried with me, weighing me down, nearly killing me . . . knowing I had killed them both."

"Dad . . . it was the Creepers."

"I've tried to convince myself of that . . . but it's not true. It was me. I was weak."

"Dad . . ."

He takes a deep breath, like he's trying to gain strength to go on. "The attack was only hours away that day. The comet . . . Imai, it was called . . . had broken up. It was moving in a strange way. I was teaching at BU but I was in the Reserves, and quietly, we were being called up. At least some knew something bad was coming. Your mother . . . she was with Melissa, was going to bring her to Children's Hospital for a checkup. Melissa had been fighting a cold for weeks and your Mom was concerned."

Something spooky happens then, for Dad's words have just unlocked a well-hidden memory. Me running around our old house in Marblehead, Melissa coughing and coughing in her bedroom, Mom trying to make me stay quiet.

"Melissa was going to see a specialist. It had taken weeks to make this appointment, and your Mom didn't want to cancel. She insisted on going. We even had a fight in the driveway . . . I almost reached in and took the keys from her car. Almost. And I hesitated. That was all it took. She started up the car, backed out of the driveway, angry at me . . . and that was the last I saw of your mom and sister."

I squeeze my arm against his. "Probably hundreds of thousands of people hesitated like that, too."

"But they weren't me." One more deep breath. "Her brother and the rest of the family's survivors never forgave me. Her brother even said if I had been more of a man, I would have stopped her . . . would have saved her life." He coughs. "Boston was hit by the tsunami later that day. I just hope . . . hope it was quick."

I keep quiet, and then he tugs my arm. "Come along. I don't want this old man to make you late."

We resume our slow pace, and I look around one more time for one soldier, and she's not here.

Near the parade ground there's a small white tent that I was told to report to, and Dad slaps me on the shoulder, and I duck into the tent, and there are a couple of officers and Colonel Kara Wallace, also in her dress uniform, and she comes over, and gives me a hug. "Good to see you, Randy. Here, want some breakfast before the show starts?"

Surprisingly enough, I'm not hungry, but I see Thor looking up at me, his brown eyes sad, and I end up with a pancake, three sausage links, and a cup of coffee. I sit with Colonel Wallace and she eats and she's the happiest I've ever seen, and she's practically bouncing up and down in the white plastic chair. One by one, the sausage links go into Thor's happy gullet.

"Look, I can't stand it," she says. "I've got to tell someone who knows me . . . look." She reaches into her uniform jacket pocket and pulls out a small envelope, creased, dirty and with one corner torn off. Her hand is shaking as she shows it to me.

"See? A letter . . . from my husband. He's alive! Still in Afghanistan . . . but damn it he's going to try to get back home. He's been there ever since the first bombs dropped . . . and he's coming home. Somehow he became a generalissimo of some Afghan province but . . . oh Christ, he's coming home."

She picks up a white napkin and holds it against her face, and a few moments pass.

After we eat, a thin woman lieutenant comes bustling into the small white tent, wearing some sort of adjutant brassard on her right shoulder. She tries to usher us out, because there's a schedule to be met, and we get up and I say, "Colonel Wallace . . . back at the orbital station."

"Make it quick, Lieutenant."

"Major Gallagher . . . she said something about having her Damascus moment. What was that about?"

She wipes her hands on a napkin. "Ah, I guess that's what comes from teaching our children about war, survival, and not much else. Saul of Tarsus lived in the time of Jesus, and he was persecuting early Christians. On the road to Damascus, he was supposedly struck by the truth of God, repented, and changed his name to Paul, and became one of the most powerful leaders of early Christianity."

The colonel drops the napkin on the round white plastic table. "Ever since then, having a Damascus moment means repenting, realizing the truth of a situation, and then trying to make it all right. That's what the major was telling us."

"Oh," I say.

We head out of the tent, and again, I feel the pang of not seeing someone I so want to see. "So when you bent down, and kissed her cheek, did you tell her you understood the Damascus story?"

Colonel Wallace puts her cover on. "No, I whispered to her that if she didn't do what she had promised, no matter how long it took, I would track down her family and slit their throats."

I stand there, a bit shocked, and with her strong even voice, she says, "I had to do it, and I would do it again. Do you understand?"

"Yes, ma'am."

The way of war. I know it so damn well.

⊕ ⊕ ⊕

The practice field has been improved and decorated with flags and bunting, and I walk along the rows of chairs, nodding and saying hello to some of my fellow troopers from Ranger Recon, but I've been away so long these faces don't look familiar at all.

I go to the front and find an empty folding chair that has my name on paper taped to the back. Colonel Wallace is there, next to me, reading that letter from her husband, still smiling.

I sit down. Thor stretches out in front of me. In front is a low riser of wood and metal, and a lectern, and an Army band starts playing a Sousa tune, and there comes a *thump-thump-thump* noise from the south.

The same thin lieutenant comes to me and says, "Your dog. If you want, I can take him someplace with shade and water."

"He's fine where he is."

"But your dog . . ."

"He stays with me, or I leave. Your choice."

She leaves. I reach out with my shiny boots and gently stroke his back.

Then they come into view, and I'm still in awe and admiration as the three Black Hawk helicopters head our way. Flying machines, taking back to the air. Power plants being re-started. Cars and trucks starting to return to the crumbling and worn highways. Asset Recovery Command, indeed. With the second station gone, and the killer stealth satellites no longer under intelligent control, the orbital space around Earth is finally safe.

Wallace leans over and says, "Looks fine, doesn't it."

"It sure does," I say. "You know, it reminds me of something Major Gallagher said . . . about whether we'd be better off staying like we were, or recreating what passed for civilization. For a long time she was convinced the Creepers were right, that it was best that we remained back in the nineteenth century."

"She was wrong, wasn't she."

The sound of the helicopters grow louder. I say, "Well, she said I was a Chosen, so that was pretty wrong."

Wallace nudges me with her elbow. "You were a chosen, Lieutenant. For the human race. Not the aliens."

The helicopters flare out and land, and in a few minutes, a cordon of people start coming over to us, including two who are holding something called *news cameras*. Television is coming back on a national level, with just one channel so far, or so I've been told. I haven't had much free time since I came back, with all the interviews and debriefing.

Now with time to think, I'm thinking of only a couple of things, the biggest being, well, what now?

Yeah.

What now.

Some Army units are being redeployed in attempts to break through the Creeper Base Domes now that they have no overhead defense, and I'm tempted to seek a transfer to one of those combat units, to feel useful again, but I just don't know.

I've been sleeping a lot, and dreaming, which doesn't leave me refreshed when I get up in the morning.

What now.

Damn good big question.

In the center of the group is an older, chubby woman, with a bright red dress, who starts smiling and waving the closer she gets to us. The Vice President of the United States, who used to be the governor of South Dakota. Earlier it was rumored the President would come here for today's ceremonies, but in a last-minute change of plans, he took one of the older Air Force One's—sprung from an aviation museum— and flew to Britain to meet with the King and his Prime Minister.

I don't mind so much. I had already met him once.

The Vice President gets up on the platform, the band kicks into the "Star Spangled Banner," and as one, we all stand up. Off in the west, there's a sparkling bright line as more orbital debris burns up reentering the atmosphere. A sour part of me thinks that up there are the atoms and molecules of the captured POWs that were in the battle station, and George, and Gwen, and Joanie. A few weeks ago a chaplain told me that no matter if I believed in God or not, at least the essence of those captured would return back to Earth, which gives me enough comfort to allow me to sleep.

The music stops, we sit down, and the Vice President begins.

There are brief remarks I ignore, and I try to be a good soldier and sit still, but every now and then I look around, and I spot Dad, and, by

God, my platoon members from Kara's Killers—Melendez, Balantic, Lileks—and then one by one, the members of the raiding force who had been up there in orbit with the colonel get up and get awarded Silver Stars.

Lots of applause, lots of cheers.

Then it's Colonel Wallace's turn, and she goes up, smiling, holding that precious dirty letter in her hand, and she gets a Silver Star as well, and something else. So she goes up to the podium as a colonel, and comes down a brigadier general.

Good for her, I think, joining in the applause.

Then it's my turn.

I forget to say "stay" to Thor and he comes up along with me, and there's laughter and some applause, and even the Vice President has a big grin on her face. I take the stairs two at a time, and with Thor next to me, I stand next to the Vice President.

She reads from a prepared statement and I ignore it, still amazed I'm alive, still amazed at what's happened to me, and I look over at the near faces, some of them familiar to me, and then there's another burst of applause, and I realize it's time.

She pins the Purple Heart to my chest. Then I step forward, lower my head, and the Vice President puts the ribbon and medal around my neck, and I stand up, shake her hands, and there's flashes of light that scare me, until I realize it's just something to do with the cameras that the newspaper people have in their hands.

I shake the Vice President's hand again, and halfway down the steps, a young woman in dirty fatigues runs up and nearly tackles me.

I fall back against the steps and start laughing, and kissing, and it's Abby Monroe, my dear Abby, whom I last saw on a hilltop in a battlefield in New York State. Lots of kissing, lots of hugging, and military personnel and civilians and other folks move around us, and I know I'm blocking the stairs, and I don't care. There's more cheers, more applause, and I realize we're the center of attention, and I don't like it.

We break apart for a moment, and I grab her hand and say, "Come."

We push our way through the crowds and I manage to find a spot near the old viewing stands for the playing fields, and we kiss again and she says, "Sorry, I was out on patrol. Tried to get back as soon as I could."

"Patrol? You?"

She laughs, points to the lieutenant chevrons on the front of her fatigues. "I got promoted, too, soldier boy. I'm no longer a combat courier. I run a platoon of the biggest group of knuckleheads and morons to ever salute the flag."

Abby then takes one hand, and then the other, and kisses each splotch of scar tissue that marked where my little fingers used to be. "Oh, you poor boy," she says. "How does it feel?"

"Feels like someone's kissing them."

That makes her laugh. Abby bends down, rubbing Thor's back. "Space dog! How come you didn't get an award? First dog to come back alive from outer space."

I laugh at that and we hug again, and now I feel pretty damn good.

Later we're sitting by ourselves at the far end of the stands, as the helicopters take off, and I even spot a military jet up higher in the sky, leaving behind a white trace of vapor. I squeeze her hand and say, "I've got thirty days leave coming to me. And then it's back for more meetings and debriefs."

"Lucky you, while I'm out crawling in the mud, looking for rogue Creepers."

"I've got an idea," I say. "You want to play along?"

"Depends what it is."

"I'm going on a trip. I want you to come with me."

What now?

The answer has just come to me.

She laughs. "For real? Even though the base commander is your uncle, you think you can pull that off?"

I slowly take off the Medal of Honor that had just been awarded to me. "Lots of things can happen if you flash this around."

Abby smiles and gives me a long, sweet kiss. "All right, then. Where are we going?"

"To California."

"California! My God, I've always wanted to go there ... what do you have in mind, Randy?"

I carefully fold up the ribbon around the medal, and gently stroke Thor's head and neck. "I need to give this to a man I've never met, and his two boys, and tell them that his wife and their mom died a hero."